ONTARIO PEOPLE:
1796–1803

ONTARIO PEOPLE:

1796–1803

Transcribed and Annotated by
E. Keith Fitzgerald

With an Introduction and Index by
Norman K. Crowder

Published by Genealogical Publishing Co., Inc.
1001 N. Calvert St., Baltimore, MD 21202
Second printing 1998
Library of Congress Catalogue Card Number 92-73802
International Standard Book Number 0-8063-1366-8
Made in the United States of America

CONTENTS

MAPS AND ILLUSTRATIONS

The 1792 map of Upper Canada compiled by James L. Morris appears on pages 4 and 5. Relevant portions are included at the beginning of the Eastern, Midland, Home and Western Districts sections.

The 1798 map of Upper Canada drawn by David William Smith appears on pages 6 and 7. Relevant portions are included at the beginning of the Eastern, Midland, Home and Western Districts sections.

Lieutenant Governor John Graves Simcoe's Proclamation of 6 April 1796 is reproduced at page 8.

ACKNOWLEDGEMENTS

Miss Patricia Kennedy of the National Archives of Canada, while acting as director of the Manuscript Division, recognized the value of RG1, L7, volume 52B District Loyalist Rolls and Others and encouraged me to undertake a project of transcribing these almost 200-year old documents. Because of their fragility they had been withdrawn from circulation and were not readily available to researchers except by means of one set of photocopies provided for use in the Archives facilities in Ottawa. Despite her heavy workload Miss Kennedy made a set of photocopies for this project and provided the archivist's descriptions of the fifteen files which have been transcribed.

Staff members of the Map Division of the National Archives assisted by locating contemporary maps of Upper Canada for the time periods covered by this transcript and their helpfulness is gratefully acknowledged.

The Reverend Orlo Miller of London, Ontario supplied much useful information on members of Butler's Rangers and residents of the Western District.

I appreciate the help and encouragement of other researchers who contributed to the completion of this project.

E. Keith Fitzgerald

INTRODUCTION

After the American Revolution several thousand families came to settle in 1784 in the western part of the colony of Quebec, later to be known as Upper Canada, then Canada West and today as Ontario. These settlers were discharged British and German servicemen, former members of American Loyalist regiments, and some civilians and refugees. A number of families were already established in the Niagara-Detroit region, headed principally by soldiers in Butler's Rangers and members of the Indian Department. In the Detroit region there were already a few hundred families, mainly of French descent.

Initially French civil law prevailed throughout all of Quebec, a situation which was unacceptable to the newcomers. This led to a decision in 1791 to divide the colony - Lower Canada in the east retaining French civil law and the seignorial land sytem, and Upper Canada in the west with British laws and freehold land grants. The first Lieutenant Governor of Upper Canada, Colonel John Graves Simcoe, arrived in late 1791 and convened the first elected Parliament in 1792 in Newark, earlier known as West Niagara and later renamed Niagara-on-the-Lake.

Simcoe was a firm believer in building up the new colony with hardy people accustomed to the rigours of frontier life and encouraged Americans to come to Upper Canada. They were offered grants of 200 acres of land on condition they would take an oath of allegiance and be loyal to the British regime. The military and Loyalist arrivals who had come earlier received larger grants, generally in relation to their services to the Crown, their rank or status, and family size. The term "Loyalist" was not well defined other than signifying someone who had remained loyal to Britain during the American Revolution. One special privilege given to Loyalists was a free grant of 200 acres of land to each son and daughter on coming of age. This attractive benefit did not apply to the children of former British and German servicemen and other settlers.

All settlers received tickets or certificates showing the location of the lots on which they were to clear land and build houses, with full title to be given at a later date when settlement duties had been performed. These tickets were exchanged fairly freely - people moved from one site to another or traded tickets for goods, services or cash. There was no central control over their circulation and no easy way of determining whether the holder of a ticket had acquired it legally. Under Simcoe's regime steps were taken to set up a land registration process, which would record all deeds from the Crown, known as patents, and subsequent changes of ownership. First, however, it was necessary to establish who had the right to obtain title deeds and on 21 August 1795 the Executive Council passed a Resolution asking that a Proclamation be issued immediately which would require Loyalists and others to surrender their certificates in exchange for title deeds and to make a statement under oath in the district court as to their right to hold them. Some months later, after dealing with legal and administrative matters, Simcoe issued a proclamation on 6 April 1796. Although in its final form it referred only to Loyalists, others also appeared in court to confirm their land rights and possibly to try to obtain Loyalist status for the benefit of their children.

Simcoe's proclamation followed the wording of an earlier one by Lord Dorchester in 1789 in limiting the definition of Loyalists to those who had "joined the Royal Standard in America, before the treaty of seperation [*sic*] in the year 1783." Joining the Royal Standard was interpreted fairly liberally to include any service to the Crown, including actual service in a Loyalist regiment. A curious and ironic twist arises from the emphasis on **in America**, which was taken to limit the Loyalists to those who had been residents of the thirteen American colonies - consequently some members of Loyalist units such as Captain George Dame of Butler's Rangers, a British officer who lived in Quebec before the Revolution, could not have their children recognized as sons and daughters of Loyalists, rendering them ineligible for the free grants of 200 acres of land on coming of age.

Subsequently thousands of settlers appeared before the magistrates in district courts and made declarations under oath. The magistrates provided additional information in the records, which have been preserved in the National Archives of Canada, and are usually called the District Loyalist Rolls of 1796. The names and relevant details of those who were not Loyalists were also noted in the documents. These rolls have been carefully transcribed by Dr. E. Keith Fitzgerald and he has supplemented the entries with further data from his historical and genealogical research. Details supplied by the settlers, the magistrates and Dr. Fitzgerald now provide a rich source of information for researchers interested in the early period of Ontario history. Some entries show, for example, relationships, deaths, military service, maiden names of married women, and remarriage of widows.

In some cases there may be a question as to the whether the persons named in the documents actually resided in Upper Canada. In those lists with a preamble stating that the applicants appeared in the court and were recognized by the magistrates, there can be little doubt that they were actually there. File 1, for example, lists numerous Eastern District residents who appeared in court from 11 October 1796 to 1 November 1796 and the majority of them were known to the various justices of the peace. Similarly File 2 shows a few more who were added to the records at sessions held from 10 October 1797 to 1 November 1797 as they were vouched for by justices. For the Midland District, File 4 provides the names of those who appeared in court from 11 October 1796 to 15 November 1796, with some additions in 1797 from 10 to 20 October. The persons listed were there in the court but they were not necessarily Loyalists. The magistrates usually indicated the status of the applicants by notations indicating whether they were considered as Loyalists or former members of the British or German forces.

In the Home District, however, there are some lists such as Files 7 and 9 which are in a very different category. They include, for example, Benedict Arnold and the Reverend Samuel Peters, neither of whom resided in Upper Canada and could not have made an appearance in court. File 8, however, specifically mentions those who attended court on 11 October 1796 and it does not include either Arnold or Peters. It may be that the magistrates or provincial officials entered the names of non-residents for reasons of their own. The Reverend Samuel Peters, for example, was the father of Hannah Peters, wife of William Jarvis, Secretary of Upper Canada. Possibly Jarvis anticipated the arrival of his father-in-law and put his name on the roll, but he did not come. There is no question as to the clergyman's loyalty to the Crown - because of his support for the British, he was driven from his charge in Connecticut and spent many years in England petitioning the British Government to aid destitute Loyalists there. After Simcoe was appointed as Lieutenant Governor of Upper Canada, Dr. Peters entertained hopes of becoming the Bishop of Canada but in this respect he was disappointed.

It is important to check each entry and footnote for a given name. In the case of Dr. Peters, for example, the footnote at entry 5965 indicates that the name was to be taken OFF. While some of the clerk's notations are cryptic, in this instance there can be no doubt that OFF meant that the name was to be deleted. Another example appears at the very end of the text on page 2 of File 15 where Peter Russell, Administrator of Upper Canada during the absence of the Lieutenant Governor, questioned the inclusion of some persons who may not have lived in one of the thirteen American colonies before the Revolution and thus their status as Loyalists was uncertain.

Some researchers may be puzzled by the district court system. In 1788, before the creation of Upper Canada, four districts were established by drawing lines due north from several points and naming them the Luneburg or Lunenburgh, Mecklenburgh, Nassau and Hesse Districts. District functions included a form of municipal government by appointed magistrates and the operation of courts. After the arrival of Lieutenant Governor Simcoe, the names were changed in 1792 to Eastern, Midland, Home and Western Districts without any change to the boundary lines. At the same time counties were created in 1792, primarily for militia, land registration, and electoral purposes - but their boundaries did not coincide with the district boundaries and as a result some counties were split between two districts. These were the boundaries and district names that were still in force at the time of the 6 April 1796 proclamation. The district boundaries were not realigned to match county boundaries until 1800; the new lines are shown in a 1798 map by David William Smith, Acting Surveyor General of Upper Canada. Consequently the reader may well be confused by finding identical districts appearing in 1788 and 1792 under two different sets of names and the new 1792 names applying to districts with different boundaries in 1792 and 1800. The situation became even more complicated in later years until in 1849 the districts were abolished and local municipal governments were established.

In 1804 David Burns, Clerk of the Court of King's Bench, the provincial high court, delivered all the district rolls to James McGill, Inspector General of Upper Canada.

Norman K. Crowder

OVERVIEW

Files 1 to 15

NATIONAL ARCHIVES OF CANADA (NAC)

UPPER CANADA (ONTARIO) DISTRICT LOYALIST ROLLS 1796-1803

Reference: NAC RG 1, L 7, vol. 52B (B as in Bravo) (Files 1 to 15)

Compiled by Proclamation of Lieutenant Governor John Graves Simcoe
6 April, 1796

INTRODUCTION

The National Archives of Canada holds originals, and in some cases copies, of Rolls of names of those who qualified as Loyalists compiled in the four Districts into which Upper Canada (Ontario) was divided in 1788. These Rolls were made by local Justices of the Peace upon orders of Lt. Gov. Simcoe - the first Lieutenant Governor of Upper Canada. In all there are just short of 8,000 entries in Files 1 to 15 - the only Files relevant to this publication.
An additional File, File 20, was also available but it is not part of the set as it was a British Army document based on Niagara in 1784/5. There are duplications of each entry at least once in the various Files; thus, there are less than 4,000 individual names/entries.

It is the contention of the transcriber that these original Rolls are the origins of all other lists of Ontario Loyalists. Their value is in the fact that they contain entries of those who wanted to be considered Loyalists - and some who did not qualify to whatever was the definition of a Loyalist in those days. Thus, the most important thing about these lists, is that these people existed in 1796/7 in Upper Canada - not that they were Loyalists. It amounts almost to a partial Census of the province at that date - inadequate as it may be.

TRANSCRIBER'S NOTES

The writing and spelling is much improved over that of the documents compiled in 1783/4 at Montreal by British Army clerks for Governor General Haldimand. Each File is duplicated (original to copy) at least once - mostly into a semi-alphabetized version; eg, File 5 is the original list of the Midland District from which File 4 was written and File 1 is the original of File 3. One may wonder if it is worthwhile transcribing both; the reader is assured that such is the case, as one

Files 1 to 15

File contains corrections and additional information not found in the others. Some valuable genealogical data is found scattered throughout the lists, eg, widows who remarried and their new names, the death of some by 1797, an indication of a few blackmen who were enumerated etc. Obviously, discharged British soldiers did not qualify as "Loyalists", nor did demobilized German mercenaries, but the Justices of the Peace recorded them anyway in the Midland District. In the case of the Western District some people felt strongly enough that the original settlers in the area, ie, prior to 1775, qualified as Loyalists just as much as the new arrivals - so they listed them. This is not only a valuable find of names but it shows the spirit at least of some of those who did qualify - a spirit the transcriber finds lacking in other Districts where sons and daughters, who obviously did not qualify, were listed in the originals.

File 3 at page 38 contains a list of those whose names were to be expunged from the lists of the Home and Midland Districts. A famous, interesting name on that list is Capt. George Dame, a company commander in Butler's Rangers; he was not a resident of one of the thirteen colonies. At page 40 of File 3 is a list of those whose names were to be added to the Rolls of the Eastern, Midland and Home Districts; some of these names cause speculation with the transcriber as to their true status as they appear to be friends or functionaries in the Government.

The reader would do well to note the following:

(a) The alphabetization of Lists 3, 7, 8, 9, 10, 12 and 14 is rough; use the list to the very end in order to not miss the name of interest. There are a few names in the Eastern District - File 3 - originally misspelled beginning with the first letter, eg. TILLABOUGH/DILLABOUGH, DERHEART/AERHEART, FOUSLER/TOOSLER, FUTTLE/TUTTLE and FETTERLY/TETTERLY which could cause some misspent efforts.

(b) Index numbers run to 7928 at the end of File 15.

Files 1 to 15

(c) Footnotes for a particular entry are indicated by an "f" supra, usually in the index column but sometimes in the body of the transcript; "ff" is used to alert the reader to more than one footnote.

(d) The Ottawa River was also known in the Eastern District as the GRAND RIVER (see File 3, page 26, footnote 6). When this river is referred to in the Home District, it obviously refers to the Grand River in Brant County that flows into Lake Erie just west of Fort Erie on the north shore.

(e) It is a pity that the Home District Files do not give a better indication of the address, ie, Township.

LIST OF FILES

FILE No.	DISTRICT	INDEX NUMBERS	ALPHA-BETIZED	COPY OF	REMARKS
1	Eastern	1 - 1335			Original Roll
2	Eastern	1341-1398			Continuation of File 1
3	Eastern	1401-2848	X	1	Added lists at end
4	Midland	3001-4033		5	By Township
5	Midland	4051-5022			Original of File 4
6	Midland	5401-5460			Additions to Midland District
7	Home or Niagara	5501-6179	X	8	
8	Home	6201-6672	X		Original
9	Home	6701-6953	X		Continuation of original - actually only 145 entries
10	Home	7001-7485	X	8	
11	Home	7501-7512			Additions to Home Roll
12	Western	7601-7641	X?	14	
13	Western	7701-7713		15	Much reduced version of File 15
14	Western	7801-7841	X?	12	
15	Western	7901-7928			An original

West Half of 1792 Map of Upper Canada

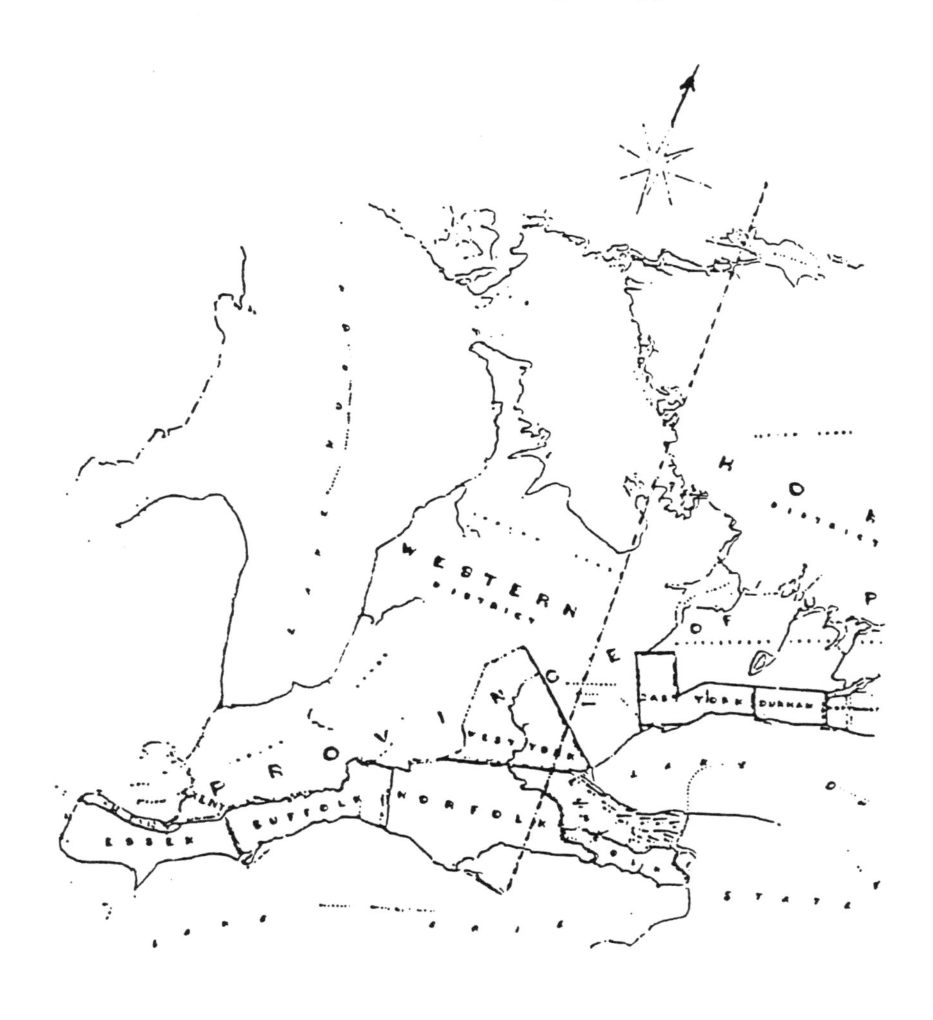

1792 Map of Upper Canada Compiled by James L. Morris

Courtesy: National Archives of Canada - National Map Collection No. 55041

East half of 1792 Map of Upper Canada

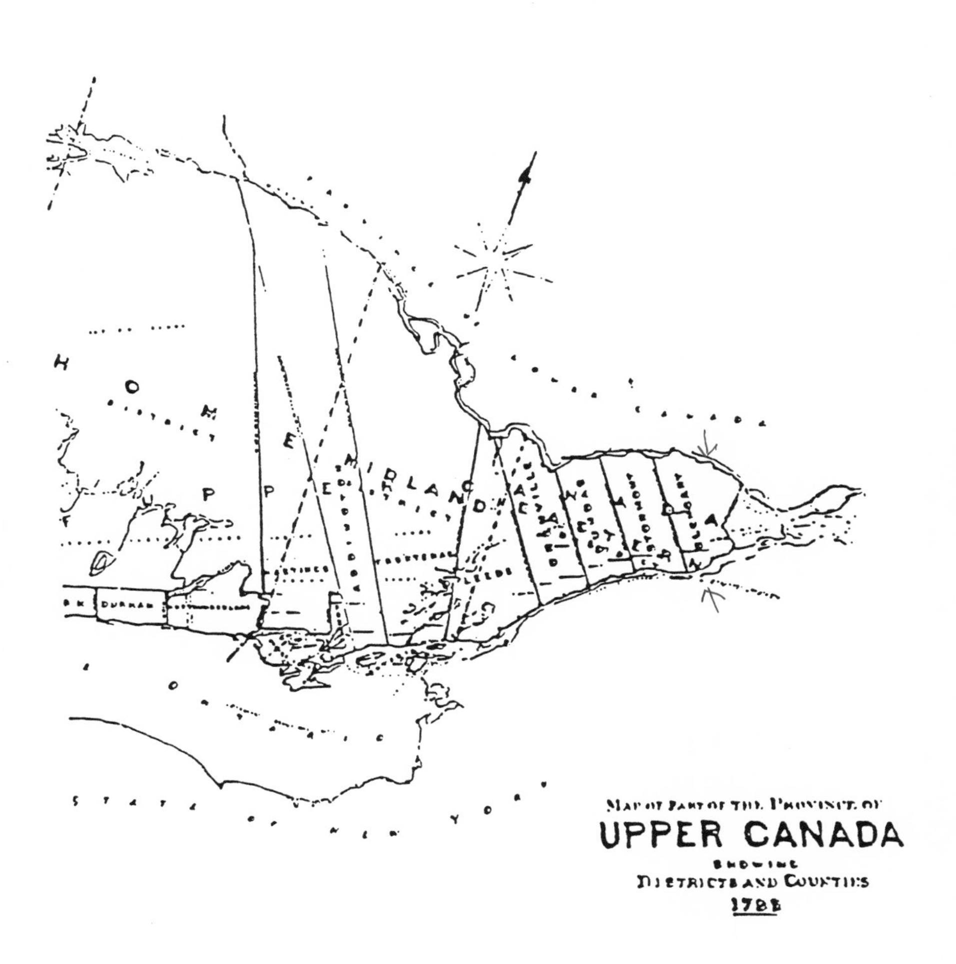

District boundaries are the same as those of 1788

Courtesy: National Archives of Canada - National Map Collection No. 55041

West Half of 1798 Map of Upper Canada

1798 Map of Upper Canada by David William Smith, Acting Surveyor General

Courtesy: National Archives of Canada - National Map Collection No. 21350

East Half of 1798 Map of Upper Canada

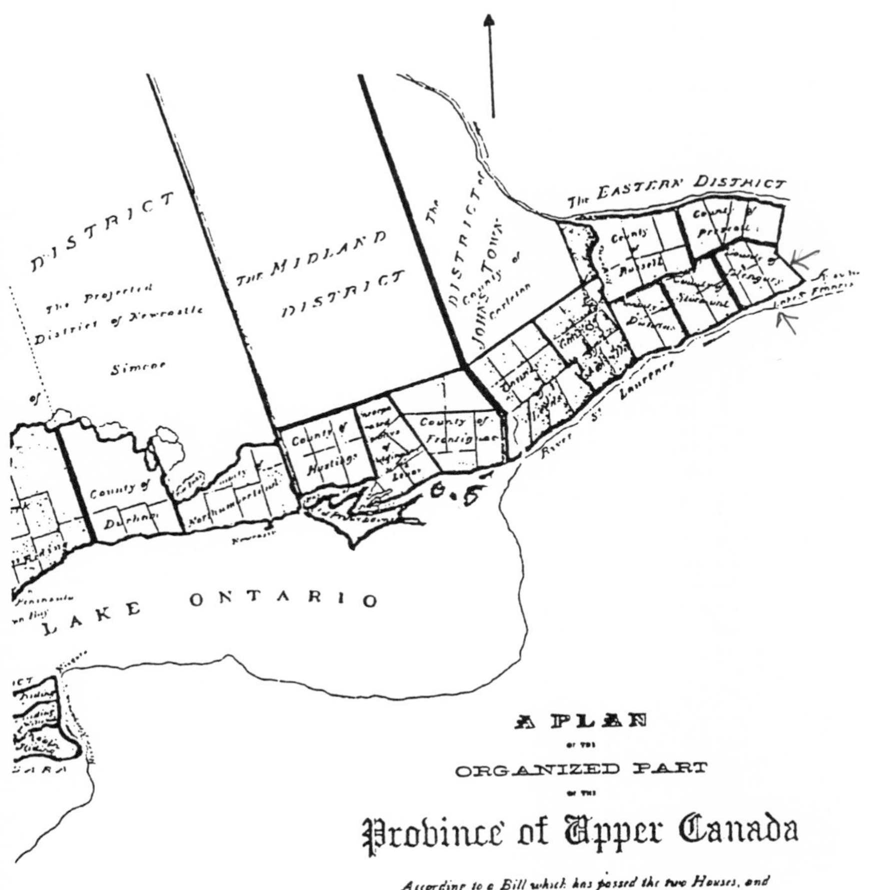

The new district boundaries were proclaimed in 1800

Courtesy: National Archives of Canada - National Map Collection No. 21350

Upper-Canada.

BY HIS EXCELLENCY JOHN G. SIMCOE, Esq.

LIEUTENANT GOVERNOR AND MAJOR GENERAL OF HIS MAJESTY'S FORCES, &c. &c. &c.

PROCLAMATION.

WHEREAS it appears by the minutes of the Council of the late Province of Quebec, dated Monday the ninth day of November 1789, to have been the deſire of his Excellency Lord Dorcheſter the Governor-General "To put a *mark of honor* upon the families who had "adhered to the Unity of the Empire, and joined the Royal Standard "in America, before the treaty of ſeperation in the year 1783," and for that purpoſe it was then "Ordered, by his Excellency in Council, that the ſeveral Land Boards (ſhould) take courſe for "preſerving a regiſtry of the names of all the perſons falling under the deſcription afore-"mentioned, to the end that their poſterity might be diſcriminated from (the then) future "ſettlers in the pariſh regiſters and rolls of the militia of their reſpective diſtricts, and other pub-"lic remembrances of the Province, as proper objects, by their perſevering in the fidelity and "conduct ſo honorable to their anceſtors, for diſtinguiſhed benefits and privileges;" but as ſuch regiſtry has not been generally made; and as it is ſtill neceſſary to aſcertain the perſons and families, who may have diſtinguiſhed themſelves as abovementioned; as well for the cauſes ſet forth, as for the purpoſes of fulfilling his Majeſty's gracious intention of ſettling ſuch perſons and families upon the lands now about to be confirmed to them, without the incidental expences attending ſuch grants:—Now KNOW YE, that I have thought proper, by and with the advice and conſent of the executive council, to direct, and do hereby direct all perſons, claiming to be confirmed by deed under the ſeal of the province in their ſeveral poſſeſſions, who adhered to the unity of the empire and joined the royal ſtandard in America, before the treaty of ſeperation in the year 1783, to aſcertain the ſame upon oath before the magiſtrates in the michaelmas quarter-ſeſſions aſſembled, now next enſuing the date of this proclamation, in ſuch manner and form, as the magiſtrates are directed to receive the ſame;—and all perſons will take notice that if they neglect to aſcertain, according to the mode above ſet forth, their claims to receive deeds without fee, they will not be conſidered as entitled, in this reſpect, to the benefit of having adhered to the unity of the empire and joined the royal ſtandard in America before the treaty of ſeperation in the year 1783.

Given under my hand and ſeal at arms, at the government houſe at York, this ſixth day of April, in the year of our Lord, one thouſand ſeven hundred and ninety-ſix, and in the thirty-ſixth year of his Majeſty's reign.

JOHN GRAVES SIMCOE.

GOD SAVE THE KING!

By his Excellency's Command,

E. B. LITTLEHALES.

SIMCOE'S PROCLAMATION OF 6 APRIL 1796

Courtesy: National Archives of Canada - Library Pamphlet No. 1796 (S)

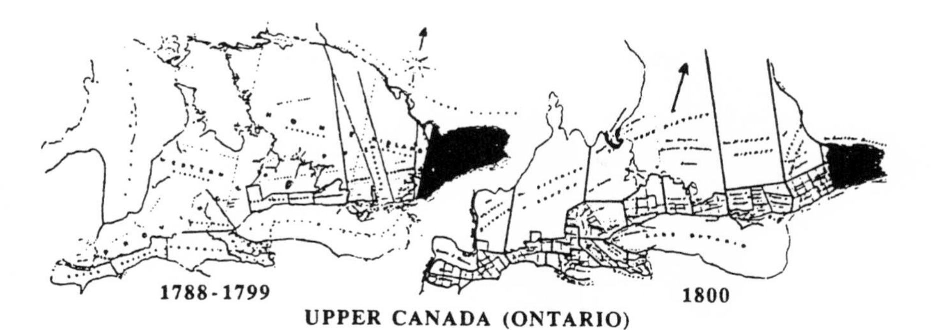

1788-1799 1800

UPPER CANADA (ONTARIO)

In 1796 the Eastern District, earlier called the Luneburgh or Lunenburgh District, comprised Stormont, Dundas, Glengarry, the southern part of Leeds, and most of Grenville Counties. The southern boundary of the district was the St. Lawrence River and the Ottawa or Grand River was the northern boundary. In 1796 it included townships which later became parts of Prescott, Russell and Carleton Counties. The district town of the Eastern District was New Johnstown. In 1800 the Johnstown District was created from Leeds and Grenville and Carleton Counties.

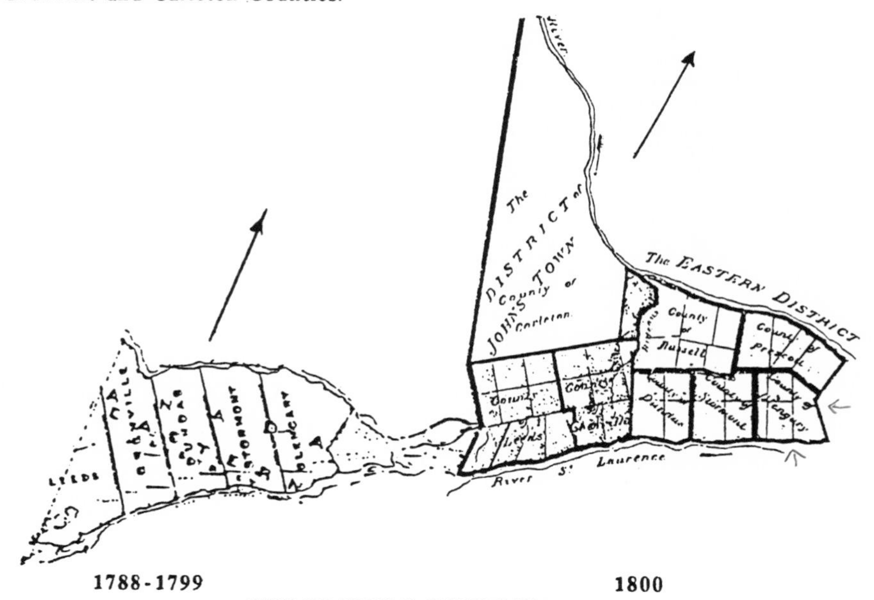

1788-1799 1800

THE EASTERN DISTRICT

Files 1, 2 and 3

NATIONAL ARCHIVES OF CANADA (NAC)

UPPER CANADA (ONTARIO) DISTRICT LOYALIST ROLLS

Reference: NAC RG 1, L 7, vol. 52B (B as in Bravo) (Files 1 to 15)

FILES 1, 2 and 3

EASTERN DISTRICT

BACKGROUND

The Eastern (formerly the Lunenburg) District Rolls are contained in Files 1, 2 and 3. This District comprised all of what is now Ontario between the Ottawa and St. Lawrence Rivers from the current Quebec boundary to a line running due North from approximately Gananoque, Ontario (just west of Brockville) on the St. Lawrence River.

MAPS

Some maps are provided to assist the reader in identifying the Townships and the Districts as they existed at that time.

ARCHIVIST'S DESCRIPTION

File 1 Endorsed "UE Roll -- Eastern District -- 1797". Contemporary copy, on paper watermarked 1795, 32x20 cm - sewn. A list of some 1277 numbered entries occupies 42 pages and is followed by 61 additional names on four more pages - 46 pp in all.

Comment: There is a mistake in the numbering at No. 146 whereby Nos. 147/8/9 are omitted; thus, there are only 1274 plus 61 additional names - total 1335 - with some of these duplicated. The writing and spelling is very good. Some spelling errors are corrected in File 3.

File 2 Endorsed "Continuation of the Roll of UEL^{s} -- Eastern District 17 Dec 1797". Original of the first addition (58 names) to the District Roll found in File 1 (pp. 43-46); paper not watermarked by date, 69x49 cm; broken on folds. Verso bears only endorsement.

Comment: Writing and spelling is good though what appears to be original signatures of J.P.s are difficult; a few phonetic spellings, eg, McGLOCLON for McLAUGHLIN that are carried over to File 1 and spelled McGLOGHLIN in File 3.

Files 1, 2 and 3

File 3 Endorsed "UE List -- Eastern District" and titled likewise. Original, on paper not watermarked by date, 49x19.5 cm; folded but not sewn into book format. An alphabetic arrangement of 1277 names from the original District Roll (see File 1), compiled between 1798 and 1803, with annotation of the numbers from the original District Roll and other details; with some additional entries. Pages 1-35 contain original list of UEs;p. 36 is the additional list repeated from File 2; p. 37 continues the index of original list;p. 38 is a list of"Names to be expunged from the Home and Midland Districts"; p. 39 is blank; p. 40 is a list of 22 names from the Eastern, Midland and Home Districts to be added.

Comment: The writing and spelling is quite good. The alphabetization is marred by indexing within the numerical order; but, even this should not be relied upon as names have been inserted after certain numbers/letters had been overlooked. Also, those additional names of File 2 appear both as 50 names at page 36 as well as alphabetically at the end of each appropriate letter without a number (they are shown as Blanks in the number column). The latest dated entry is at No. 907 (File 1) - 31 July 1811 - for all three Files.

TRANSCRIBER'S NOTES TO AID THE USER

(1) There are only a few letters that can not be interpreted clearly.

(2) File 1 is divided into five columns in the original: N°.; Names of Persons; Lot; Concession; Township. As the 3rd & 4th columns were not used, they have been omitted. A similar format has been used for File 2. The format of File 3 is as in the original.

(3) A column, "NUMBER", has been added on the left hand side of each File for indexing purposes; these numbers run consecutively through the entire volume.

(4) Everything between the double lines is as it appears in the original. Anything outside these lines are the transcriber's annotations.

(5) The asterix, "*", is used to denote "sic", or, as written.

(6) The Grand River is the Ottawa River.

Files 1, 2 and 3

(7) In File 3, the Remarks Column is seldom used and when it is the entry usually starts in the Township Column or even further left.

(8) When an entry is made in the Township Column, it appears that "ditto" is not written for all entries below it that correspond; rather it is simply left blank until a change is necessary. The user is cautioned, however, in that all these Township entries are not correct; as many as possible have been substantiated in the Notes. The land allocations have been checked against McNiff's Map of Townships 1, 2,3, 4, 5 and Lake (Lancaster) made in 1786 and found at NAC Map Collection H2/400/1786. Judge J.F. Pringle's book, Lunenburgh or the Old Eastern District, which has a listing of these land allocations based on McNiff's map, is also used.

(9) The Township "ELIZABETHTOWN" was initially read as "ELISABETHTOWN" and is written that way throughout most of these Files.

(10) It is quite obvious that all these people were not "True" Loyalists - but were sons or daughters of Loyalists; however, in the intervening 13 years since the end of the Revolutionary War, these sons and daughters had become of age and the parents did not want them to be overlooked in any benefits that they might be entitled to.

(11) The reader should note that there could be some importance attached to the order and close association of the names to one another in File 1. Relationships are likely to be together.

(12) Footnotes to entries are indicated by an "f" supra, usually with the index number but sometimes in the body of the transcript; double ff's indicate more than one footnote for an entry.

File 1 Page 1

EASTERN DISTRICT

(COPY)

A Roll of Loyalists or Persons names who adhered to the Unity of the Empire by joining the Royal Standard in America before the Treaty of Peace in the year one thousand seven hundred and eighty three, taken and made pursuant to His Excellency Lieut. Governor Simcoes* Proclamation bearing date the sixth day of April in the year one thousand seven hundred and ninety six, at the Michaelmas General Quarter Sefsions of the Peace, holden* in and for the Eastern District of the Province of Upper Canada on the eleventh day of October, in the thirty sixth year of His Majesty's Reign, and in the year of our Lord one thousand seven hundred and ninety six.

NUMBER	N°	NAMES OF PERSONS	TOWNSHIPS
1	1	Richard Smith	Osnabruck
2	2	Jonathan Black	Augusta
3	3	Michael Cook	Edwardsburg
4	4	David Elliot	Elisabethtown
5	5	John McDonell	Edwardsburg
6	6	William Appleby	Edwardsburg
7	7	David Lee	Bastard
8	8	Paul Terry	Elisabethtown
9	9	David Munroe	Cornwall
10	10	Philip Patton	Matilda
11	11	Nicholas Mattice	Elisabethtown
12	12 f	London Derry	Edwardsburg
13	13	Samuel Munroe	Yonge
14	14	John Valentine	Yonge
15	15	Mitchel Landrie	Elisabethtown
16	16	Joseph McNish	Elisabethtown

NOTES:
1. The asterix, "*", means "sic", or, as written though as an error.
2. All between the double lines is a transcription of the original as best can be interpreted.
3. At the top of the page are some indecipherable annotations that are faded, eg, top left "(copy of II/wo)".
4. This first page (or Folio) is partially destroyed along its right border - but the reading is not impaired.
5. McNiff's 1786 map shows "LONDONDERRY* (a negro)" allotted Lot 27 (all) of the 2nd (actually 3rd) Concession of Lake (later called Lancaster) Township. See No. 12 above.

File 1 Page 2

NUMBER	N^o	2 NAMES OF PERSONS	TOWNSHIPS
17	17	Elijah Whitney	Elisabethtown
18	18	Joseph Falkner	Elisabethtown
19	19	Charles Bush	Osnabruck
20	20	William Livingston	Augusta
21	21	John Livingston	Augusta
22	22	David Henderson	Elisabethtown
23	23	William Davies	Elisabethtown
24	24	Matthew Gosley*	Yonge
25	25	Eleazar Fairchild	Yonge
26	26	Daniel Burrit	Augusta
27	27	James Keeler	Augusta
28	28	Adoniram Burrit	Augusta
29	(29)	Ichial Hurd	Augusta
30	30	Gersham Wing	Elisabethtown
31	31	Joseph Bissle	Augusta
32	32 f	Samuel Emberry	Augusta
33	33	John Booth	Augusta
34	34	Elisha*Baker	Augusta
35	35	Stephen Howard	Elisabethtown
36	36	Dan Throop	Augusta
37	37	John Wooly	Elisabethtown
		(space lined - no No./name)	Elisabethtown*
38	38	Freelove Butler senior	Elisabethtown
39	39	Freelove Butler junior	Augusta
40	40	James McNish	
41	41	John Pottier	
42	42	Jonathan Fulford sen^r.	
43	(43)	Jonathan Fulford jun^r.	
44	(44)	Levius Wickwire	
45	(45)	Jonathan Wickwire	

NOTES:

1. Brackets on some numbers indicate a loss of the left-hand border of the folio.
2. The lower case "z" is written like a modern day written lower case "R" - nothing below the line; the lower case "r" is written like an inverted "i" without the dot. Hence, confusion on No. 25 and the spelling of Elizabethtown throughout this transcription where ELISABETHTOWN is used.
3. Large ink blot over last two letters of surname No. 33.

File 1 Page 3

NUMBER	N°	NAMES OF PERSONS	TOWNSHIPS 3
46	46f	Jonathan Millschurch	
47	47	Timothy Buel*	
48	48	Bemsley Buel*	
49	49	Jonathan Buel*	
50	50	Samuel Buel*	
51	51	Abel Fulford	
52	52	Daniel McArtheren	
53	53	Stephen Jod Beach	
54	54	Matthew*Howard	
55	55	Stephen Howard	
56	56	John Howard	
57	57	Dier* Howard	
58	58	Peter howard	
59	59	Caleb Henderson	
60	60	Bartholomew Carley	
61	61f	Conrodt*Peterson	
62	62f	Andrew Naughton	Grand River
63	63	Philander Naughton	
64	64	Josiah Case	
65	65	Archibald McLaren	
66	66	Peter McLaren	
		I do hereby vouch for the twenty nine names last above mentioned.	
		(Signed) Wm. Buel J.Pf.	
67	67f	Edward Jefsup Esquire	Augusta
68	68	Louis Mosher	
69	69	Robert Nicholson	
70	70	Nicholas Mosher	
71	71	Joseph Knapp	
72	72	Isaac Haftail	
73	73	William Leaky junr.	
74	74	Ezechial Spicer	

NOTES:
1. No. 46 - otherwise JONATHAN MILLS CHURCH, and so indexed.
2. GRAND RIVER is the Ottawa River - see File 3, page 26, Note 6, re: No. 806.
3. The certification by Wm. Buel implies that all the missing township designations from No. 40 should read Augusta as he is from there.
4. No. 67 - the old written double "S" is as written here, "fs".
5. For township see Note 1, Page 7.

File 1 Page 4

NUMBER	4 N°	NAMES OF PERSONS	TOWNSHIPS
75	75	Justus Sherwood Esquire	
76	76	Thomas Brown	
77	77	Nathaniel Brown	
78	78[f]	Caleb Clafson (CLASSON)	
79	79	James Campbell	
80	80	John Bryan	
81	81	Doctor Sparam	
82	82	Duncan Grant	
83	83	Daniel Jones	
84	84	Ephraim Jones Esquire	
85	85	Solomon Jones	
86	86	Valentine Herman	
87	87	Peter Carrigan	
88	88	John Difson (DISSON)	
89	89	Peter Hodogan*	
90	90	David Jones	
91	91[f2]	Benond* W(iltsy)	
92	92[f]	Oliver Sw(eet)	
93	93	Phili(p) Hard	
94	94	James Hard	
95	95	Henry Crofs (CROSS)	
96	96	Elijah Bottom Ensign	
97	97	Abijah Hawley	
98	98	John Earheart	
99	99	Corporal Bennet	
100	100	Thomas Jones	
101	101	Benoni Smith	
102	102	Joseph Ávery	
103	103	John Jones Esquire	
104	104	Henry Mooth	

NOTES:
1. The double "S" as "fs" is shown.
2. Nos. 91 & 92 - a large ink blot obscures these surnames.
3. No. 91 - the first name is otherwise spelled BENONI/BENONIE in lists in Haldimand Papers (OGS Publication, Loyalist Lists - 1985).
4. The asterix means sic= as written.
5. For township see Note 1, Page 7.

File 1 Page 5

NUMBER	N°	NAMES OF PERSONS	TOWNSHIPS 5
105	105	Major Watson	
106	106	Enoch Mallery	
107	107	Afsa Landen (ASSA)	
108	108	Justus Sealey	
109	109	Beeches Heirs	
110	110	Joseph Sealey	
111	111	Alexander Berrard	
112	112	Daniel Dunham	
113	113	Alexander Campbell	
114	114	Samuel Batman	
115	115	John Gray	
116	116	Christopher Quinn	
117	117	James Chambers	
118	118	Charles Shibbarn*	
119	119	Moses Stratford	
120	120	Cary Pitman	
121	121	John Shoults	
122	122	Edward Elveston	
123	123	James Cluny	
124	124	John Glafsford (GLASSFORD)	
125	125	Oliver Everts	
126	126	Rofswell Everts (ROSSWELL)	
127	127	Benjamin Knight	
128	128	Joel Smades	
129	129	John Chester	
130	130	Daniel Spicer	
131	131	John Bunker	
132	132	Nathaniel Corbin	
133	133	Bathael* Bunker	
134	134	Thomas Barton	
135	135	Dennis Smith	
136	136	Israel Thompkins	
137	137	Silas Hamblin	
138	138	Samuel Sheet	
139	139	Moses Halabart	
140	140	Paul Heck	

NOTES: 1. The asterix, "*" means sic = as written.
2. For township see Note 1, Page 7.

File 1 Page 6

NUMBER	6 N°	NAMES OF PERSONS	TOWNSHIPS
141	141	William Graham	
142	142	Philip Dulmage	
143	143	John Lorence	
144	144	Paul Glafsford (GLASSFORD)	
145	145 f	Lyttle Glafsford	
146	146	Francis Scotte	
147	150*	Christopher Beygar	
148	151	Thomas Stratford	
149	152	Charles Sweet	
150	153	Guellies* Stamp	
151	154	Richard Jones	
152	155	Samuel Hick	
153	156	John Hick	
154	157	Charles McArther	
155	158	Abraham Leaky	
156	159	Stephen Burrit	
157	160 f	William Leaky	
158	161 f	John Arkenbrack	
159	162	James Kelsey	
160	163	William Kelsey	
161	164 f	David Hunter	
162	165 f	Abraham Pannal	
163	166	Nicholas Loucks	
164	167	John Dunham	
165	168	James Dunham	
166	169	Hagard Wilcox senior	
167	170	Hagard Wilcox junior	
168	171	William Wilton	
169	172	Ezekiel Shue junior	
170	173	John Dulmage	
171	174 f	Elias Dulmage	
172	175	Abraham Louck(s)	
173	176	Samuel Sherwood	

NOTES:
1. Nos. 147 to 149 missing in original; no effect on list.
2. Nos. 161/2 - large ink blot on surnames.
3. No. 165 - one wonders if this name is now spelled PENNAL.
4. Nos. 166 & 175 - an old German Palatine name otherwise spelled LAUXS.
5. For township see Note 1, Page 7.

File 1 Page 7

NUMBER	N°	NAMES OF PERSONS	TOWNSHIPS 7
174	177	David Hamblin	
175	178	Jonathan Wickwire	
176	179	Simon Coville	
177	180	Thomas Stratford	
178	181	Samuel Weatherhead	
179	182	James Chambers	
180	183	Herman Landen	
181	184	Joseph Jefsup (JESSUP)	
182	185	Henry Jefsup (JESSUP)	
183	186	Edward Jefsup (JESSUP)	
184	187	Mary Jones senior	
185	188	Mary Jones junior	
		I do hereby vouch for	
		the one hundred and twent	y
		two names last above ment	ioned
		(Signed) Eph[m]. Jones J.P.[f]	
186	189	Allan Campbell	Elisabethtown
187	190	David Shipman	Elisabethtown
188	191	David Bissle	Augusta
189	192	David Manhart	Elisabethtown
190	193 [f]	Jeremiah Birdsall	Elisabethtown
191	194	John Chisholm	one seventh Cornwall
192	195	Benjamin Andrews eighteen	third Elisabethtown
193	196	Ichida De Boyce*	Elisabethtown
194	197	Joseph Barton	Augusta
195	198	Silas Judson	Elisabethtown
196	199 [f]	Daniel Pattison	Yonge
197	200	Hugh McIlmoyle	Edwardsburg
198	201	Thomas McIlmoyle	Edwardsburg
199	202	Capt. Thomas Fraser	Edwardsburg
200	203	Thomas Fraser	Edwardsburg
201	204	William Fraser senior	
202	205	William Fraser junior	
203	206	Thomas Gooseberry	
204	207	Hugh Fraser	

NOTES:
1. The certification after No. 188 indicates that all the Townships for Nos. 66 to 188 are Augusta.
2. The figures refer to the Lot and Concession number, ie, No. 194, JOHN CHISHOLM would be Lot 1, Concession 7. McNiffs 1786 map confirms this allocation as does Judge J.F. Pringles book.
3. From No. 200 to 289 it appears all are from Edwardsburg.

File 1 Page 8

NUMBER	B N°	NAMES OF PERSONS	TOWNSHIPS
205	208	Capt. William Fraser	
206	209	William Fraser	
207	210	Thomas Fraser	
208	211	William Robertson	
209	212	John McKenzie	
210	213	Joseph Robertson	
211	214	David Hunter	
212	215	John Sharp	
213	216	Archibald McNiel	
214	217	Abraham Saunders	
215	218	William Saunders	
216	219	Thomas Armstrong	
217	220	Richard Bolton	
218	221	John Armstrong	
219	222	Thomas Armstrong junr.	
220	223 f	Duncan Cameron	
221	224 f	Joel Adams	
222	225	Benjamin (McCar)bin	
223	226	John Ruderback	
224	227	Simon Ruderback	
225	228	John Lampson	
226	229	James Lampson	Edwardsburg f
227	230	William Lampson	
228	231 f	William Welsh	
229	232	Jacob Bonistal	
230	233	Thomas Marlotte	
231	234 f	John Marlotte	
232	235	Denowe	
233	236	Joseph Robertson	
234	237	Thomas McIlmoyle	
235	238	Thomas Boid* senior	
236	239	Thomas Boid* junior	
237	240	James Boid	

NOTES:

1. Nos. 224/5 - large ink blot spoils surnames.
2. No. 232 - JACOB "BONISTEEL", from NYS, member Jessup's Rangers per Haldimand Papers (OGS Publication; Loyalist Lists - 1985). See index this publication. Spelling varients are BOHNESTIEL/BONESTIEL from PINE PLAINS, Dutchess County, New York State.
3. No. 235 - no first name.
4. From No. 200 to 289 it appears all from Edwardsburg.

File 1 Page 9

NUMBER	N°	NAMES OF PERSONS	TOWNSHIPS 9
238	241	Henry Anderson	f
239	242	Thomas Main	
240	243	Matthew Main	
241	244	John McIlmoyle	
243	246	Ephraim Curry	
244	247	Archibald Montgomery	
245	248	Alexander Ferguson	
246	249	Andrew McDonell	
247	250	Samuel Rose	
248	251	Aaron Rose	
249	252	Ezray Adams	
250	253	Constant King	
251	254	Charles Peebles	
252	255	Dennis Smith	
253	256	Daily* Silk*	
254	257	Duncan Grant	
255	258	Daniel McIntosh	
256	259	David Rose	
257	260	James Humphrey	
258	261	John Galbreath*	
259	262	Henry Jackson	
260	263	Hugh Munroe	
261	264	Wil^m. Saml. Adams	
262	265	James Adams	
263	266	James Froom senior	
264	267	James Curry	
265	268	James Fullarton*	
266	269	James Grant	
267	270	James Jackson	
268	271	James Main	
269	272	Thomas Peters	
270	273	John McIntosh	
242	245	James McIlmoyle	(omitted in proper order above)

NOTES: 1. The asterix, "*", means sic=as written.
2. From No. 200 to 289 it appears all are from Edwardsburg; see Note 1 on Page 11.

File 1 Page 10

NUMBER	10 N°	NAMES OF PERSONS	TOWNSHIPS
271	274	Alexander McIntosh	
272	275	Peter Jackson	
273	276	Richard David	
274	277	Chevaleur Lorimier*	
275	278	Samuel Rose	
276	279	Thomas Maine* senior	
277	280	Allan Campbell	
278	281	Alexander Campbell jun	
279	282	James Campbell	
280	283	Alexander Campbell Esquire	
281	284	Ezechiel Rose	
282	285	John Fraser	
283	286	William Fraser	
284	287	Thomas Fraser	
285	288	William Grant	
286	289 f	Peter Grant	
287	290 f	James Miller	Elisabethtown
288	291	Adam Cole	
289	292	Archibald McNeal	
290	293	John McNeal	
291	294	Ruben Motte	
292	295	Joseph Griffin	
293	296	Isaac Griffin	
294	297	George Belton	
295	298	William Clew*	
296	299	Henry Clow*	
297	300	George Gardiner*	
298	301	John Whitley	
299	302	Allan Grant	
300	303	Allan McDonell	
301	304	John Whitley	
302	305	Peter Thomas	

NOTES: 1. Nos. 290 & 291 - large ink blot obscures surnames.
2. The asterix, "*", means sic= as written.
3. From No. 200 to 289 it appears all are from Edwardsburg; see Note 1 on Page 11.

File 1 Page 11

NUMBER	N°	NAMES OF PERSONS	TOWNSHIPS 11
303	306	James Wright	
304	307	Jacob Van Camp	Matilda
305	308	John Van Camp	
306	309	John Boyce	
307	310	Philip Servos	
308	311	Peter Van Camp	
		I do hereby vouch for the hundred and ten names last above mentioned.	
	(Signed)	Tho. Fraser J.P.	
309	312	Samuel Pennick	Elisabethtown
310	313	Samuel Landen	Augusta
311	314	Moses Reid	Elisabethtown
312	315	Benjamin Kilburn	
313	316	Nathan Dayton	Leeds
314	317	James Brackenridge	
315	318	Joel Stone	
		I do hereby Certify for the three names last above mentioned	
	(Signed)	Joel Stone J.P.	
316	319	Elisha Stephens	
317	320	Frederick Fell	Augusta
318	321	William Rood	
319	322	Jefse (JESSE) McIntyre	
320	323	Joachim* Denault	
321	324	Rachel Mosher	
322	325	Chloe Vanvolkenburgh	
323	326[f]	John Haegaerman	Elisabethtown
324	327	Timothy Hodge	Augusta
325	328	John McVee	Elisabethtown
326	329[f]	John White	Augusta[f]
327	330	John Covil	
328	331	Archibald Gilchrist	

NOTES:
1. The certification below No. 311 seems to imply that all from No. 200 to 289 are from Edwardsburg unless otherwise defined.
2. No. 326 - anglicized to HAGERMAN.
3. Nos. 329 to 357 - see Note 1, Page 13; these are Augusta.

File 1 Page 12

NUMBER	12 N°	NAMES OF PERSONS	TOWNSHIPS
329	332	David Leaken*	
330	333	John Livingston	
331	334	William Livingston	
332	335	Philimon* Pennock	
333	336	Daniel McDonell	
334	337	Carlmon Michel	
335	338	Harvey Michel	
336	339	Philip Wickwire	
337	340[f]	Joshua Bostwick	
338	341	John Crine*	
339	342	Henry Morrison	
340	343	Asa Landen	
341	344	John McDougall	
342	345	Thomas Stratford	
343	346	Duncan Campbell	
344	347	Ami Campbell	
345	348	Daniel Thompson	
346	349	John Smith	
347	350	Roger Stephens	
348	351	Jefse (JESSE) Brown senior	
349	352	Leberry* Wilcox	
350	353	George Campbell	
351	354	Joseph White junior	
352	355	John Laird	
353	356	Joseph White senior	
354	357[f]	Henry French	
355	358	Basil Rorrison*	Elisabethtown[f]
356	359	Charles Peebles	
357	360	David Hamblyn	
358	361	Francis Hamblyn	
359	362	David Brackenridge	
369	363	Archibald McIlmoyle	
361	364	Jefse (JESSE) Brown senior	

NOTES:
1. No. 341 - just as positively, this name is spelled CRONE in the index (File 3).
2. Nos. 329 to 357 - see Note 1, Page 13; these all Augusta. No. 358 to 376 at least Elisabethtown - maybe to 388.

File 1 Page 13

NUMBER	N°	NAMES OF PERSONS	TOWNSHIPS 13
362	365	John Booth senior	
363	366	Zeaks Booth	
364	367	Abner Booth	
365	368	Bethia* Booth	
366	369	Phebe Booth	
367	370	Charles Booth	
368	371	Samuel Booth	
369	372	Vincent Booth	
370	373	Isaac Booth	
371	374	Rebecca Gorman	
372	375	Lida Hoskins	
373	376	Benoni Wiltsey junior	
		I do hereby vouch for the forty eight names last above mentioned	
	(Signed)	Alex.r Campbell J.P.	
374	377	Peter Drummond Esquire	
375	378	William Lamson	
376	379	William Snyder sen.r	
377	380	William Snyder jun.r	
378	381	Robert Smith	
379	382 f	Stephen Smith	
380	383	Encrease* Smith	
381	384	James Smith	
382	385	William Wright	
383	386	Samuel Wright junior	
384	387 f	Sylvester Wright	
385	388	Berecci* Beeck*	
386	389	Joseph Sealey	Augusta
387	390	Justus Sealey	Elisabethtown
388	391 f	Peter McLarin*	
389	392 f	Ruggles Mutchimson*	Yonge
390	393	Stephen Duclen*	Elisabethtown

NOTES:
1. The certification below No. 376 indicates that Nos. 329 to 357 are all Augusta; No. 358 to 376 Elisabethtown.
2. No. 383 - the only letter in doubt is the third; thus, a good 2nd choice is ENEREASE. In File 3 definitely ENCREASE.
3. No. 388 - name quite distinct as shown; in File 3, just as definitely BUCK.
4. Nos. 392 & 393 -correspond with File 3.
5. Nos. 377 to 419 all Elisabethtown; see Note 6, Page 14.

File 1 Page 14

NUMBER	14 N°	NAMES OF PERSONS	TOWNSHIPS
391	394	Baria Chiltsey*	
392	395	Sealvenus* Everitt	
393	396	James Brown	
394	397	Thomas Wood	
395	398	Samuel Caswell	
396	399	Oliver Graham	
397	400	William Howard	
398	401	George Buck	
399	402	Timothy Buel*	
400	403 f	John Aerheart	
401	404	Lia or Lix Hitcher	
402	405 f	George Campble*	
403	406	Jefse (JESSE) Brown	
404	407	John Waicoff	
405	408	Peter Freen	Yonge
406	409 f	Thomas Smyth*Esquire	Yonge
407	410 f	George Smyth*	Elisabethtown
408	411 f	Terence Smyth	
409	412	Daniel McArtherer	
410	413	James Kelsie	
411	414 f	Coonradt* Peterson	
412	415	Jacob Thomas	
413	416	Joseph White junior	
414	417	James McNish	
415	418	Jonathan Fulford sen	
416	419 f	David Peet	
		I do hereby vouch for the forty three names last above mentioned	
	(Signed)	Saml Wright J.P.	
417	420	Henry Larue	Yonge
418	421	William Larue	Escotte

NOTES:
1. No. 403 - in File 3, listed under "DERHEART", stroked through and corrected to above.
2. No. 405 - a common spelling error; File 3 spelled CAMPBELL.
3. No. 409/410/411 - spelled as above here; File 3, SMITH.
4. No. 414 - COONRADT spelled with one "O" in File 3.
5. No. 419 - good 2nd choice is PEEL; definitely PEET in File 3.
6. Nos. 377 to 419 appear to be all Elisabethtown except where otherwise noted.

File 1 Page 15

NUMBER	N°	NAMES OF PERSONS	TOWNSHIPS 15
419	422	Alexander McDonell	Charlottenburg[f]
420	423	Kenneth McDonell	
421	424	William McLeod	
422	425	Alexander Grant	
423	426	John Murchison	
424	427	Finlay Rofs (ROSS)	
425	428	Andrew Summers	
426	429	Allan McDonell	
427	430	Alexander McDonell	
428	431	Allan McDonell	
429	432	Jacob Summers	
430	433	Archibald Grant	
431	434	Alexander McLaughlin	
432	435	Alexander McDonell	
433	436	John McDonell	
434	437	John McGregor	
435	438	John Caldwell	
436	439	Alexander Grant	
437	440	John Cameron	
438	441	Murdock McLean	
439	442	Donald McLean	
440	443	William McLean	
441	444	Donald McLean Jun.[r]	
442	445	John McKay	
443	446	William Dickey	Charlottenburg[f]
444	447	William Robins	
445	448	Allan Grant	
446	449	Duncan Grant	
447	450	Peter McGregor	
448	451	Charles Rose	
449	452	William Rose	
450	453	Alexander Rose	
451	454	Peter Grant	

NOTES:
1. All this page appear to be from Charlottenburg; the names are quite familiar to the transcriber.

File 1 Page 16

NUMBER	16 N°	NAMES OF PERSONS	TOWNSHIPS
452	455	John Grant	Charlottenburg
453	456	Frederick Goose	Cornwall
454	457	Henry Runion	
455	458	James Forsyth	
456	459	Thomas Robertson	
457	460	Donald McGregor	
458	461	Nicholas Mattice	
459	462	John Mattice	
460	463	Adam Mattice	
461	464	Jacob Sheets senior	
462	465	George Sheets	
463	466	William Sheets	
464	467	Henry Empey[f]	
465	468	Christian Sheek	
466	469	John Cameron junior	
467	470	Alexander Cameron senior	
468	471	Mickle Van Koughnet[f]	
469	472	Ebenezer Wright	
470	473	David Wright	
471	474	George Barnhart	
472	475	Jacob Barnhart	
473	476	Nicholas Barnhart	
474	477	David McCuin* senior	
475	478	David McCuin* junior	
476	479	William Carr	
477	480	George Mictchell*	
478	481	Christopher Empey[f]	
479	482	Jacob Empey[f]	
480	483	William Empey[f]	
481	484	Philip Empey senior[f]	
482	485	Philip Empey sen.[f][f]	
483	486	Elisha Anderson	
484	487	James Anderson	
485	488	Cyrus Anderson	

NOTES:

1. All the EMPEYs on this page served in 1KRRNY EXCEPT HENRY; he was born 1767 at Stone Arabia in the Mohawk Valley as were all his brothers listed here as sons of PHILIP Snr. They were all allotted land in Cornwall Twsp. PHILIP Snr.'s petitions in the Haldimand Papers attest to the fact that HENRY & his next oldest brother, PETER, were too young to serve. Thus, these two were SUEs NOT UEs themselves.
2. MICHAEL VAN KOUGHNET married ANNA EVA, eldest d/o PHILIP Snr.

File 1 Page 17

NUMBER	N^{o}	NAMES OF PERSONS	TOWNSHIPS 17
486	489	Thomas G. Anderson	
487	490	George Anderson	
488	491	John Farlinger senior	
489	492	John Farlinger junior	
490	493	Nicholas Farlinger	
491	494	George Johnston	
492	495	William McLaughlin	
493	496	Ephraim Putman	
494	497	Henry Gallinger	
495	498	John Smith senior	
496	499	John Smith junior	
497	500	Jacob Smith	
498	501	Daniel Smith	
499	502	John Pascod senior	
500	503	John Pascod junior	
501	504	John McCaffrey	
502	505	Joseph Anderson	
503	506	Ebenezer Anderson	
504	507 f	Francis Clerke*	
505	508	William Toosler (DUSLER)	
506	509	Stephen Miller	
507	510 f	Daniel Robertson	
508	511 f	Donald McDonell	Four fifth
509	512 f	Duncan McDonell	six fifth
510	513 f	John Link	
511	514	Matthias Link	
512	515	Capt. John McDonell	Scothouse
513	516	Colon^{l}. James Gray	
514	517	Jacob Ferrand Esquire	
515	518 f	Robert J.D. Gray Esquire	
516	519 f	Widow C. Valentine	
517	520 f	Capt. Samuel Anderson	
518	521	John Anderson senior	
519	522	John Anderson junior	

NOTES:
1. No. 508 - see File 3.
2. No. 511/2 - this means Lot 4, 5th Concession; Lot 6, 5th Con.
3. No. 513 - JOHANNES GOTTFRIED LINK, married MARIA, youngest born of PHILIP EMPEY Snr. & MARIA ELISABETH BARBARA SCHULTS.
4. No. 519 - her husband the Adjutant of 1KRRNY.
5. No. 520 - a Company Commander of 1KRRNY and later Justice of the Peace at Cornwall Town; attestor of some of these lists.

File 1 Page 18

NUMBER	18 N°	NAMES OF PERSONS	TOWNSHIPS
520	523	John van* Koughnet	
521	524	Adam Johnston	
522	525	Robert Johnston	
523	526	Richard Anderson	
524	527	John Hartle	
525	528	Capt. Miles McDonell	
526	529	Ranald McDonell Esquire	
527	530	Donald McDonell	twelve sixth
528	531	Mathias Snetsinger	
529	532	Gilles McBane	
530	533	John Quin*	
531	534	Michael Quin*	
532	535	George Bender	
533	536	Thomas Ross	
534	537	George Wait	
535	538	Joseph Waite*	
536	539	Adam Hartle	
537	540[f]	Hermanus Cryderman	
538	541	James Lynch	
539	542	John Cryderman	
540	543[f]	George Gallinger	
541	544	Christian Hartle	
542	545	Solomon Tuttle	
543	546	George Crites	
544	547	John Dewitt*	
545	548	John Wood	
546	549	Frederick Bough sen[r].	
547	550	Frederick Bough jun[r].	
548	551	John Bough	
549	552	Garrit Dewitt*	
550	553	Jacob Waggoner senior	
551	554	John Hawn	
552	555	Dennis Bender (Tunis)*	
553	556	Barny Hart	
554	557	Jacob Waggoner Junior	

NOTES:
1. No. 540 - Herman Cryderman allotted Cornwall Lot 11E/II.
2. No. 543 - George Gallinger allotted Cornwall Lot 11E/IV.
3. These and many other land allocations confirm this as Cornwall Twsp.

File 1 Page 19

NUMBER	N^o	NAMES OF PERSONS	TOWNSHIPS 19
555	558	Henry Waggoner	
556	559	Elisha Hollister	
557	560	James Buttersworth	
558	561	John Christie senior	
559	562	Abijah Christie	
560	563	John Christie junior	
561	564 f	Nathan Parks sen^r.	
562	565	Robert Park*	
563	566 f	Nathan Park* junior	
564	567	Joseph Cryderman	
565	568	Philip Amor	
566	569	Josiah Wood	
567	570	Peter Amor	
568	571	Christian Gallinger	
569	572	Mich^l. Gallinger junior	
570	573 f	Michael Clyne*	
571	574 f	John Cline*	
572	575 f	George Cline*	
573	576	Luke Bready*	
574	577	Allan Cameron	
575	578	Alex^r. Cameron junior	
576	579	Hugh Cameron junior	
577	580	Daniel Cameron	
578	581	John Cameron junior	
579	582	Hugh Cameron senior	
580	583	Michael Gallinger sen^r.	
581	584 f	Widow Christ. Austin	
582	585	John Hartle senior	
583	586 f	Widow Catha^n. Cryderman	
584	587	John Fyke	
585	588	James Johnston	
586	589	William Ferguson	
587	590	James Knight	
588	591	Daniel Campble*	
589	592 f	Jacob Algire* senior	

NOTES:
1. Nos. 564 & 566 - the junior & senior are reversed; this is relative to File 3 and is of no significance.
2. No. 592 - otherwise spelled ALGUIRE.
3. Nos. 573/4/5 - note the change in spelling in these three lines.
4. Nos. 584 & 586 - McNiff's 1786 map shows both of these women as widows as of that date; both Cornwall Twsp. - AUSTIN Lot 9E/III and CRYDERMAN Lot 12E/III.

File 1 Page 20

NUMBER	20 Nº	NAMES OF PERSONS	TOWNSHIPS
590	593	Martin Algire	
591	594	Jacob Algire	
592	595	Patrick McGuire	
593	596	William Cumming	
594	597	Benjamin Anderson	Brother of Samuel
595	598	Martin Selmser	
596	599	Nicholas Selmser	
597	600	Benjamin Easton*	
598	601	John Milroy see the Petition of William Milroy Read 31 October 1809	
599	602	Levy*Baily	
600	603	Nadab Eastman*	
601	604 f	John Baily	
602	605 f	Angus McDonell	eighteen fourth
603	606 f	Angus McDonell	fourteen eighth
604	607 f	John McDonell	A Eleventh
605	608 f	John McDonell	7 fifth
606	609	John McDonell	nine dº
607	610 f	James McGriger*	
608	611	John McDonell	twenty fourth
609	612	Duncan McDonell	nineteen fourth
610	613 f	Donald McMillan	
611	614	John McDonell	seventeen fourth
612	615	Allan McPhee	
613	616	Archibald McDonell	five fifth
614	617	Widow Isable* Fraser	
615	618	Mary McGrigor	
616	619	Christian McGruer	
617	620 f	Donald McGruer	
618	621	John McDonell	ten fifth
619	622	William Fraser	
621	624	Donald Cameron	fifteen fifth
622	625	William Cameron	
623	626	Alexander McDonell	eight fifteenth
620	623	Donald Fraser (omitted from sequence above)	

NOTES:
1. There are six JOHN McDONELLs on this page.
2. No. 600 - definitely EASTON;definitely EASTMAN in File 3.
3. No. 603 - definitely EASTMAN.
4. No. 617 - the spelling seems to have been corrected in File 3 both here and in many other instances.
5. The figures refer to Lot & Concession numbers to help in identifying all the McDONELLs.

File 1 Page 21

NUMBER	N[o]	NAMES OF PERSONS	TOWNSHIPS 21
624	627	Hugh McDonell	C fourth Roxbury
625	628	Ranald McDonell	Fourteen ninth Cornwall
626	629	Alexander McDonell	
627	630[f]	Donald McDonell	twenty two fourth
628	631[f]	Duncan McDonell	seventeen fourth
629	632[f]	Kenneth McDonell	twenty two fourth
630	633	Abraham Marsh	
631	634	John McNarin*	
632	635	Evan Roise senior	
633	636	Evan Roise junior	
634	637	John Annabal	
635	638	Godfrey Warner	
636	639[f]	Andrew Milross (MILROFS)	
637	640	Michael Warner sen[r].	
638	641	John Milross (MILROFS)	
639	642	Thomas Milross (MILROFS)	
640	643	Michael Warner jun[r].	
641	644	William Milross (MILROFS)	
642	645	John Dixon	
643	646	John Helmer	
644	647[f]	Jacob Stoneburner	
645	648	William Wood	
646	649	Henry Hawn	
647	650	Hermanius* Hawn	
648	651[f]	John McDonell	Eleven fifth
649	652[f]	Donald McDonell	twelve fifth
650	653[f]	Alexander McDonell	twelve fifth*
651	654[f]	Hugh McDonell	one eight*
652	655	Peter Fitzpatrick	
654	657	John Hare	
655	658	Barny Hare	
656	659	William Hare	
657	660	Lieut. William Fraser	
658	661	John McIntyre	
653	656	William Fitzpatrick (omitted from sequence above)	

NOTES:

1. No. 639 - Andrew Milross allotted Cornwall 29E/I & 22W/IV.
2. No. 647 - Jacob Stoneburner allotted Cornwall 26W/IV.
3. Nos. 630/1/2 - these allocations do not check with McNiff's map; nor does No. 654. Nos. 651/2/3 do check out.

File 1 Page 22

NUMBER	22 N°	NAMES OF PERSONS	TOWNSHIPS
659	662[f]	Lieut. Neil Robertson	
660	663	John McDonell	A ninth
661	664	William McDonell	B ninth
662	665	Jacob Hawn	
663	666	Christian Hawn	
664	667	Jeremiah French Esq[r].	
665	668	Albert French	
666	669	Benjamin French	
667	670	Duncan Murchison	Lancaster
668	671	John Cameron	
669	672	Alexander Rofs (ROSS)	
670	673	Thomas Rofs (ROSS)	
671	674	George Rofs (ROSS)	
672	675	Alexander McDonell	
673	676	John McDougald	
674	677	Paul Glafsford (GLASSFORD)	
675	678	Alexander Cameron	
676	679	Jeremiah Snyder	
677	680	William Murchison	
678	681	Donald Rofs (ROSS)	
679	682	Thomas Ben Rofs (ROSS)	
680	683	Jacob Snyder	
681	684	John Snyder	
682	685	Stephen Miller	Cornwall
683	686[f]	Thomas Swan Esq[r].	
684	687	Caleb Peek	
685	688	John Knight	
686	689[f]	Levi Willard	
687	690	John Emerson	
688	691	William Branan	
689	692	Angus Fraser	
690	693	John Hare	Osnabruck
691	694	John McIntyre	Williamsburg

NOTES:

1. No. 686 - a THOMAS SWAN allotted Cornwall Lot A east½/IV.
2. No. 662 - a Lieut. Neil Robertson allotted 1350 acres in the 6th Concession Cornwall.
3. No. 689 - a Levi Willard allotted part Lots 18 & 19 of 6th Concession Cornwall.
4. No. 700 (Page 23) - this is Sgt. ADAM EMPEY, s/o PHILIP Snr & step-father of JAMES & HENRY HARE listed above him, even though they were allotted land in different townships.

File 1 Page 23

NUMBER	Nº	NAMES OF PERSONS	TOWNSHIPS 23
692	695	John McKee	Osnabruck
693	696	Lieut. Peter Everitt	
694	697	Lieut. Gersham French	Cornwall
695	698	James Hare	Lancaster
696	699	Henry Hare	
697	700 f	Adam Empey	Osnabruck
698	701	Angus McDonell	eight twelfth Cornwall
699	702	Richard Mandaville*	
700	703	Peter Davies	
701	704	Frederick Weaver	
702	705	Philip Crysler	
703	706	John Crysler junr.	
704	707	(blank) Crysler	
705	708	Adam Snyder	
706	709	Conradt Snyder	
707	710	Peter Weaver	
708	711	John Weaver	
709	712	George Thompson	Matilda
710	713	Jno. A. Shevertfeger*	Williamsburg
711	714	Michael Hains	
712	715	Jacob Weeger	
713	716 f	Capt. William Claus	Cornwall
714	717	John Loeney	Charlottenburg
715	718	Edward Loeney	
716	719	William Loeney	
717	720	Samuel Loeney	
718	721	John Cashin*	
719	722	Allan McDonell	
720	723	William Emery senior	
721	724	John Emery	
722	725	William Emery junior	
723	726	Thomas Emery	
724	727 f	John Empey senior	Osnabruck
		(No. 700 - footnote on Page 22)	

NOTES: 1. No. 716 - a Lieut. William Claws was allotted Cornwall land - Lot 27 & East half 28/I.
2. No. 727 - one of the mysteries of the EMPEY family is why three of PHILIP Snr.'s sons (JOHN F., Sgt. ADAM & PETER) were allotted land in Osnabruck, when he and his five other sons were in Cornwall. This JOHN Snr. was the eldest, b. 8 June 1748 at Stone Arabia, Mohawk Valley; he had the designation "Snr." relative to his cousin, Sgt. JOHN W. Jnr.

File 1 Page 24

NUMBER	24 N^o	NAMES OF PERSONS	TOWNSHIPS
725	728	John Hoople	
726	729	Henry Hoople	
727	730	Jacob Merkle	
728	731	Christopher Servos	
729	732	Samuel Mofs (MOSS)	
730	733	Andrew Wert	
731	734	John Redick	
732	735	John Cadman Senr.	
733	736	John Cadman Junr.	
734	737	James Stuart	
735	738	George Stuart	Son of James
736	739	Henry Stuart	do
737	740	Gilbert Stuart	do
738	741	Jacob Aman	
739	742	Philip Frymire	
740	743	John Aman	
741	744	Padar Ruport	
742	745	David Jacocks	
743	746	Conradt Devoe	
744	747	Philip Stata	
745	748	Henry Merkle	
746	749	Joseph Stoneburner	
747	750	Leonard Stoneburner	
748	751	John Stoneburner	
749	752	John Coons	
750	753 f	Peter Empey	
751	754	Jacob Rofs (ROSS)	
752	755 f	John Empey junr.	
753	756	David Summers	
754	757	Francis Albrant	
755	758 f	Adam Empey jun.	
756	759	William Empey Senr.	
757	760	William Empey junr.	
758	761	Richard Empey	

NOTES:

1. The most significant information on this page is the last two EMPEYs - both sons of WILLIAM Snr. born 1772 & 1774 respectively; thus, sons of a UE but not UEs themselves.
2. No. 758 - ADAM Jnr. (junior to No. 700 on Page 23) s/o WILLIAM Snr., served in 1KRRNY. No.755 could be his brother, Sgt. JOHN W. Jnr., or his second cousin s/o JOHN Snr. (No. 727 on Page 23).
3. No. 753 - PETER, s/o PHILIP Snr. (2nd youngest son).

File 1 Page 25

NUMBER	N°	NAMES OF PERSONS	TOWNSHIPS 25
759	762 f	Nicholas Alt*	
760	763	Joseph Loucks	
761	764 f	James Dougharty	
762	765 f	John Wert junior	
763	766	Conradt Weart*	
764	767	John Cough	
765	768	Philip Moak	
766	769	Jacob Rambough	
767	770	Amos Rambough	
768	771	John Rambough	
769	772	David Rambough	
770	773	John Bradshaw	
771	774	Jacob Countryman jun.r	
772	775	Jacob Countryman sen.r	
773	776	Conradt Countryman	
774	777	Henry Winter	
775	778 f	Peter Winter	
776	779	Rudolph Pepst	
777	780	Laurence Amon	
778	781	Jacob Fenner	
779	782	Adam Baker sen.r	
780	783	Adam Baker jun.r	
781	784	John Baker	
782	785	William Baker	
783	786	Martin Baker	
784	787	John McWilliams	
785	788	Martin Meddough	
786	789 f	William Crouder Sen.r	
787	790	James Crouder	
788	791	Anthony Crouder	
789	792 f	Isaac Crouder	
790	793	William Crouder jun.r	

NOTES:

1. No. 762 - otherwise spelled "AULT".
2. Nos. 765 & 766 - note spelling variations. "Coend. Wert" allotted Osnabruck Lot 5/I; Andrew Wert allotted Lot 5E/I.
3. No. 779 - "Rhdol. Papist" allotted Osnabruck Lot 12W/II.
4. Nos. 790 & 793 -"Isaac Crowder" (Lot 17 E) and "James Crowder" (Lot 17W) allotted land in second concession of Osnabruck.
5. This page and preceding one at least is for Osnabruck.

File 1 Page 26

NUMBER	26 N°	NAMES OF PERSONS	TOWNSHIPS
791	794	John Crouder	
792	795	William Crouder	
793	796	George Warner	
794	797	Conradt Warner	
795	798 f	Col. Archild. McDonell	
796	799	Asel Wright	
797	800	Amos Wright	Augusta
798	801 f	Simon Derheart	Edwardsburg
799	802	Richard Dingman	Osnabruck
800	803 f	William Lovelass	Grand River f
801	804	John Wragg	
802	805	Archibald Lovelass	
803	806	John Platt	
804	807	Josiah Case junior	
805	808	Peter Case	
806	809	Walter Case	
807	810	James Perrigor	
808	811	John Tipple	Osnabruck
809	812	Cornelius Bulson	Williamsburg
810	813	William McCue	Escotte
811	814	Widow Cruickshank	
812	815	Col. Alexr. McDonell	Charlottenburg
813	816 f	Col. John McDonell	
814	817	Capt. Hugh McDonell	
815	818	Lieut. Chichester McDonell	
816	819 f	Capt. Richard Norton Wilkinson	
817	820	Walter Wilkinson	
818	821	Capt. John McKenzie	Williamsburg
819	822	Lieut. Kenneth* McKenzie	Cornwall
820	823	Timothy Painting	Augusta
		I do hereby vouch for the four hundred and two names last above mentioned	
	(Signed)	S. Anderson J.P.	

NOTES:

1. Nos. 798 & 816 - in File 3 are changed to Lieutenant Colonel
2. Nos. 803 to 810 are believed to be all Grand River, ie, the Ottawa River. (See File 3, P-26, Note 6.
3. No. 819 - NORTON inserted with an inverted "v".
4. No. 801 - apparently should be AERHEART.
5. No. 811 - apparently should be TEEPLE.

File 1 Page 27

NUMBER	N°	NAMES OF PERSONS	TOWNSHIPS 27
821	824	Sir John Johnson K.B.	
822	825	Major Will.m Hogan	Cornwall
823	826f	William Byrnes* Esquire	Charlottenburg f
824	827	John McGruer	
825	828	Daniel Campbell senior	
826	829	Daniel Campbell junior	
827	830	John Dingwell	
828	831	James Dingwell	
829	832	Alex.r McGruer	
830	833	Alex.r McPherson	
831	834	James McPherson	
832	835	Murdock McPherson	
833	836	John Murchison	
834	837	Keneth* Murchison	
835	838	Daniel Prentis	
836	839	John Cain	
837	840	Donald McGilles sen.r	
838	841	Donald McGilles jun.r	
839	842	Duncan McGilles	
840	843	Hugh McGilles	
841	844	John Livingston	
842	845	Neil Livingston	
843	846	Hugh McDonell	
844	847	Alex.r McDonell	
845	848	Rev.d John Bethune	
846	849	Alex.r McDonell	
847	850	Donald McDonell	
848	851	John McDonell	
849	852	Roderick McDonell	
850	853	John McDonell	
851	854	Hugh McDonell	
852	855	John McDonell	
853	856	Tinnan McDonell	

NOTES: 1. No. 826 - 2nd choice BYRNE.

2. All after No.826 believed to be Charlottenburg.

File 1 Page 28

NUMBER	28 N°	NAMES OF PERSONS	TOWNSHIPS
854	857	Roderick McDonell	
855	858[f]	John Bane McDonell	
856	859[f]	Donald* McDonell*	
857	860[f]	John Duen*McDonell	
858	861	Donald McDonell	
859	862	John McNaughton	
860	863	Donald McNaughton	
861	864	John McKenzie	Charlottenburg
862	865	Duncan McKenzie	
863	866	Angus Cameron	
864	867	Archibald Cameron	
865	868	Alexander Cameron	
866	869	Duncan Cameron	
867	870	William Cameron	
868	871	Donald Cameron	
869	872	Alexander Ferguson sen[r].	
870	873	Alexander Ferguson jun[r].	
871	874	Peter Ferguson	
872	875	William Ferguson	
873	876	Donald Grant sen[r].	
874	877	Lewis Grant sen[r].	
875	878	Lewis Grant jun[r].	
876	879	Donald Grant jun[r].	
877	880	Duncan Grant	
878	881	Alexander Grant	
879	882	Allan Grant	
880	883	Duncan Grant	
881	884	John Grant	
882	885	Finlay Grant	
883	886	Angus Grant	
884	887	Donald McGilles	
885	888	Daniel McIntosh	
886	889	Benjamin McIntosh	

NOTES:

1. No. 859 - in File 3 the first name and the surname (less the "Mc") have been reversed; this (File 1) is more likely the correct version.
2. No. 860 - the middle name is "DUE" in File 3; this is the more likely correct version, ie, File 1 is correct. "DUE" was a very common abbreviation, even in 1797, for "Daughter of a United Empire Loyalist".

File 1 Page 29

NUMBER	N°	NAMES OF PERSONS	TOWNSHIPS 29
887	890	James Clark	
888	891	Peter Smith Senior	
889	982	Peter Smith Junior	
890	893	James Smith	
891	894	Hugh McLaren	
892	895	Peter Finney	
893	896	George Finney	
894	897 f	Angus Bethune	
895	898	Mary Livingston alias Mutchman	
896	899	Hugh Munroe	
897	900	Thomas Munroe	
898	901	John Dunn	Lancaster
899	902	Duncan McIntyre sen^r.	
900	903	Duncan McIntyre jun^r.	
901	904	John McIntyre	
902	905	Donald McIntyre	
903	906 f	William Colders*	
904	907 f	William Urquhart	Charlottenburg - (see?) Petition of John his son filed 31 July 1811
905	908	Alexander Urquhart	
906	909	Alexander Kenedy*	
907	910	Donald Chisholm	
908	911	Lewis Chisholm	
909	912	Duncan Chisholm	
910	913	William Chisholm	
911	914	Hugh Chisholm	
912	915	Allan Chisholm	
913	916	Alexander Chisholm sen^r.	
914	917	Alexander Chisholm	
915	918	Donald Rofs (ROSS)	
916	919	John Rofs (ROSS)	
917	920	Donald McKay	
918	921	Angus McKay	
919	922	William McKay	

NOTES: 1. No. 898 - poor 2nd choice MULCHMAN, though that is first choice in File 3.
2. No. 907 - this gives the latest (?) date recorded for some entries/changes in these documents.

File 1 Page 30

NUMBER	30 N°	NAMES OF PERSONS	TOWNSHIPS
920	923 f	Hugh McKay	
921	924	James Young	
		I hereby vouch for the one hundred and one names last above mentioned	
	(Signed)	Willm Byrne J.P.	
922	925	Ralph Falkner	Lancaster
923	926	John McLelan*	Cornwall
924	927	Peter Grant	Charlottenburg
		I do hereby vouch for the three names last above mentioned	
	(Signed)	Arch^d. McDonell J.P.	
925	928	William Sowils senior	Matilda
926	929	William Sowils junior	
927	930	John Sowils	
928	931 f	Frederick Bouk*	Williamsburg
930	933 f	Christian Bouk* sen^r.	
931	934	George Weart	
932	935	Henry Stata	
933	936	Farquhar McDonell	
934	937	Henry Strader	
935	938	Giles Stamp	
936	939	Peter Brouse	
937	940	George Brouse	
938	941	Jacob Coons	
939	942	Conradt Coons	
940	943	Henry Wellery	
941	944	Edward Foster	
942	945	John Foster	
943	946	George Reddick	Williamsburg
929	932 f	Adam Bouk* (omitted from sequence above)	

NOTES:
1. No. 924 - the attestor under No. 924 is at No. 826 on Page 27.
2. Nos. 931/2/3 - otherwise spelled "BOUCK/BOUCH".

File 1 Page 31

NUMBER	N[o]	NAMES OF PERSONS	TOWNSHIPS 31
944	947	Christopher Reddick	
945	948	Adam Reddick	
946	949	Henry Baker	Matilda
947	950	Joseph Avery	
948	951	John Everser	Williamsburg
949	952	John Shaver	Williamsburg
950	953	William Franks	
951	954	Conradt Baker	
952	955	John Marcellis	
953	956[f]	Michael Ault	Matilda
954	957[f]	John Ault	
955	958[f]	Everhart Ault	
956	959	Simon Strader	
957	960	William Strader	
958	961	John Strader	
959	962	Anthony Walliser	
960	963	John Shaver	
961	964	Adam Shaver	
962	965	Edward Gay	
963	966	John Walliser	
964	967	Anthony Walliser junior	
965	968	George Carman	
966	969[f]	Luke Bowen	
967	970	John Mercle	Williamsburg
968	971	Peter Fetterly	Williamsburg
969	972	Henry Fratts	
970	973[f]	John Collison*	Matilda
971	974	Jacob Carns*	
972	975	Christian Carns	
973	976	John Meddough jun.[r]	
974	977	John Meddough sen.[r]	

NOTES: 1. Nos. 956/7/8 - allottments Matilda are recorded as: JOHN Lot 19E/I; EDWARD Lot 19W/I; MICHAEL 20W/I - all AULT.
2. No. 969 - LUKE BOWEN allotted Matilda Lot 14W/II.
3. No. 973 - as definitely as this is COLLISON, in File 3 it is CALLISON just as definitely.

File 1 Page 32

NUMBER	32 N°	NAMES OF PERSONS	TOWNSHIPS
975	976 f	John Parlow	
976	979 f	Peter Prunner jun.r	
977	980 f	Peter Prunner sen.r	
978	981 f	Ludwig Frederick	
979	982	Barnet Frederick	
980	983	Philip Shaver jun.r	
981	984	William Stanford	
982	985	Martin Stealey	
983	986	Lucis* Feader	
984	987	Peter Dorn	
985	988	Martin Walter	
986	989	Aver Berkeley	Williamsburg
987	990	Philip Shaver sen.r	Matilda
988	991	Adam Shaver	
989	992 f	Jacob Shaver	
990	993 f	Jacob Dorin	
991	994 f	David Dorin	
992	995 f	Jeremiah Dorin	
993	996	George Loucks	Williamsburg
994	997	Richard Loucks	Williamsburg
995	998	Henry Mercle	
996	999	Michael Cook	
997	1000	George Cook	
998	1001 f	George Storin	
999	1002 f	John Saver	Matilda
1000	1003	John Service	
1001	1004	Henry Albrant	
1002	1005	John Benedict	
1003	1006	Joseph Benedict	
1004	1007	John Crouse	
1005	1008	Philip Walter	
1006	1009	Michael Piller	Williamsburg

NOTES:

1. Nos. 993/4/5 - spelled as "DORRING", McNiff's 1786 map shows Matilda Lot 26W/I allotted JACOB; Lot 28W/I DAVID; Lot 26E/I to JERMY.
2. No. 1002 - McNiff's map shows JOHN SAVER Lot 35W/I Matilda.
3. No. 979/80 - McNiff's map shows PETER PRUNNER allotted OSNABRUCK 15W/II; Pringle omits this name altogether.
4. No. 981 - allotted Lot 16E/I Matilda.

File 1 Page 33

NUMBER	N°	NAMES OF PERSONS	TOWNSHIPS 33
1007	1010	Jacob Anderson	
1008	1011	Adam Nudale	
1009	1012	Jacob Mercle sen.r	
1010	1013f	Christopher Mercle	
1011	1014f	Henry Mercle	
1012	1015	Jacob Mercle junior	
1013	1016	Josip* Brouse	Matilda
1014	1017	Peter Brouse	
1015	1018f	Gaspar Coons	
1016	1019f	Christian Tillebough jun.r*	
1017	1020f	Suffrinus* Cafsleman	
1018	1021f	Christian Tillebough jun.r*	Williamsburg
1019	1022	Abraham Hopper	
1020	1023	John McKitchie	
1021	1024	Jacob Rosenbarger	
1022	1025	John Glafsford (GLASSFORD)	Matilda
1023	1026	Robert Glafsford	
1024	1027	Michael Carman sen.r	
1025	1028	Michael Carman jun.r	
1026	1029	Martin Walliser	
1027	1030	William Rufsell (RUSSELL)	
1028	1031	Nicholas Frymire	
1029	1032	Jacob Garlough	
1030	1033f	John Crysler sen.r	
1031	1034f	Peter Garlough sen.r	
1032	1035f	Peter Garloch* jun.r	
1033	1036f	Henry Garloch*	
1034	1037	Jacob Vanallen	Matilda
1035	1038	Warner Cafsleman	Williamsburg
1036	1039	Henry Cafsleman (CASSLEMAN)	
1037	1040	Andrew Sipes	Matilda
1038	1041	Jacob Carman	
1039	1042	Jefse (JESSE) Wright	

NOTES:
1. No. 1014 - one of two HENRY MERKLEYs in Williamsburg; one became an MLA (1808-1812) and fought in the Militia at the Battle of Crysler's Farm November 1813.
2. Nos. 1019 & 1021 - one must be "Senior"; not much difference.
3. Nos. 1034/5/6 - note change in spelling; File 3 is consistent with "GARLOUGH".

File 1 Page 34

NUMBER	34 N°	NAMES OF PERSONS	TOWNSHIPS
1040	1043	Richard Cafsleman	Williamsburg
1041	1044	Florence McKarty	Matilda
1042	1045	John Helmer	Williamsburg
1043	1046	John Shell	
1044	1047	Benjamin Shell	Matilda
1045	1048	Daniel Shell	Williamsburg
1046	1049 f	Peter Tillibough	Williamsburg
1047	1050	Mary Alingdelp*	Williamsburg
1048	1051	Christopher Hains	
1049	1052	Joseph Hains	
1050	1053	John Hains	
1051	1054	Alexander Rose	
1052	1055	Saffrenus* Cafsleman jun^r.	
1053	1056	Conradt Cafsleman	
1054	1057	John McDonell	Matilda
1055	1058	Alexander McDonell	
1056	1059	James McDonell	
1057	1060	Martin Tillibough	
1058	1061	George Johnson	
1059	1062 f	Michael Mercle	Williamsburg
1060	1063	John Hicky	
1061	1064 f	Frederick Mercle	
1062	1065	John Shaver	Matilda
1063	1066	Conradt Shaver	
1064	1067	Nathan Brown	Augusta
1065	1068 f	Nicholas Ridman	Matilda
1066	1069	Jonas*Hood*	Williamsburg
1067	1070 f	Henry Waggoner	Matilda
1068	1071	Michael Rufsill* (RUSSILL)	
1069	1072	John Crouder	Osnabruck
1070	1073	Nicholas Miller	Williamsburg
1071	1074	John Dorin	Matilda
1072	1075	John Bishop	

NOTES:
1. No. 1069 - in File 3 spelled JONAH WOOD SNR. formerly of Williamsburg, now of Cornwall.
2. No. 1065 - JOHN SHAVER allotted Matilda 15W/I.
3. No. 1071 - MICHAEL RUSSEL allotted Matilda 21W/I.
4. No. 1063 - JOHN HICKEY allotted Williemsburg Lot 3E/I.
5. No.1050 - same spelling Files 1 & 3.

File 1 Page 35

NUMBER	N^{o}	NAMES OF PERSONS	TOWNSHIPS 35
1073	1076	Elias Butler	
1074	1077	Robert Averall	
1075	1078^{f}	John Pearse	Williamsburg
1076	1079^{f}	The Honble. John Munro*	Matilda
1077	1080^{f}	Hugh Munroe*	
1078	1081^{f}	Cornelius Munroe*	
1079	1082^{f}	John Munroe* junior	
1080	1083^{f}	Henry Munroe	
1081	1084^{f}	William Munroe	
1082	1085^{f}	Cornelia Munro*/alias Paterson	
1083	1086	Richard Duncan Esquire	Williamsburg
1084	1087	Allan McDonell	Matilda
1085	1088^{f}	Malcolm McMartin	Williamsburg
1086	1089^{f}	Thomas Castleman*	
1087	1090^{f}	Christie Munroe*/alias Mount	
		I do herby vouch for the hundred and sixty names last above mentioned	
	(Signed)	Allan Paterson J.P.	
1088	1091	Abel Stephens	Bastard
1089	1092	Dennis Burges	
1090	1093	Joseph Slack	
1091	1094	James Finch	Kitley
1092	1095	Benjamin Randolph	Yonge
1093	1096	Juber*Landers	
1094	1097	Samuel Scovils	Bastard
1095	1098	William Church	Yonge
1096	1099	Edward Haus	Kitley
1097	1100	John Yates	Bastard
1098	1101	Darius Crippon	
1099	1102	Jacob Hewit*	Yonge

NOTES:
1. No. 1079 to 1085 & No. 1090 - see spelling variations of MUNRO(E); is ALLAN PATERSON, the attestor at No. 1090, the second husband of CORNELIA MUNRO whose first husband was The Honourable JOHN MUNRO ? Capt. JOHN MUNRO allotted Lots 1 & 2/I of Matilda.
2. No. 1088 - Lieut. McMartin allotted Lot 26E & all 27/I of Williamsburg per McNiff's 1786 map.
3. No. 1089 - another spelling varient of CASSLEMAN.

File 1 Page 36

NUMBER	36 N°	NAMES OF PERSONS	TOWNSHIPS
1100	1103	John Munroe	
1101	1104	William Lochart	Escotte
1102	1105	Pennuel* Stephens	Bastard
1103	1106	James Stark	Elisabethtown
1104	1107	Asa Hutchinson	Yonge
1105	1108	Jonathan Tuttle	
1106	1109	Phoeneas* Baldwin	Lansdown
1107	1110	Zebeda* Miller	
1108	1111	Isaiah Cain	Yonge
1109	1112	Thomas Naulton	Elisabethtown
1110	1113	Kaleb* Simmons	
1111	1114	Joshua Bostwick	Augusta
1112	1115	Edmond Mott	Yonge
1113	1116	Moses Rose	Bastard
1114	1117	James Butler	Elisabethtown
1115	1118	Matthew Snyder	
1116	1119	Alexander McLean	
1117	1120	Thomas Hubert	Kitley
1118	1121	Thomas Elliot	Elisabethtown
1119	1122	Walter Davis	
1120	1123	Nathaniel Mallery	Yonge
1121	1124	William McNiel	Elisabethtown
1122	1125	Peter Trumble	Augusta
1123	1126	Dodley* Moor	
1124	1127	Jeremiah Fraser	
1125	1128	Simon Storey	Elisabethtown
1126	1129	Peter Dopp	Montague
1127	1130	William Martin	Augusta
1128	1131	John Cole	
1129	1132	Nathaniel Nettleton	
1130	1133	Jacob Elliot	Elisabethtown
1131	1134[f]	James Wilsie*	Yonge
1132	1135	John Barton	Augusta

NOTES:
1. No. 1134 - otherwise spelled WILTSIE/WILTSEY et var.

File 1 Page 37

NUMBER	N°	NAMES OF PERSONS	TOWNSHIPS 37
1133	1136	William Barton	Elisabethtown
1134	1137	William Reid	Yonge
1135	1138f	Amos Nettleton	Augusta
1136	1139	Joseph Easton*	Elisabethtown
1137	1140	George Mitchell	
1138	1141	Zalmon* Mitchell	
1139	1142	Harcuey* Mitchell	
1140	1143	Samuel Tuttle	
1141	1144	Henry French	
1142	1145	Peter Tuttle	
1143	1146	Charles Ward	
1144	1147	James Walker	
		I do hereby vouch for the eight names last above mentioned	
	(Signed)	Ephm. Jones J.P.	
1145	1148	Joseph Proctor	Yonge
1146	1149	Ranald McDonell	
1147	1150	George Starrs	
1148	1151	Henry Sanders	
1149	1152	Nathan Tuttle	
1150	1153	Duncan McAlpin*	
1151	1154	Thomas McKnight	
1152	1155	Ezekiel Parish	
1153	1156	John Thompson	
1154	1157	Samuel Adams	
1155	1158	Lieut. Gideon Adams	
1156	1159	Daniel Munro	
1157	1160	Samuel Rose	
1158	1161	John Wickoff	
1159	1162	Ezekiah* Brown	
1160	1163	Chese Pine	

NOTES: 1. One wonders who vouched for No. 1091 to 1139.

File 1 Page 38

NUMBER	38 N°	NAMES OF PERSONS	TOWNSHIPS
1161	1164	John Brundage	
1162	1165	John Scott sen.[r]	
1163	1166	Mosa Moor	
1164	1167	Andrew Adams	Edwardsburg
1165	1168	Elijah Curtis Adams	
1166	1169	James Froom junior	
1167	1170	David Froom	
		I do hereby vouch for the four names last above mentioned	
	(Signed)	Hugh Munro J.P.	
1168	1171	William Falkner Esq.[r]	Lancaster
1169	1172	Joseph Falkner	
1170	1173	Ralph Falkner Sen.[r]	
1171	1174	Walter Sutherland Esquire	
1172	1175	John Johnson Sutherland	
1173	1176	Thomas Sutherland	
1174	1177	Alexander Sutherland	
1175	1178	George Sutherland	
1176	1179	Donald Rofs (ROSS)	
1177	1180	Thomas Graham	
1178	1181	Murdock Graham	
1179	1182	John Graham	
1180	1183	Donald Culbert	Charlottenburg
1181	1184	William Grant	Lancaster
1182	1185	Alexander Grant	Charlottenburg
1183	1186	John Grant	Lancaster
1184	1187	John Dunn junior	
1185	1188	James Dunn	
1186	1189	John Curry	
1187	1190	James Curry	
1188	1191[f]	John Flynn	

NOTES:

1. No. 1191 - after the number in the first column, written astride the line separating that column from the "Names" column are the digits "33"; what the meaning is is unknown.
2. The writing on this and the preceding page is particularily large and clear.

File 1 Page 39

NUMBER	N^{o}	NAMES OF PERSONS	TOWNSHIPS 39
1189	1192	George Curry	
1190	1193	Margaret Curry / alias Picard	
1191	1194 f	Margaret Blakeley / alias Flynn	
1192	1195	John Gibson	
1193	1196	John Leman	
1194	1197 f	David McFall	
1195	1198	Capt. Willm. Morrison	
1196	1199	William Morrison	
1197	1200	Mary Morrison	
1198	1201	Richard Fountain	
1199	1202	Samuel Brown	
1200	1203 f	Thomas Busby	
1201	1204	Mary Edge Widow	
1202	1205	Samuel Teynick	
1203	1206	John Powell	
1204	1207	Donald McDonell	
1205	1208	Alexander Campbell	
1206	1209	Isabella Graham / alias McDonell	
1207	1210	Allan Campbell	
1208	1211	William Bland	
1209	1212 f	Elisabeth Campbell Widow	
1210	1213	Peter McIntosh	
1211	1214	Benjamin McIntosh	Charlottenburg
1212	1215	John Castles	Lancaster
1213	1216	Hugh McKay	Charlottenburg
1214	1217	John McKay	
1215	1218	Duncan Cameron	
1216	1219	John McDonell	
1217	1220	Ranald McDonell	
1218	1221	Alexander Grant	
1219	1222	Nelly McDonell Widow	
1220	1223 f	John Mustard	

NOTES:
1. No. 1197 - Lieut. D. McFall allotted Lot 4(all)/I Lancaster.
2. No. 1212 - Widow Campbell allotted Lot 12(all)/I Lancaster.
3. No. 1203 - Thomas Busby allotted Lot 16(all)/I Lancaster.
4. No. 1194 - Widow Blakeley allotted Lot 15(all)/II Lancaster.
5. No. 1194 - a John Flynn allotted Lot 10(all)/III Lancaster.
6. No. 1223 - John Mustard allotted Lot 57W/ I Concession north of the River aux Raisins.

File 1 Page 40

NUMBER	40 N°	NAMES OF PERSONS	TOWNSHIPS
1221	1224	Alexander Grant	Charlottenburg
1222	1225	David Gunn	Lancaster
1223	1226	William Noble	
1224	1227	Hugh Cameron	Charlottenburg
1225	1228	William Dixon	
1226	1229	Robert Dixon senior	
1227	1230	Robert Dixon junior	
1228	1231	John McArther* sen.r	
1229	1232	Donald McArther*.	
1230	1233	John McArther J.r*	
1231	1234	Duncan McArther	
1232	1235	Peter McArther	
1233	1236	Archibald McArther	
1234	1237	John Hagard	
1235	1238	Peter Hagard	
1236	1239	John Cameron Sen.r	
1237	1240	John Cameron Jun.r	
1238	1241	Duncan Grant	
1239	1242	Hugh McGregor	
1240	1243	John McMartin	
1241	1244	Malcolm McMartin	
1242	1245	Peter Grant	
1243	1246	Philip Rofs (ROSS)	
1244	1247	Alexander Rofs (ROSS)	
1245	1248	Thomas Munroe	
1246	1249 f	John McLeland jun.r*	
1247	1250 f	John McLeland jun.r*	
1248	1251	Keneth* McLeland	
1249	1252	Richard McBane	
1250	1253	Augustus Sealye*	Lancaster
1251	1254 f	Isabella McBane / alias McD. / (McDonell ?)	Charlottenburg
1252	1255 ff	William McLeod	

NOTES:
1. Nos. 1249/50 - File 3 corrects there being two "Juniors".
2. No. 1255 - there is a digit "2" after the No. 1255 - meaning?
3. No. 1254 - Widow McBane allotted Lot 21W/II Concession south of River aux Raisins in Charlottenburg.
4. No. 1255 - Sgt. William McLeod allotted Lot 13W/ Concession south of the South Branch of the River aux Raisins.

File 1 Page 41

NUMBER	N^{o}	NAMES OF PERSONS	TOWNSHIPS 41
1253	1256	Isabella McLeod Widow	
1254	1257	Thomas McLeod	
1255	1258	Alexander McDonell	
1256	1259	Duncan McArther	
1257	1260	David Whealer	
1258	1261	Joseph Fitchet	
1259	1262	Peter McIntosh	Lancaster
1260	1263	John Fraser	
1261	1264	Mary Fraser / alias McNeal	
1262	1265	Thomas Fraser	
1263	1266	Robert Gordon	Charlottenburg
1264	1267	Benjamin Baker	Lancaster
1265	1268	Alexander Ferguson	Edwardsburg
1266	1269	Robert Parker	
1267	1270	Thomas Taylor Rofs (ROSS)	Lancaster
1268	1271	James Sealey	
1269	1272	Michael Whalin	Charlottenburg
1270	1273	John Stuart Sutherland	
1271	1274	Walter Sutherland	
1272	1275	John Scaret	
1273	1276	John Grant	
		I do hereby vouch for the one hundred and six names last above mentioned	
	(Signed)	Walter Sutherland J.P.	
1274	1277	Roswell Rufsell (RUSSELL)	
		I do hereby vouch for the above named Roswell Rufsell	
	(Signed)	Thos. Fraser J.P.	

NOTES:

File 1 Page 42

42

We do hereby Certify that the foregoing Roll containing twelve hundred and seventy seven names of Loyalists or U.E.[s] has been duly taken and made pursuant to His Excellency Lieutenant Governor Simcoes* Proclamation bearing date the sixth day of April last, before us the subscribers and others our afsociates Justices of our Sovereign Lord the King afsigned to keep the Peace &c[a] at the Michaelmas Court of General Quarter sefsions of the Peace holden* at the Town of New Johnstown in and for the Eastern District of the Province of Upper Canada on the second Tuesday the eleventh day of October in the year of our Lord one thousand seven hundred and ninety six and continued by Adjournment till the third Tuesday the fifteenth day of November in the same year.

In Testimony whereof we have hereunto set our hands and affixed the seal of the said court at New Johnstown aforesaid this fifteenth day of November in the year of our Lord one thousand seven hundered* and ninety six.

Signed / Ephr.[m] Jones Chairman
Tho.[s] Fraser J.P.
Allan Paterson J.P.

A Copy from the Original in the Crown Office.

David Burns
Clk of the Crown &c.

TRANSCRIBER'S NOTE:

This certification is part of the journal and is on a page lined as all the foregoing pages; these columns have not been duplicated here as they would impair the transcription and the reading.

File 1 Page 43

NUMBER	N^{o}	NAMES OF PERSONS	TOWNSHIPS 43
	A Contin	uation of the Roll of U.E.^{s}	or Loyalists for the
	Eastern	District, taken and made at	a Court of General
	Quarter	Sefsions of the Peace, hold	en* in and for the said
	District	on the tenth day of October	1797 and from that day
	to the f	irst day of November in the	same year in pursuance
	of an Or	der from His Honor Peter Ru	fsell Esquire
	Administ	rator of the Province of Up	per Canada for extending
	the time	untill* the said first day	of November, for the
	enrollin	g of such U.E.^{s}, as had not	been enrolled under the
	Proclama	tion of His Excellency Lieu	tenant Governor Simcoe,
	bearing	date the sixth day of April	1796
1275	1	Jonathan Mills Church	Elisabethtown
1276	2	Levy Salvester	
1277	3	Ebenezer King	
1278	4	Abijah Hawley	
1279	5	John McLeane	
1280	6	William Campbell	
		I do hereby vouch for the	
		six names last above menti	oned
	/Signed/	Thos. Campbell J.P.	
1281	7	Edward Brown	Augusta
		I do hereby vouch for the	
		person last above mentione	d
	/Signed/	Gideon Adams J.P.	
1282	8	Roger Stevens	
		I do hereby vouch for the	
		above named Roger Stevens	
	/Signed/	Saml. Wright J.P.	

NOTES:

File 1 Page 44

NUMBER	44 N°	NAMES OF PERSONS	TOWNSHIPS
1283	9f	Robert McLean	Elisabethtown
1284	10f	Thadeus Carter*	Augusta
1285	11f	John Snyder	Augusta
1286	12f	John Myres*	Elisabethtown
1287	13f	Abraham Brown	Augusta
1288	14f	Johial Mitchel	Bastard
1289	15f	Nicholas Haskins	
1290	16f	John Wiltsie*	Yonge
1291	17f	Western Allan	
1292	18f	Duncan McLean	Augusta
1293	19	Frederick Johnson	Yonge
1294	20	John Gardiner	
1295	21	John Dawson	
		I do hereby vouch for the two names last above mentioned /Signed/ Ephr^m. Jones J.P.	
1296	22	Sylvester More	
1297	23	David Haskins	
		I do hereby vouch for the two names last above mentioned /Signed/ W^m. Fraser J.P.	
1298	24	Cornelius Losee*	Matilda
1299	25	William Parish	Yonge
1300	26	Margaret Armstrong alias Welch	Edwardsburg
1301	27	Rebecca Deforrest	Leeds
		I do hereby vouch for the two names last above mentioned /Signed/ Alex^r. Campbell J. P.	

NOTES:

1. Nos. 9 to 19 not vouched for by anyone.
2. These added names are found in File 3 at the end of each alphabetical listing as "blanks" in the Numbers Column.
3. No. 10 - in File 3, spelling is "CURTIS".

File 1 Page 45

NUMBER	N°	NAMES OF PERSONS	TOWNSHIPS 45
1302	28	William Wood	
1303	29	John Wood	
1304	30	Benjamin Wood	
1305	31	Roger Wood	
1306	32	Stephen Wood	
1307	33	Jonas Wood jun.r	
1308	34	Nathaniel Wood	
1309	35f	David Morrison	
1310	36f	Robert McGloclon*	
1311	37	David McGloclon*	
1312	38	Michael Myres	
1313	39f	Adam Papts*	
1314	40	Nicholas Schaffer *	
1315	41	Gottlieb Otto	
1316	42	William Baxter	
1317	43	John Lang	
1318	44	Peter Carpenter	
1319	45	David Sheek	
1320	46	William Bruce	
1321	47	David Bruce	
1322	48f	Tunis Bender	
1323	49	Margaret Bruce	
1324	50	Richard Mandaville	
1325	51f	Alexander Bruce	
1326	52	Margaret Bruce J.r	
1327	53	Sally Bruce	
1328	54	Richard Wragg	
1329	55	Thomas Wragg	
1330	56	William Fortune	Hawkesbury
1331	57	Joseph Fortune	
		I do hereby vouch for the thirty names last above mentioned	
		/Signed/ S. Anderson J.P.	

NOTES:

1. Nos. 36/7 - a phonetic spelling never seen before by this transcriber; otherwise spelled 'McLAUGHLIN' et var.
2. No. 52 - note another of this name at No. 49 - thus, the use of the designation "Junior" for a woman.
3. No. 40 - this would be the root spelling of SHAFFER/SHAVER.

File 1 Page 46

NUMBER	46 N°	NAMES OF PERSONS	TOWNSHIPS
1332	59*[f]	David McCready I do hereby vouch for the name last above mentioned Tho.[s] Fraser J.P.	Elisabethtown
		We do hereby Certify that the foregoing Roll of U.E.[s] containing fifty eight names, has been duly taken and made at the Michaelmas General Quarter sefsions of the Peace, holden* in and for the Eastern District, on the tenth day of October, one thousand seven hundred and ninety seven; And also after that Court untill* the first day of November in the same year.	
	SEAL	In testimony whereof we have hereunto set our hands and caused the seal of the said Court to be hereunto affixed at Edwardsburg, in the said District the fifteenth day of December in the year 1797.	
	/Signed/	J. Farrand Clk. P East. Dist.	/Signed/ Hugh Munro Presiding J. W.[m] Fraser J.P. Tho.[s] Fraser J.P.
1333	(blank)	Thomas Sherwood) by order of Council	17th June 1798
1334	(blank)	George Hintner)	
1335	(blank)	David Jacocks)	

NOTES:

1. No. 58 - does not exist; note the certification is only for 58 names not 59.
2. File 1 - consists of Pages 1 to 46 inclusive; pages 47 to 55 are blank; page 56 is the cover and reads "U.E. Roll/ Eastern District/ - 1797 -"

File 2

A Continuation of the Roll of U.E.^{s} or Loyalists for the Eastern District, taken and made at a Court of General Sefsions of the Peace holden* in and for the said District on the tenth day of October 1797, and from that day to the first day of November in the same year, in pursuance of an order from His Honor Peter Rufsell Esquire, Administrator of the Province of Upper Canada, for extending the time, untill* the said first day of November, for the enrolling of such U.E.'s as had not been enrolled under the proclamation of his Excellency Lieutenant Governor Simcoe, bearing date the sixth day of April 1796.

We do hereby certify that the foregoing Roll of U.E.'s containing fifty eight names, has been duly taken and made at the Michaelmas General Quarter Sefsions of the Peace, holden* in and for the Eastern District, on the tenth day of October, one thousand seven hundred and ninety seven; And also after that Court untill* the first day of November, in the same year.

In testimony whereof, we have hereunto set our hands, and caused the seal of the said Court to be hereunto affixed, at Edwardsburg, in the said District, the fifteenth day of November, in the year 1797.

Hugh Munro Presiding J.
J. Farrand Clk. P — W^{m}. Fraser J.P.
East. Dist:- — Thos. Fraser J.P.

NOTES:

1. The continuation paragraph first above is found at the top of the list beginning on Page 2 of this File. It is placed here purely for convenience.
2. The lower certification is also extracted from its proper position which is at the lower right of the page.
3. The liberal use of punctuation in these two paragraphs surprised the transcriber also.
4. The cover of File 2 is simply labelled " Continuation of the Roll of U.E.L.^{s} Eastern District 15 Dec 1797."

File 2

NUMBER	Nº	NAMES OF PERSONS	TOWNSHIPS
1341	1	Jonathan Mills Church	Elizabethtown
1342	2	Levy Salvester	
1343	3	Ebenezer King	
1344	4	Abija* Haley*	
1345	5	John McLean	
1346	6	William Campbell	
		I do hereby vouch for the six names last above mentioned	
		Alexr. Campbell J.P.	
1347	7	Edward Brown	Augusta
		I do hereby vouch for the person last above mentioned	
		Gidn. Adams J.P.	
1348	8	Roger Stevens	
		I do hereby vouch for the above named Roger Stevens	
		Saml. Wright J.P.	
1349	9	Robert McLean	Elizabethtown
1350	10	Thadeus Carter*	Augusta
1351	11	John Snyder	Augusta
1352	12	John Myres*	Elizabethtown
1353	13	Abraham Brown	Augusta
1354	14	Ichial Mitchel	Bastard
1355	15	Nicholas Haskins	
1356	16	John Wiltsie	Yonge
1357	17	Western Allan	
1358	18	Duncan McLean	Augusta
1359	19	Frederick Johnson	Yonge
1360	20	John Gardiner	
1361	21	John dauson*	
		I do hereby vouch for the two names last above mentioned	
		Ephm. Jones J.P.	

NOTES:

1. Except for a few spelling variations, this is the same as Pages 43/4/5/6 of File 1. The writing is much poorer than File 1 and is obviously the original as some of the signatures are almost unreadable.
2. The "Z" of Elizabethtown flows with a tail below the line here; in File 1 & 3 it is more like an "s" or "r". Thus, the difference in this spelling between Files 1/3 & 2.

File 2

NUMBER	N^{o}	NAMES OF PERSONS	TOWNSHIPS
1362	22	Sylvester More	Edwardsburg
1363	23	david* Haskins	Augusta
		I do hereby vouch for the two names last above mentioned	
		W^{m}. Fraser J.P.	
1364	24	Cornelius Losee	Matilda
1365	25	William Parish	Yonge
1366	26	Margaret/armstrong*/alias Welch/	Edwardsburg
1367	27	Rebecca deforrest*	Leeds
		I do hereby vouch for the two names last above mentioned	
		Alex^{r}. Campbell J.P.	
1368	28	William Wood	
1369	29	John Wood	
1370	30	Benjamin Wood	
1371	31	Roger Wood	
1372	32 f	Stephen Wood	
1373	33 f	Jonas Wood Ju^{r}.	
1374	34	Nathaniel Wood	
1375	35	David Morrison	
1376	36 f	Robert McGoclon*	
1377	37 f	David McGloclon*	
1378	38	Michael Myres	
1379	39	Adam Papts	
1380	40	Nicholas Schaffer	
1381	41	Gottleib Otto	
1382	42	William Baxter	
1383	43	John Lang	
1384	44	Peter Carpenter	
1385	45	David Sheek	
1386	46	William Bruce	
1387	47	David Bruce	
1388	48	Tunis Bender	
1389	49 f	Margaret Bruce	
1390	50	Richard Mandaville	
1391	51	Alexander Bruce	
1392	52 f	Margaret Bruce J^{r}.	
1393	53	Sally Bruce	

NOTES:

1. No.32 - this ends the first column; No. 33 starts 2nd col^{n}.
2. No. 36/7 - note the spelling error even in this phonetic spelling of McLaughlin.
3. Nos. 49 & 52 - use of junior with women's names.

File 2

NUMBER	N°	NAMES OF PERSONS	TOWNSHIPS
1394	54	Richard Wragg	
1395	55	Thomas Wragg	
1396	56	William Fortune	Hawksbury *[f]
1397	57	Joseph Fortune	
		I do hereby vouch for the thirty names last above mentioned	
		J. Anderson J.P.	
1398	58[f]	David McCready	
		I do hereby vouch for the name last above mentioned	
		Thos. Fraser J.P.	
		(The certification on Page 1 next follows in the lower part of the third & fourth columns).	

NOTES:

1. Note that the omission of No. 58 and its substitution by No. 59 does not occur in File 2 (the original) as it does in File 1, Page 46.
2. There is even a variation in the spelling of Hawk(e)sbury between here and File 1.

File 3 Page 1

A 1

An Alphabetical List of UE Loyalists in the Eastern District

NUMBER	N°	NAMES	TOWNSHIP	REMARKS
1401	6	Appleby William	Edwardsburg	
1402	102	Avery Joseph	Augusta	
1403	161	Arkenbrack John	do	
1404	195	Andrews Benjamin	Elisabethtown	
1405	219	Armstrong Thomas	Edwardsburg	
1406	221	Armstrong John		
1407	222	Armstrong Thomas Junr.		
1408	224	Adams Joel		
1409	241	Anderson Henry		
1410	252	Adams Ezray		
1411	264	Adams Will. Samuel		
1412	265	Adams James		
1413	486	Anderson Elisha	Cornwall	
1414	487	Anderson James	son of Samuel	
1415	488	Anderson Cyrus	do	
1416	489	Anderson Thomas G.	do	
1417	490	Anderson George	do	
1418	505	Anderson Joseph	do	
1419	506	Anderson Ebenezer	do	
1420	520	Anderson Capt. Sam.[1]		
1421	521	Anderson John Senr.	son of Benjamin	
1422	522	Anderson John Junr.	son of Samuel	
1423	526	Anderson Richard	son of Benjamin	
1424	568	Amor Philip		
1425	570	Amor Peter		
1426	584	Austin Christ.[r] Widow		
1427	592	Algire Jacob Senr.		
1428	593	Algire Martin		
1429	594	Algire Jacob		
1430	597	Anderson Benjamin	Brother of Samuel	
1431	637	Anable* John		
1432	741	Aman Jacob	Osnabruck	
1433	743	Aman John		
1434	757	Albrant Francis		
1435	762	Alt Nicholas		

NOTES:
1. Under the word "District" in the heading are the faint words "To be arranged alphabetically - W.C."
2. The "Remarks" column is seldom used as such; the "Township" column is used in lieu and the writing flows as needed.
3. The last named township appears to apply without use of dittoes until a change is necessary.
4. The asterix "*" is used to indicate "sic" = as written.

File 3 Page 2

	A			2
NUMBER	N°	NAMES	TOWNSHIP	REMARKS
1436	(780)[f]	Amon Laurence		
1437	950	Avery Joseph	Matilda	
1438	956	Ault Michael	do	
1439	957[f]	Ault John	do X omitted[f]	
1440	958	Ault Everhart	do	
1441	1004	Albrant Henry	do	
1442	1010	Anderson Jacob	Williamsburg	
1443	1050	Alingdelp Mary		
1444	1077	Averall Robert	Matilda	
1445	1157	Adams Samuel	Yonge	
1446	1158	Adams Gideon Lieut.		
1447	1167	Adams Andrew	Edwardsburg	
1448	1168	Adams Elijah Curtis		
1449	403	Aerheart* John	Elisabethtown	
1450	801	Aerheart Simon	Edwardsburg	
1451	(blank)	Allan Western		
1452	(blank)	Armstrong Margaret alias Welch	Edwardsburg	

NOTES:
1. No. 957 "omitted" faint writing; likely by Campbell.
2. No. (780) - the brackets indicate this is assumed as paper destroyed.
3. *= sic
4. No. 957 - the "X" or "X omitted" appear to have been added by some functionary post 1797; they seem to question tha accuracy of the name as a true UEL.

File 3 Page 3

B 3

NUMBER	N^o	NAMES	TOWNSHIP	REMARKS
1453	2	Black Jonathan	Augusta	
1454	19	Bush Charles	Osnabruck	
1455	26	Burrit Daniel	Augusta	
1456	28 f	Burrit Adoniram	do	
1457	31	Bissle Joseph	do	
1458	33	Booth John	do	
1459	34	Baker Elishua	do	
1460	38	Butler Freelove Senior	Elisabethtown	
1461	39 f	Butler Freelove Junr	Augusta	
1462	47 f	Buel Timothy		
1463	48 f	Buel* Bemsley		
1464	49	Buel Jonathan		
1465	50	Buel Samuel		
1466	53	Beach Stephen Jod		
1467	76	Brown Thomas		
1468	77	Brown Nathaniel		
1469	80	Bryan John		
1470	96 f	Bottom Elijah, Ensign		
1471	99	Bennet Corporal		
1472	111	Berrard Alexander		
1473	114	Batman Samuel		
1474	131	Bunker John		
1475	133	Bunker Bathael		
1476	134	Barton Thomas		
1477	150	Beygar* Christopher		
1478	159 f	Burrit Stephen		
1479	191	Bissle David		
1480	193	Birdsall Jermiah	Elisabethtown	
1481	197	Barton Joseph	Augusta	
1482	220	Bolton Richard	Edwardsburg	X omitted
1483	232	Bonistal Jacob		
1484	238	Boid* Thomas Senr.		
1485	239	Boid* Thomas Jun.		
1486	240	Boid* James		
1487	297	Belton George	Elisabethtown	
1488	309 f	Boyce John	Matilda	
1489	317	Brackenride* James	~~Leeds~~ ~~Duke of Leeds~~	
1490	340 f	Bostwick Joshua	Augusta	
1491	351 f	Brown Jesse Senr.		(see footnote
1492	362	Brackenridge David	Elisabethtown	page 3 contd.)

NOTES:

1. Page 3 continued.
2. Nos. 31 & 191 spelled BIFSLE.
3. Nos. 47,48 & 49 otherwise spelled BUELL.
4. No. 99 - no first or given name shown.
5. No. 317 - "Leeds" & "Duke of Leeds" stroked through. This entry has been inserted between Nos. 309 & 340. Compare two spellings of this name, ie, Nos. 317 & 362.

File 3 Page 3 cont'd

NUMBER	N°	NAMES	TOWNSHIP	REMARKS
1493	364[f]	Brown Jesse Sen[r].		
1494	366	Booth Zeaks		
1495	367	Booth Abner		
1496	368	Booth Bethia*		
1497	369	Booth Phebe		
1498	370	Booth Charles		

NOTES: 1. Nos. 364 & 351 - identical entries; same person with two entries or two persons of same name ? One could be a mistake for junior.

File 3 Page 4

	B			4
NUMBER	N°	NAMES	TOWNSHIP	REMARKS
1499	371	Booth Samuel	Elisabethtown	
1500	372	Booth Vincent		
1501	373 f	Booth Isaac		
1502	388 f	Buck Berecci*	X	
1503	396	Brown James		
1504	401 f	Buck George	X	
1505	402 f	Buel* Timothy		
1506	406	Brown Jesse		
1507	474	Barnhart George	Cornwall	
1508	475	Barnhart Jacob		
1509	476	Barnhart Nicholas		
1510	535	Bender George		
1511	549	Bough Frederick Senr		
1512	550	Bough Frederick Junr		
1513	551	Bough John		
1514	555	Bender Tunis	son of Geo.	
1515	560	Buttersworth James	X	omitted
1516	576	Bready Luke		
1517	602	Baily* Levi*		
1518	604	Baily John Son of Levi		
1519	691	Branan William		
1520	773	Bradshaw John	Osnabruck	
1521	782	Baker Adam Senior		
1522	783	Baker Adam Junr.		
1523	784	Baker John		
1524	785	Baker William		
1525	786	Baker Martin		
1526	812	Bulson Cornelius	Williamsburg	
1527	826	Byrne William Esquire	Charlottenburg	
1528	848	Bethune John Rev(erend)		
1529	897 f	Bethune Angus		
1530	931 f	Bouk Frederick	Williamsburg	
1531	932 f	Bouk Adam		
1532	933 f	Bouk Christian Senr		
1533	939 f	Brouse Peter		
1534	940	Brouse George		
1535	949	Baker Henry	Matilda	
1536	954	Baker Conradt	Williamsburg	
1537	969	Bowen Luke	Matilda	
1538	989	Berkeley Aver	Williamsburg	

NOTES:
1. Page 4 continued.
2. No. 388 - good 2nd choice BERECEL.
3. No. 402 - see page 3. Repeat ?
4. Nos. 931/2/3 - otherwise written BOUCH/BOUCK.
5. No. 939 - a PETER BROUSE was allotted Matilda I/22W per McNiff's 1787 map. See No. 1017 on Page 4 contd.
6. See note 4 on Page 2 re: "X".
7. "*"= sic. 8. No. 388 - on File 3 no doubt it is BEECK.

File 3 Page 4 cont'd

NUMBER	N°	NAMES	TOWNSHIP	REMARKS
1539	1005	Benedict John	Matilda	
1540	1006	Benedict Joseph		
1541	1016 f	Brouse Joseph		
1542	1017	Brouse Peter		
1543	1067	Brown Nathan	Augusta	
1544	1075	Bishop John	Matilda	
1545	(10)76	Butler Elias		

NOTES: 1. No. 1017 - see page 4, Note No. 5.

File 3 Page 5

5

NUMBER	Nº	NAMES	TOWNSHIP		REMARKS
1546	1092	Burges Dennis	Bastard		
1547	1109	Baldwin Phoenias	Lansdown		
1548	1114	Bostwick Joshua	Augusta		
1549	1117	Butler James	Elisabethtown		
1550	1135	Barton John	Augusta		
1551	1136	Barton William	Elisabethtown		
1552	1162	Brown Erekiah	Yonge		
1553	1164	Brundage John			
1554	1194[f]	Blakeley Margaret	Lancaster		(alias Flynn)
1555	1202	Brown Samuel			
1556	1203	Busby Thomas			
1557	1211	Bland William			
1558	1267	Baker Benjamin			
1559	109[f]	Beache's Heirs	Augusta	X	
1560	(blank)	Brown Edward	ditto		
1561	(blank)	Brown Abraham			
1562	(blank)	Baxter William			
1563	(blank)	Bruce William	Cornwall		
1564	(blank)	Bruce David	ditto		
1565	(blank)	Bender Tunis	ditto		
1566	(blank)	Bruce Margaret	ditto		
1567	(blank)	Bruce Alexander	ditto		
1568	(blank)	Bruce Margaret Jun[r].	ditto		
1569	(blank)	Bruce Sarah	ditto		
1570	(blank)	Buck Mihitable	(blank)		

NOTES:

1. No. 1194 - from other information in the Haldimand Papers, Mrs.Margt. BLAKELEY was a widow Sept./Oct. 1784 with three daughters under 10 years of age at Montreal; her husband, a member of Jessup's Corps, had abandonned her there and she was shown "in great distress". She apparently remarried a man named FLYNN.
2. No. 109 shows spelling there as "BEECHES".
3. See note 4, page 2 re:"X".

File 3 Page 6

C 6

NUMBER	N°	NAMES	TOWNSHIP	REMARKS
1571	3	Cook Michael	Edwardsburg	
1572	60	Carley Barthalomew	Augusta	
1573	64[f]	Case Josiah	Grand River	
1574	78	Classon Caleb	Augusta	
1575	79	Campbell James		
1576	187	Carrigan Peter		
1577	95[f]	Crass Henry		
1578	113	Campbell Alexander		
1579	117	Chambers James		
1580	123	Cluny James		
1581	129	Chester John		
1582	132	Corbin Nathaniel		
1583	179[f]	Covill Simeon		
1584	182	Chambers James		
1585	189	Campbell Allen	Elisabethtown	
1586	194	Chisholm John	Cornwall	
1587	223	Cameron Duncan	Edwardsburg	
1588	246	Curry Ephraim		
1589	267	Curry James		
1590	280	Campbell Allan		
1591	281	Campbell Alexander Junior		
1592	282	Campbell James		
1593	283	Campbell Alexander Esq[r].		
1594	291	Cole Adam	Elisabethtown	
1595	298[f]	Clew William*		
1596	299[f]	Clow Henry*		
1597	330	Covil John	Augusta	
1598	341[f]	Crone John		
1599	346	Campbell Duncan		
1600	347	Campbell Ami		
1601	353	Campbell George		
1602	394	Chiltsey Baria	Elisabethtown	
1603	398	Caswell Samuel		
1604	405	Campbell George		
1605	438	Caldwell John	Charlottenburg	
1606	440	Cameron John		
1607	469	Cameron John Jun[r].	Cornwall	
1608	470	Cameron Alexander Sen[r].		

NOTES:
1. Page 6 continued.
2. No. 95 - spelled "CROSS" at No. 95. (CRAFS/CROFS).
3. No. 179 - good 2nd choices are CAVILL/CEVILL.
4. Nos. 298/9 - interpreted as written.
5. No. 341 -good 2nd choice CRANE.
6. No. 64 - see footnote No. 6 on page 7. See Note No. 6 on Page 26.

File 3 Page 6 cont'd

NUMBER	N°	NAMES	TOWNSHIP	REMARKS
1609	479	Carr William		
1610	507	Clerke Francis		
1611	540	Cryderman Hermanus		
1612	542	Cryderman John		
1613	561	Christie John Sen.r		
1614	562	Christie Abijah		
1615	563	Christie John Jun.r		
1616	(5)67	Cryderman Joseph		

NOTES:

File 3 Page 7

C 7

NUMBER	N°	NAMES	TOWNSHIP	REMARKS
1617	573	Cline Michael		
1618	574	Cline John Son of Michael		
1619	575	Cline George ditto		
1620	577	Cameron Allan		
1621	578	Cameron Alexander jun^r.		
1622	579	Cameron Hugh Junior		
1623	580	Cameron Daniel		
1624	581	Cameron John Junr.		
1625	582	Cameron Hugh Senr.		
1626	591	Campbell Daniel		
1627	596	Cumming William		
1628	624	Cameron Donald (lot) 15	5th concefsion	
1629	625	Cameron William		
1630	671	Cameron John	Lancaster	
1631	678	Cameron Alexander		
1632	705	Crysler Philip	Cornwall	
1633	706f	Crysler John Junr.		
1634	707	Crysler (no 2nd name)		
1635	721	Cashier John	Charlottenburg	
1636	735	Cadman John Senior	Osnabruck	
1637	736f	Cadman John Junr.		
1638	752f	Coons John		
1639	767f	Cough John		
1640	774f	Countryman Jacob jun^r.	son of Jacob Senr.	
1641	775f	Countryman Jacob Senr.		
1642	776f	Countryman Conradt	son of Jacob Senr.	
1643	789	Crouder William Senr.		
1644	790	Crouder James		
1645	791	Crouder Anthony		
1646	792	Crouder Isaac		
1647	793	Crouder William Junr.		
1648	794f	Crouder John		
1649	795f	Crouder William 3^d		
1650	807f	Case Josiah Junr.	Grand River	
1651	808	Case Peter		
1652	809	Case Walter		

NOTES:
1. Page 7 continued.
2. No. 707 - no 2nd name at original list No. 707.
3. No.752 - COONS is the anglicization of the German name KUHNS.
4. Nos. 774/5/6 - COUNTRYMAN is anglicization of LAND(E)MAN.
5. No. 795 - son of JAMES (No. 790 above) and UE in his own right.
6. No. 807 - see No. 64 on page 6 . Same name - father & son ? This Grand River is the Ottawa River.

File 3 Page 7 cont'd

NUMBER	N°	NAMES	TOWNSHIP	REMARKS
1653	814f	Cruickshanks Widow	Escotte	
1654	828	Campbell Daniel Senr.	Charlottenburg	
1655	829	Campbell Daniel Junr.		
1656	839	Cain John		
1657	866	Cameron Angus		
1658	867f	Cameron Archibald		
1659	868f	Cameron Alexander	X 4th	
1660	869	Cameron Duncan		omitted
1661	870	Cameron William		
1662	871	Cameron Donald		

NOTES:
1. No. 814 -"The Widow Crook Shanks" is shown in the Haldimand Papers (FAMILIES 24:Vol.1;p8) at Montreal Sep./Oct. 1784 with three daughters - one over 10 - "Man lately dead. Family in distress".
2. No. 868 - see note 4, page 2 re:"X". The "4th" likely means the 4th time a name of these words has appeared on these rolls.

File 3 Page 8

C

8

NUMBER	N°	NAMES	TOWNSHIP	REMARKS
1663	890	Clark James	Charlottenburg	
1664	906	Colders* William	Lancaster	
1665	910	Chisholm Donald		
1666	911	Chisholm Lewis		
1667	912	Chisholm Duncan		
1668	913	Chisholm William		
1669	914	Chisholm Hugh		
1670	915	Chisholm Allan		
1671	916	Chisholm Alexander Sen[r].		
1672	917	Chisholm Alexander		
1673	941	Coons Jacob	Williamsburg	
1674	942	Coons Conradt		
1675	968	Carman George		
1676	973	Callison John		
1677	974	Carns Jacob		
1678	975	Carns Christian		
1679	999	Cook Michael	Williamsburg	
1680	1000	Cook George		
1681	1007	Crouse John	Matilda	
1682	1018	Coons Gaspar		
1683	1020[f]	Cassleman Suffrenus		
1684	1027	Carman Michael Sen[r].		
1685	1028	Carman Michael Jun[r].		
1686	1033	Crysler John Sen[r].		
1687	1038[f]	Cafsleman Warner*	Williamsburg	
1688	1039[f]	Cafsleman* Henry		
1689	1041	Carman Jacob	Matilda	
1690	1043[f]	Cafsleman Richard	Williamsburg	
1691	1055[f]	Cafsleman Suffrenus Jun[r].		
1692	1056[f]	Cafsleman Conradt		
1693	1072	Crouder John	Osnabruck	
1694	1089[f]	Castleman Thomas	Williamsburg	
1695	1098	Church William	Yonge	
1696	1101	Crippon Darius	Bastard	

NOTES:

1. Page 8 continued.
2. The spelling of CAFSLEMAN/CASSLEMAN on this page is as in the original in each instance - and exemplifies how the double "s" was written in the 1700s; in some cases, the single "s" was written as a lower case "f" in modern writing.
3. No. 1089 - another spelling variation of CASSLEMAN.
4. "*"= sic.

File 3 Page 8 cont'd

NUMBER	N°	NAMES	TOWNSHIP	REMARKS
1697	1111	Cain Isaiah	Yonge	
1698	1131	Cole John	Augusta	
1699	1183 f	Culbert Donald	Charlottenburg	
1700	1189 f	Curry John	Lancaster	
1701	1190 f	Curry James		
1702	1192 f	Curry George		
1703	1193	Curry Margaret	alias Picard	
1704	1208	Campbell Alexander		
1705	1210	Campbell Allan		
1706	1212 f	Campbell Elisabeth	(Widow)	
1707	1215	Castles John		
1708	1218	Cameron Duncan	Charlottenburg	

NOTES:

1. No. 1212 - The note "(Widow)" is in the "NAMES" Column.
2. It is assumed all the "CURRYs" are located in Lancaster Twsp. as are all those named after them, ie, the dittoes are missing.

File 3 Page 9

C 9

NUMBER	N°	NAMES	TOWNSHIP	REMARKS
1709	(12)27	Cameron Hugh	Charlottenburg	
1710	(12)39	Cameron John Sen.r		
1711	(12)40	Cameron John Jun.r		
1712	586	Cryderman Catherine	Widow Cornwall	
1713	(54)6	Crites George		
1714	(71)6	Claus William Captain		
1715	(blank)	Church Jonathan Mills f	Elisabethtown	
1716	(blank)	Campbell William	ditto	
1717	(blank)	Curtis Thadeus	Augusta	
1718	(blank)	Carpenter Peter	Cornwall	
		(This is the end of the "C"s; the lower half of page 9 continues with the "D"s - see page 9 contd.)		

NOTES: 1. The edges of the original page have been destroyed - hence some writing in "N°" column is in brackets.
2. Entry after No. 716 - this name written elsewhere in this transcription as possibly "Jonathan Churchmills".

File 3 Page 9 cont'd

NUMBER	N°	NAMES	TOWNSHIP	REMARKS
		D		
1719	12	Derry London	Edwardsburg	
1720	23[f]	Daviss William	Elisabethtown	
1721	88	Disson John	Augusta	
1722	112	Dunham Daniel		
1723	142	Dulmage Philip		
1724	167	Dunham John		
1725	168	Dunham James		
1726	173	Dulmage John		
1727	174	Dulmage Elias		
1728	196[f]	Deboyce Ichida	Elisabethtown	
1729	235	Denowe (no 2nd name)	Edwardsburg	
1730	276	Davies Richard		
1731	316	Dayton Nathan	Leeds	
1732	323	Denault Joachim	Augusta	
1733	377	Drummond Peter	Elisabethtown	
1734	393	Duclen Stephen		
1735	~~403~~[f]	~~Derheart John~~	vide Aerheart	
1736	446	Dicky William	Charlottenburg	
1737	547	Dewit John	Cornwall	
1738	552[f]	Dewitt Perton		

NOTES:
1. No. 23 - at No. 23 this is spelled "DAVIES".
2. No. 196 - at No. 196 this is spelled "De Boyce".
3. No. 552 - at No. 552 the 2nd name is "Garrit". The 2nd "t" of last name may be stroked through here.
4. No. 403 - the entire entry in N° & NAMES columns stroked through.

File 3 Page 10

10

NUMBER	N°	NAMES	TOWNSHIP	REMARKS
1739	645[f]	Dixson* John Senior	Cornwall	
1740	703	Davies Peter		
1741	746	Devoe Conradt	Osnabruck	
1742	764	Dougharty James		
1743	801	Derheart Simon	Edwardsburg	vide Aerheart
1744	802	Dingman Richard	Osnabruck	
1745	830	Dingwell John	Charlottenburg	
1746	831	Dingwell James		
1747	901	Dunn John	Lancaster	
1748	987[f]	Dorn Peter	Matilda	
1749	993	Dorin Jacob*		
1750	994	Dorin* David		
1751	1074	Dorin* John		
1752	1086	Duncan Richard Esquire	Williamsburg	
1753	1122	Davis Walter	Elisabethtown	
1754	1129	Dopp Peter	Montague	
1755	1187	Dunn John Jun.r	Lancaster	
1756	1188	Dunn James		
1757	1228	Dixon William	Charlottenburg	
1758	1229	Dixon Robert Sen.r		
1759	1230	Dixon Robert Jun.r		
1760	995	Dorin Jeremiah	Matilda	
1761	(blank)	Dawson* John		
1762	(blank)	Deforrest Rebecca	Leeds	

NOTES:
1.No. 645 - at No. 645 "DIXSON" is spelled "DIXON".
2.No. 987 - a JEREMIAH DORN was allotted Matilda V/3E & V/10W per McNiff's 1787 map. SEE No.995 - is DORN and DORIN the same name?
3. "*"= sic.

File 3 Page 11

	E			11
NUMBER	N^o	NAMES	TOWNSHIP	REMARKS
1763	4	Elliot David	Elisabethtown	
1764	32	Emberry Samuel	Augusta	
1765	98	Earheart John		
1766	122	Elveston Edward		
1767	125	Everts Oliver		
1768	126	Everts Rosswell		
1769	395	Everitts* Sealvenus*	Elisabethtown	
1770	457	Empey Henry++	Cornwall	(s/o PHILIP Sr)
1771	481	Empey Christopher		(s/o Philip Sr)
1772	482	Empey Jacob		(s/o Philip Sr)
1773	483 f	Empey William		(s/o Philip Sr)
1774	484 f	Empey Philip Senr.		
1775	485	Empey Philip Senr.		(s/o Philip Sr)
1776	600	Eastman Benjamin		
1777	603	Eastman Nadab*		
1778	690	Emerson John		
1779	696	Everitt Peter (Lieut)	Osnabruck	
1780	700	Empey Adam (Sgt - Snr ?)		(s/o Philip Sr)
1781	723	Emery William Senior	Charlottenburg	
1782	724	Emery John		
1783	725	Emery William Junr.		
1784	725	Emery Thomas		
1785	727	Empey John Senr.	Osnabruck	(s/o Philip Sr)
1786	753 f	Empey Peter++		(s/o Philip Sr)
1787	755	Empey John Junr.*		(s/o Wm. Snr)
1788	758 f	Empey Adam junr.		(s/o Wm. Snr)
1789	759	Empey William Senr.		
1790	760	Empey William Junr.++	Son of Wm. Senior	
1791	761	Empey Richard++		(s/o Wm. Snr)
1792	951	Everser John	Williamsburg	
1793	1121	Elliot Thomas	Elisabethtown	
1794	1133	Elliot Jacob		
1795	1139	Easton Joseph		
1796	1204	Edge Mary (Widow)	Lancaster	

NOTES: 1. Nos. 484 & 485 - the father, PHILIP Snr. died between 7 Aug 1795 & 27 Feb 1796 per his Will. His 2nd son, JOHANN PHILIP, assumed the designation "Senior" at this time (& the Will also used that term); thus, two PHILIP Snrs. here. Six of PHILIP Snr.'s sons served in 1KRRNY: JOHN Snr.; John PHILIP (both as Corporals); WILLIAM Jnr.; Sgt. ADAM; CHRISTOPHER; JACOB. There is no record of military service for PETER or HENRY (b. 1765 & 1767 respectively) as they were too young. All of PHILIP Snr.'s sons settled in Cornwall Twsp. except JOHN Snr., PETER and Sgt. ADAM (who was at The Cedars in PQ - near Le Coteau). Marks++= too young.

2. No. 759 - WILLIAM Snr. was the (younger ?) brother of PHILIP Snr. (29 Apr 1728 - 5 Dec 1803) who married MARIA MARGARET LOUCHS/LAUXS. Their sons were: Sgt. JOHN WILLIAM, aka JOHN Jnr.; Pte. ADAM (both 1KRRNY); WILLIAM born c1772; & RICHARD, b1774. No. 755 could be Sgt. JOHN W. or the eldest s/o JOHN Snr. as Sgt. JOHN W. did not come to Upper Canada until 1795 as he was a blacksmith with the Indian Department until then. The point made here is that all these EMPEYs were not "TRUE" UELs - some were sons of UELs - as are likely many others on these Rolls. See FAMILIES 22:213-219 (1983) and others of that volume.

3. John PHILIP (above) was known as PHILIP Jnr. originally - being junior to his father. Later known as PHILIP Snr; later still, PHILIP PHILIP.

File 3 Page 12

12

F

NUMBER	N°	NAMES	TOWNSHIP	REMARKS
1797	18	Falkner Joseph	Elisabethtown	
1798	25	Fairchild Eleazar	Yonge	
1799	42	Fulford Jonathan Sen.r	Augusta	
1800	43	Fulford Jonathan Jun.r		
1801	51	Fulford Abel		
1802	202	Fraser Thomas Capt.n	Edwardsburg	
1803	203	Fraser Thomas Jun.r son of Wm. Sen.r Capt.n		
1804	204	Fraser William Sen.r		
1805	205	Fraser William Jun.r son of Thomas Sen.r Capt.n		
1806	207	Fraser Hugh		
1807	208	Fraser William Captain		
1808	209	Fraser William		
1809	210	Fraser Thomas		
1810	248	Ferguson Alexander		
1811	266	Froom James Sen.r		
1812	268	Fularton James		
1813	285	Fraser John		
1814	286	Fraser William		
1815	287	Fraser Thomas		
1816	320	Fell Frederick	Augusta	
1817	357	French Henry		
1818	408[f]	Freen Peter	Elisabethtown*	(there is faint unreadable writing in this column - ends in Freen - 2 words)
1819	418	Fulford Jonathan Sen.r		
1820	458	Forsyth James	Cornwall	
1821	491	Farlinger John Senior		
1822	492	Farlinger John junior*		
1823	493	Farlinger Nicholas		
1824	508[f]	~~Fousler William~~ vide William Toosler		omitted ent.d Solomon
1825	517	Farrand Jacob Esquire		
1826	545[f]	~~Futtle Solomon~~ vide Solomon Tuttle		
1827	587	Fyke John		
1828	589	Ferguson William		
1829	617	Fraser Isabella (widow)		
1830	622	Fraser William		
1831	623	Fraser Donald		

NOTES:
1. No. 408 - at No. 408 reads Yonge Twsp.
2. Nos. 508 & 545 - first names lined through.
3. Page 12 continued.
4. "*"= sic.

File 3 Page 12 cont'd

NUMBER	N^{o}	NAMES	TOWNSHIP	REMARKS
1832	655	Fitzpatrick Peter		
1833	656	Fitzpatrick William		
1834	660 f	Fraser William Lieu^{t}.		
1835	667 f	French Jermiah* Esqr.		
1836	668	French Albert Son of	Jerimiah*	
1837	669	French Benjamin d^{o}.		
1838	692	Fraser Angus		
1839	697	French Gersham (Lieu^{t}.)	(Lower Canada)	
1840	742	Frymire Philip	Osnabruck	
1841	781	Fenner Jacob		
1842	872	Ferguson Alexander Senr.	Charlottenburg	
1843	873	Ferguson Alexander Junr.		

NOTES: 1. Nos. 667 & 668 - note the copying error of JERIMIAH, yet same person.

File 3 Page 13

F 13

NUMBER	N^{o}	NAMES	TOWNSHIP	REMARKS
1844	874	Ferguson Peter		
1845	875	Ferguson William		
1846	895	Finney Peter		
1847	896	Finney George		
1848	925	Falkner Ralph	Lancaster	
1849	944	Foster Edward	Williamsburg	
1850	945	Foster John		
1851	953	Franks William		
1852	972	Fratts Henry		
1853	981	Frederick Ludwig	Matilda	ent^{d}. Fredrick
1854	982 f	Frederick Barnet		
1855	986	Feader Lucas		
1856	1031	Frymire Nicholas		
1857	1094	Finch James	Kitley	
1858	1127	Fraser Jeremiah	Augusta	
1859	1144	French Henry		
1860	1169	Froom James jun^{r}.*	Edwardsburg	
1861	1170	Froom David		
1862	1171 f	Falkner William Esqr.	Lancaster	
1863	1172	Falkner Joseph Son of	William	before
1864	1173 f	Falkner Ralph Senr.		
1865	1191	Flynn John		
1866	1201	Fountain Richard		
1867	1261	Fitchet Joseph	Charlottenburg	
1868	1263	Fraser John	Lancaster	
1869	1264	Fraser Mary (alias McNeil)		
1870	1265	Fraser Thomas		
1871	1268	Ferguson Alexander	Edwardsburg	
1872	971	Fetterly Peter	Williamsburg	ent^{d}. UE List Tetterly
1873	1194	Flynn Margaret alias Blakeley	Lancaster Ent^{d}.	before in B.
1874	(blank)	Fortune William	Hawkesbury	
1875	(blank)	Fortune Joseph	ditto	

NOTES:
1. No. 1172 - "before" likely means entered before.
2. No. 1191 - is this the 2nd husband of MARGARET BLAKELEY at No. 1194? See Note 1 on Page 5.
3. No. 986 - in original German, this named spelled "VEDDER" et var. Modern spelling is "FADER".

File 3 Page 14

G

14

NUMBER	Nº	NAMES	TOWNSHIP	REMARKS
1876	24	Gosley Mathew	Yonge	
1877	82	Grant Duncan	Augusta	
1878	115	Gray John		
1879	124	Glasford John		
1880	141	Graham William		
1881	144	Glasford Paul		
1882	145	Glasford Lyttle		
1883	206	Gooseberry Thomas	Edwardsburg	
1884	257	Grant Duncan		
1885	261	Galbreath* John		
1886	269	Grant James		
1887	288	Grant William		
1888	289	Grant Peter		
1889	295	Griffin Joseph	Elisabethtown	
1890	296	Griffin Isaac		
1891	300	Gardiner George		
1892	302	Grant Allan		
1893	331	Gilchrist Archibald	Augusta	
1894	374	Gorman Rebecca	Elisabethtown	
1895	399	Graham Oliver		
1896	425	Grant Alexander	Charlottenburg	
1897	433	Grant Archibald		
1898	439	Grant Alexander		
1899	448	Grant Allan		
1900	449	Grant Duncan		
1901	454	Grant Peter		
1902	455	Grant John		
1903	456	Goose Frederick	Cornwall	
1904	497	Gallinger Henry		
1905	516	Gray James (Colonel)		
1906	518	Gray Robert J.D. Esquire		
1907	543	Gallinger George		
1908	571	Gallinger Christian		
1909	572	Gallinger Michael Junr.		
1910	583	Gallinger Michael Senr.		

NOTES: 1. The asterix "*"= sic.
2. Page 14 continued.

File 3 Page 14 cont'd

NUMBER	N°	NAMES	TOWNSHIP	REMARKS
1911	677	Glasford Paul	Lancaster	
1912	876	Grant Donald Senior	Charlottenburg	
1913	877	Grant Lewis Sen.r		
1914	878	Grant Lewis Jun.r		
1915	879	Grant Donald Jun.r		
1916	880	Grant Duncan		
1917	881	Grant Alexander		
1918	882	Grant Allan		
1919	883	Grant Duncan		
1920	884	Grant John		
1921	885	Grant Finlay		
1922	886	Grant Angus		

NOTES:

File 3 Page 15

G 15

NUMBER	N[o]	NAMES	TOWNSHIP	REMARKS
1923	927	Grant Peter		
1924	965	Gay Edward	Matilda	
1925	1025	Glasford John		
1926	1026	Glasford Robert		
1927	1032	Garlough Jacob		
1928	1034	Garlough Peter Sen[r]		
1929	1035	Garlough Peter Jun[r]		
1930	1036	Garlough Henry		
1931	1180	Graham Thomas	Lancaster	
1932	1181	Graham Murdock		
1933	1182	Graham John		
1934	1184	Grant William		
1935	1185	Grant Alexander	Charlottenburg	
1936	1186	Grant John	Lancaster	
1937	1195	Gibson John		
1938	1209	Graham Isabella (alias	McDonell)	
1939	1221[f]	Grant Alexander	Charlottenburg	
1940	1224	Grant Alexander	ditto	not Ent[d]
1941	1225	Gunn David	Lancaster	
1942	1241	Grant Duncan	Charlottenburg	
1943	1245	Grant Peter		
1944	1266	Gordon Robert		
1945	1276	Grant John		
1946	(blank)	Gardener John		

NOTES: 1. Nc.1224 - presumed to mean "Not entered" ... on UE List.

File 3 Page 16

	H			16
NUMBER	N°	NAMES	TOWNSHIP	REMARKS
1947	22	Henderson David	Elisabethtown	
1948	29	Hurd Ichial	Augusta	
1949	35	Howard Stephen	Elisabethtown	
1950	54	Howard Mathew	Augusta	
1951	55 f	Howard Stephen	do	
1952	56	Howard John		
1953	57	Howard Dier*		
1954	58	Howard Peter		
1955	59	Henderson Caleb		
1956	72	Haftail Isaac		
1957	86	Herman Valentine		
1958	89	Hodogan* Peter		
1959	93	Hard Phili(p?)		
1960	94	Hard James		
1961	97	Hawley Abijah		
1962	109	Heirs Beaches vide	letter B	
1963	137	Hamblin Silas		
1964	139	Halabart Moses		
1965	140	Heck Paul		
1966	155	Hick Samuel		
1967	156	Hick John		
1968	164	Hunter David		
1969	177	Hamblin David		
1970	214	Hunter David	Edwardsburg	
1971	260	Humphrey James		
1972	326 f	Hagaerman* John	Augusta	
1973	327	Hodge Timothy		
1974	360	Hamblyn David	Elisabethtown	
1975	361	Hamblyn Francis		
1976	375	Hoskins Lida		
1977	400	Howard William		
1978	404 f	Hitcher Lix*		
1979	527	Hartle John	Cornwall	
1980	539	Hartle Adam		
1981	544 f	Hartle Christain*		
1982	554	Hawn John		
1983	556	Hart Barney		
1984	559	Hallister Elisha		
1985	585	Hartle John Senr.		
1986	649	Hawn Henry		
1987	650	Hawn Hermanus*		

NOTES:
1. No. 55 - the "do" is quite faint.
2. No. 326 - at No. 326 it is spelled "HAEGAERMAN"
3. No. 404 - at No. 404 it is spelled "LIA".
4. No. 544 - at No. 544 it is spelled "CHRISTIAN".
5. Page 16 continued.

File 3 Page 16 cont'd

NUMBER	N°	NAMES	TOWNSHIP	REMARKS
1988	657 f	Hare John		
1989	659* f	Hare William		
1990	658* f	Hare Barney		
1991	665	Hawn Jacob		
1992	666 f	Hawn Christain*		
1993	693	Hare John	Osnabruck	

(ADDITIONAL FOOTNOTE:

Maryly Penrose in her book, Mohawk Valley in the Revolution, at page 257, shows HENRY HARE married ALITA VROOMAN 15 Apr 1765 - per Reformed Dutch Church, Stone Arabia, p. 175. Their children were: JOHANNES, b. 22 Nov 1767 (RDSA:72); FAULKY; ALBY; WILLIAM; PETER; BARENT; CATY and gives as an additional reference her other book, BAUMANN/BOWMAN Family of the Mohawk, Susquehanna & Niagara Rivers - Franklin Park, N.J., 1977).

(And further:

The Record, NYG&B Society, vol. 117, No. 1 of January 1986 page20, has a "List of Prisoners in the Hands of the Congress belonging to the Corps of Rangers Royalists and their families". On this list is ... "Family of Henry Hare - Mrs. Hare, Children: Alby, John, Faulky, William, Peter, Barent and Caty". There is no JAMES or HENRY.

NOTES: 1. Nos. 656 (657 & 659) - a Lieut. Henry Hare was hanged as a spy at Canajoharie (Mohawk Valley) in July 1779 by Clinton's men along with a Sgt. Newberry, both of Butler's Rangers. There are many references for this story - one , The Mark of Honour by Hazel C. Mathews, UofT Press. Hare's widow remarried, 1st, Sgt. ADAM EMPEY & 2nd, VROOMAN after EMPEY died in 1803 at the Cedars. Sgt. ADAM EMPEY petitioned (PAC RG 1 L3L, Vol.81, Reel C-2524) stating Lieut. HENRY HARE'S children were: JOHN; WILLIAM; BARNABY; PETER; & CATHERINE. (Contd p.17)

File 3 Page 17

H

17

NUMEER	N°	NAMES	TOWNSHIP	REMARKS
1994	698	Hare James	Lancaster	
1995	699	Hare Henry		
1996	714	Hains Michael	Williamsburg	
1997	728	Hoople John	Osnabruck	
1998	729	Hoople Henry		
1999	825 f	Hogan William (Major)	Cornwall	
2000	1022	Hoopper* Abraham	Williamsburg	
2001	1045	Helmer John		
2002	1051	Hains Christopher		
2003	1052	Hains Joseph		
2004	1053	Hains John		
2005	1063	Hicky John		
2006	1069	Hood Jonas (This name is (who resided	supposed to be Jona at one time in this	h Wood Senior) Township)
2007	1099	Haus Edward	Kitley	
2008	1102	Hewit Jacob	Yonge	
2009	1107	Hutchinson Asa		
2010	1120	Hubert Thomas	Kitley	
2011	1237	Hagard John	Charlottenburg	
2012	1238	Hagard Peter		
2013	646	Helmer John	Cornwall	
2014	(blank)	Hawley Abijah	Elisabethtown	
2015	(blank)	Haskins Nicholas	son of Abel	
2016	(blank)	Haskins David		

NOTES: 1. No. 1022 - at No. 1022 it is spelled "HOPPER".

NOTE 1. (Cont'd from page 16). Sgt. ADAM PHILIP EMPEY (s/o PHILIP Snr.) and ALLADA (OLIVE) HARE EMPEY'S children were:PHILIP; AULLY; ELIZABETH; and ELATTA per the same Lower Canada Land Petition. These EMPEYs lived at The Cedars running a hotel at a portage point just inside Quebec below the Upper Canada border. The two daughters married after 1807 two French Canadians; both daughters were dead by 1817 per UCLPs of their cousin, JACOB WILLIAM EMPEY.

File 3 Page 18

I[f] 18

NUMBER	N°	NAMES	TOWNSHIP	REMARKS
2017	67	Jessup Edward Esquire	Augusta	
2018	83	Jones Daniel		
2019	84	Jones Ephraim Esquire		
2020	85	Jones Solomon		
2021	90	Jones David		
2022	100	Jones Thomas		
2023	103	Jones John Esquire		
2024	154	Jones Richard (Son of Daniel)		
2025	184	Jessup Joseph		
2026	185	Jessup Henry		
2027	186	Jessup Edward		
2028	187	Jones Mary Senior		
2029	188	Jones Mary Junior		
2030	198	Judson Silas		
2031	262	Jackson Henry	Edwardsburg	
2032	270	Jackson James		
2033	275	Jackson Peter		
2034	494	Johnston George	Cornwall	
2035	524	Johnston Adam		
2036	525[f]	Johnston Robert		
2037	588	Johnson* James		
2038	745[f]	Jacocks David	Osnabruck	
2039	824	Johnson Sir John K.B.	Augusta	
2040	1061	Johnson George	Matilda	
2041	(blank)	Johnson Frederick	Yonge	
2042	(blank)	Jacocks David		
2043	(blank)	Jones Sarah Widow		

NOTES:
1. Page 18 continues with the "K"s on the lower half of the page; see Page 18 contd.
2. No. 528 - at No. 588 it is spelled "JOHNSTON".
3. No. 745 - DAVID JACOCKS also appears 2nd from the bottom. On McNiff's 1787 map, MARGARET JEACOCKS is allotted Osnabruck II/34E. There was a Corporal DAVID JAYCOCKS in 1KRRNY; this could be his widow.
4. While this page is indexed "I" it is all "J"s; there are no names beginning with "I".

File 3 Page 18 cont'd

NUMBER	N°	NAMES	TOWNSHIP	REMARKS
		K		
2044	27	Keeler James	Augusta	
2045	67	Knapp Joseph		
2046	127	Knight Benjamin		
2047	162	Kelsey James		
2048	163	Kelsey William		
2049	253	King Constant	Edwardsburg	
2050	315	Kilburn Benj^m.	Elisabethtown	
2051	413	Kelsie James		
2052	590	Knight James	Cornwall	
2053	688	Knight John		
2054	909	Kennedy Alexander	Lancaster	
2055	(blank)	King Ebenezer	Elisabethtown	
2056	(blank)	Kenter George		

NOTES:

File 3 Page 19

19

L

NUMBER	N^o	NAMES	TOWNSHIP	REMARKS
2057	15	Landrie Mitchel	Elisabethtown	
2058	7*	Lee David	Bastard	
2059	20	Livingston William	Osnabruck	
2060	21	Livingston John	Augusta	
2061	73 f	Leaky William junior	alias Lehy	
2062	107	Landen Assa* (AFSA)		
2063	143	Lorence* John		
2064	158	Leaky Abraham) alias	Lehy	
2065	160	Leaky William) alias	Lehy	
2066	166	Loucks Nicholas		
2067	173	Loucks Abraham		
2068	183	Landen Herman		
2069	228	Lampson John	Edwardsburg	
2070	229	Lampson James		
2071	230	Lampson William		
2072	277	Lorimier Chevaleur		
2073	313 f	Landen Samuel	Augusta	
2074	332	Leaken* David		
2075	333	Livingston John		
2076	334	Livingston William		
2077	343	Landen Asa		
2078	355 f	Laird John		
2079	378	Lamson* William	Elisabethtown	
2080	420	Larue Henry	Yonge	
2081	421	Larue William	Escotte	
2082	513	Link John	Cornwall	
2083	514	Link Mathew		
2084	541	Lynch James		
2085	717	Loeney John	Charlottenburg	
2086	718	Loeney Edward son of John		
2087	719	Loeney William d^o		
2088	720	Loeney Samuel d^o		
2089	763	Loucks Joseph	Osnabruck	

NOTES:
1. No. 107 - AFSA/ASSA/ASA are equivalent spellings.
2. No. 378 - spelled this way at No. 378; compare with Nos. 228 & 229.
3. No. 332 - an unusual name. Could this be "LEAKE"?
4. Page 19 continues.

File 3 Page 19 cont'd

NUMBER	N°	NAMES	TOWNSHIP	REMARKS
2090	803[f]	Lovelass William	Grand River	
2091	805[f]	Lovelass Archibald		
2092	844	Livingston John	Charlottenburg	
2093	845	Livingston Neil		
2094	996	Loucks George	Williamsburg	
2095	997	Loucks Richard		
2096	1096[f]	Landers Jaber*	Yonge	
2097	1104	Lochart William	Escotte	
2098	1196	Leman John	Lancaster	
2099	898	Livingston Mary alias Mulchman	Charlottenburg	
2100	(blank)[f]	Losee Cornelius	Matilda	
2101	(blank)	Lang John		
		Continued to folio 37		
		(Under "M"s on folio 37 is one entry under "L")		
2102	(blank)	Livingston Daniel deceased O.C. 26 July 1798		

NOTES:
1. Nos. 803 & 805 - written LOVELAFS.
2. No. 1096 - at No. 1096 spelled JUBER - quite definite.
3. (blank) Losee - more likely LOZEE.

File 3 Page 20

M 20

NUMBER	N°	NAMES	TOWNSHIP	REMARKS
2103	5	McDonell John	Edwardsburg	
2104	9	Munroe David	Cornwall	
2105	11	Mattice Nicholas	Elisabethtown	
2106	13	Munroe Samuel	Yonge	
2107	16	McNish Joseph	Elisabethtown	
2108	40f	McNish James	Augusta	
2109	46f	Millschurch Jonathan		Entered in C
2110	52f	McArtheren* Daniel		
2111	65	McLaren Archibald		
2112	66	McLaren Peter		
2113	68	Mosher Louis*		
2114	70	Mosher Nicholas		
2115	104	Mooth Henry		
2116	106f	Mallery Enoch		
2117	157f	McArther* Charles		
2118	192	Manhart David	Elisabethtown	
2119	200	McIlmoyle Hugh	Edwardsburg	
2120	201	McIlmoyle Thomas		
2121	212	McKenzie John		
2122	216	McNeil Archibald		
2123	225	McCarbin Benjamin		
2124	233	Marlotte Thomas		
2125	234	Marlotte John		
2126	237	McIlmoyle Thomas		
2127	242	Main Thomas		
2128	243	Main Mathew		
2129	244	McIlmoyle John		
2130	245	McIlmoyle James		
2131	247	Montgomery Archibald		
2132	249	McDonell Andrew		
2133	258	McIntosh Daniel		
2134	263	Munroe Hugh		
2135	271	Main James		
2136	273	McIntosh John		
2137	274	McIntosh Alexander		
2138	279	Main Thomas Senr.		

NOTES:
1. No. 46 - this name is otherwise JONATHAN MILLS CHURCH.
2. Nos. 52 & 157 - both spelled as written at their respective entries.
3. Page 20 continues.

File 3 Page 20 cont'd

NUMBER	N°	NAMES	TOWNSHIP	REMARKS
2139	290 f	Miller James	Elisabethtown	
2140	292 f	McNeal* Archibald (McNeal)		
2141	293 f	McNeal* John (McNeal)		
2142	294	Motte Ruben (Ruben)		
2143	303 f	McDonell Allan		
2144	322	McIntyre Jesse (McIntyre)	Augusta	
2145	324	Mosher Rachel		
2146	328	McVee John	Elisabethtown	
2147	336	McDonell Daniel	Augusta	
2148	337	Michel* Carlmon*		
2149	338	Michel Harvey		

NOTES:

1. The asterix "*"= sic.
2. Nos. 292, 293, 294 & 322 had rewrites of some names for purposes of clarity by the original writer.

File 3 Page 21

M 21

NUMBER	N°	NAMES	TOWNSHIP	REMARKS
2150	342	Morrison Henry	Augusta	
2151	344	McDougall John[d]		
2152	363	McIlmoyle Arch.	Elisabethtown	
2153	391[f]	McLarin* Peter		
2154	392	Mutchimson* Ruggles	Yonge	
2155	412	McArtheren Daniel	Elisabethtown	
2156	417	McNish James		
2157	422	McDonell Alexander	Charlottenburg	
2158	423	McDonell Kenneth		
2159	424	McLeod William		
2160	426	Murchison John		
2161	429	McDonell Allan		
2162	430	McDonell Alexander		
2163	431	McDonell Allan		
2164	434	McLaughlin Alexander		
2165	435	McDonell Alexander		
2166	436	McDonell John		
2167	437	McGregor John		
2168	441	McLean Murdock		
2169	442	McLean Donald		
2170	443	McLean William		
2171	444	McLean Donald Jun.[r]		
2172	445	McKay John		
2173	450	McGregor Peter		
2174	460	McGregor Donald	Cornwall	
2175	461	Mattice Nicholas		
2176	462	Mattice John		
2177	463	Mattice Adam		
2178	477	McCuin* David Sen.[r]		
2179	478	McCuin* David Jun.[r]		

NOTES:
1. No. 392 - one wonders if this was not intended to be HUTCHINSON; though it is spelled as written including original No. 392.
2. Page 21 continues.

File 3 Page 21 cont'd

NUMBER	N^{o}	NAMES	TOWNSHIP	REMARKS
2180	480[f]	Mictchel George*		
2181	495	McLaughlin William		
2182	509	Miller Stephen		
2183	511	McDonell Donald	4-5th Con	
2184	512	McDonell Duncan	6-5th d^{o}	
2185	515	McDonell Captn John	Scothouse	
2186	528	McDonell Captn Miles		not entered
2187	529	McDonell Ranald Esqr		
2188	530	McDonell Donald	12-6th Con	
2189	532	McBane Gillis		
2190	595	McGuire Patrick		
2191	601	Milroy John see the Petition of William Milroy Read 31 October 1809		
2192	605	McDonell Angus	N.º 18-4th Con.	
2193	606	McDonell Angus	14-5th d^{o}.	
2194	607	McDonell John	A-11th d^{o}	
2195	608	McDonell John	7-5th d^{o}	
2196	609	McDonell John	9-5th d.^{o}	
2197	610	McGregor James		
2198	611	McDonell John	20-4th d^{o}	
2199	612	McDonell Duncan	19-4th d.^{o}	
2200	613	McMullin Donald		

NOTES: 1. No. 480 - spelled as written at original No. 480.

File 3 Page 22

M 22

NUMBER	N°	NAMES	TOWNSHIP	REMARKS
2201	614	McDonell John	N°.17-4th Con	
2202	615	McPhee Allan		
2203	616	McDonell Archibald	5-5th Con	
2204	618 f	McGrigor Mary		
2205	619	McGruer Christain		
2206	620	McGruer Donald		
2207	621	McDonell John	10-5th Con	
2208	626 f	McDonell Alexander	8-15th d°	
2209	627	McDonell Hugh G-4th Con	Roxbury	
2210	628	McDonell Ranald 13-9th do	Cornwall	
2211	629	McDonell Alexander		
2212	630	McDonell Donald	N°.22-4th Con.	
2213	631	McDonell Duncan	17-4th d°	
2214	632	McDonell Kenneth	22-4th d°	
2215	633	Marsh Abraham		
2216	639	Millross Andrew		
2217	641	Millross John		
2218	642	Millross Thomas		
2219	644	Millross William		
2220	651	McDonell John	11-5th Con	
2221	652	McDonell Donald	12-5th d° Wes	t half
2222	653	McDonell Alexander	12-5th d° Eas	t half
2223	654	McDonell Hugh	1-8th d°	
2224	661	McIntyre John		
2225	663	McDonell John	A-9th Con.	
2226	664	McDonell William	B-9th Con.	
2227	670	Murchison Duncan	Lancaster	
2228	675	McDonell Alexander		
2229	676	McDougald* John		
2230	680	Murchison William son	of Duncan	

NOTES:
1. No. 619 - at original No. 619 spelled CHRISTIAN.
2. No. 627 - Roxbury now Roxborough Twsp. - at rear of Cornwall Twsp.
3. Page 22 continues.

File 3 Page 22 cont'd

NUMBER	N°	NAMES	TOWNSHIP	REMARKS
2231	685	Miller Stephen	Cornwall	
2232	694	McIntyre John	Williamsburg	
2233	695	McKee John	Osnabruck	
2234	701 f	McDonell Angus 8-12th	Con. Cornwall	
2235	702	Mandaville* Richard		
2236	722	McDonell Allan	Charlottenburg	
2237	730	Merkle Jacob	Osnabruck	
2238	732	Moss Samuel		
2239	748	Merkle Henry		
2240	768	Moak Philip		
2241	787 f	McWilliams, John		
2242	798	McDonell Lt. Col Archd.		
2243	813	McCue* William	Escotte	
2244	815	McDonell Alexander (Colonel)	Charlottenburg	
2245	816 f	McDonell John Lt. Col.		
2246	817	McDonell Hugh Captn.		not entd.
2247	818	McDonell Chichester Lieut.		not entd.
2248	821	McKenzie John Captn.	Williamsburg	

NOTES: 1. No. 702 - a Sgt.Richard Mandeville served in 1KRRNY and was allotted Lot 22W/I & II Williamsburg.
2. No. 798 & 816 - in original ranks written as COLONEL in both cases.

File 3 page 23

M 23

NUMBER	N°	NAMES	TOWNSHIP	REMARKS
2249	822 f	McKenzie Keneth*	Cornwall	
2250	827	McGruer John	Charlottenburg	
2251	832	McGruer Alexander	Charlottenburg	
2252	833	McPherson Alexander		
2253	834	McPherson James		not ent.d
2254	835	McPherson Murdock		
2255	836	Murchison John		
2256	840	McGilles Donald Senr.		
2257	841	McGilles Donald Junr.		
2258	842	McGilles Duncan		
2259	843	McGilles Hugh		
2260	846	McDonell Hugh		
2261	847	McDonell Alexander		
2262	849	McDonell Alexander		
2263	850	McDonell Donald		
2264	851	McDonell John		
2265	852	McDonell Roderick		
2266	853	McDonell John		
2267	854	McDonell Hugh		
2268	855	McDonell John		
2269	856	McDonell Tinnan		
2270	857	McDonell Roderick		
2271	858	McDonell John Bane		
2272	859 f	McDonald Donell		
2273	860 f	McDonell John Due		
2274	861	McDonell Donald		
2275	862	McNaughton John		
2276	863	McNaughton Donald		
2277	864	McKenzie John		
2278	865	McKenzie Duncan		
2279	887	McGilles Donald		
2280	888	McIntosh Daniel		
2281	889	McIntosh Benjamin		

NOTES:
1. Page 23 continues.
2. No. 822 - at No. 822 spelling is KENNETH.
3. Nos. 859 & 860 - see Notes 1 & 2 in File 1, Page 28.

File 3 page 23 cont'd

NUMBER	N^o	NAMES	TOWNSHIP	REMARKS
2282	894	McLaren Hugh		
2283	896	Munroe Hugh		
2284	900	Munroe Thomas		
2285	902	McIntyre Duncan Senr	Lancaster	
2286	903	McIntyre Duncan Junr.		
2287	904	McIntyre John	Charlottenburg	
2288	905	McIntyre Donald		
2289	920	McKay Donald		
2290	921	McKay Angus		
2291	922	McKay William		
2292	923	McKay Hugh		
2293	926	McLelan* John	Cornwall	
2294	936	McDonell Farquhar	Williamsburg	
2295	955	Marcellis John		

NOTES:

File 3 page 24

M 24

NUMBER	N^{o}	NAMES	TOWNSHIP	REMARKS
2296	970[f]	Mercle John	Williamsburg	
2297	976	Meddough John Junr	Matilda	
2298	977	Meddough John Senr.		
2299	998	Mercle Henry	Williamsburg	
2300	1012	Mercle Jacob Senr.		
2301	1013	Mercle Christopher		
2302	1014	Mercle Henry		
2303	1015	Mercle Jacob Junr.		
2304	1023	McKitchie John		
2305	1044	McKarty* Florence	Matilda	
2306	1057	McDonell John		
2307	1058	McDonell Alexander		
2308	1059	McDonell James		
2309	1062	Mercle Michael	Williamsburg	
2310	1064	Mercle Frederick		Ent^{d}. Merkle
2311	1073	Miller Nicholas		
2312	1079	Munroe John (Honble)	Matilda	
2313	1080	Munroe Hugh		
2314	1081	Munroe Cornelius		NE [f]
2315	1082	Munroe John Junr.		
2316	1083	Munroe Henry		
2317	1084	Munroe William		
2318	1085[f]	Munroe Cornelia	alias Paterson	NE [f]
2319	1087	MacDonell Allan		
2320	1088[f]	McMartin Malcom*	Williamsburg	
2321	1090	Munroe Christie	(alias Mount)	NE [f]
2322	1103	Munroe John	Yonge	
2323	1110	Miller Zebeda	Lansdown	
2324	1115	Mott Edmond	Yonge	
2325	1119	McLean Alexander	Elisabethtown	

NOTES:

1. Page 24 continues.
2. The letters "NE" assumed to mean "Not Entered"...on UE List.
3. No. 970 et seq - MERCLE spelling varients include: MARKLE/MERKLEY/MARKLAND/MERQUEL etc.
4. No. 1085 - the remarks "alias Paterson" also written in names column but stroked through.
5. No. 1088 - actually spelled "McMirtin" here, but McMARTIN at No. 1088. Note common misspelling of MALCOLM.

File 3 page 24 cont'd

NUMBER	N[o]	NAMES	TOWNSHIP	REMARKS
2326	1123	Mallery Nathaniel	Yonge	
2327	1124	McNeil William	Elisabethtown	
2328	1126[f]	Moor Dodley	Augusta	
2329	1130	Martin William		
2330	1140	Mitchell George		
2331	1141[f]	Mitchell Zalmon*		
2332	1142[f]	Mitchell Harcuey*		
2333	1149	McDonell Ranald	Yonge	
2334	1153	McAlpine Duncan		
2335	1154	McKnight Thomas		Ent[d]. McNight
2336	1159	Munroe Daniel		
2337	1166	Moor Mosa*		
2338	1197	McFall David	Lancaster	
2339	1198	Morrison William Capt[n].		
2340	1199	Morrison William		
2341	1200	Morrison Mary		

NOTES:
1. No.1126 - in both entries 1st name spelled as above NOT "DUDLEY"
2. No. 1141 - could be "ZABNON".
3. No. 1142 - no doubt as to spelling both entries.

File 3 Page 25

M 25

NUMBER	N°	NAMES	TOWNSHIP	REMARKS
2342	1207	McDonell Donald		
2343	1213	McIntosh Peter		
2344	1214	McIntosh Benjamin	Charlottenburg	see 889
2345	1216	McKay Hugh		
2346	1217	McKay John		see 445
2347	1219	McDonell John		
2348	1220[f]	McDonell Ranald		omitted 4
2349	1221[f]	Angus MacDonell		
2350	1222	McDonell Nelly Widow		
2351	1223	Mustard John		
2352	1231	McArther John Sen[r].		
2353	1232	McArther Donald		
2354	1233	McArther John Jun[r].		
2355	1234	McArther Duncan		
2356	1235	McArther Peter		
2357	1236	McArther Archibald		
2358	1242	McGregor Hugh		
2359	1243	McMartin John		
2360	1244	McMartin Malcolm		
2361	1248	Munroe Thomas		
2362	1249	McLeland* John Jun[r].		
2363	1250	McLeland John Senior		
2364	1251	McLeland Kenneth		
2365	1252	McBane Richard		
2366	1254[f]	McBane Isabella (alias	McD)	
2367	1255	McLeod William		
2368	1256	McLeod Isabella Widow		
2369	1257	McLeod Thomas		
2370	1258	McDonell Alexander		
2371	1259	McArther Duncan		omitted
2372	1262	McIntosh Peter	Lancaster	
2373	504	McCaffrey John	Cornwall	
2374	788	Meddough Martin	Osnabruck	
2375	634	McNarin* John	Cornwall	
2376	898	(Mutchmore The Widow) (Mary alias Livingston)	Charlottenburg	Ent[d]. as Livingston
2377	837	Murchison Kenneth	ditto	

NOTES:
1. No. 1220 - the meaning of the "4" is unknown; it could be a tick mark used to tick-off each name with an extra cross through it.
2. No. 1221 - this entry is squeezed in between Nos. 1220 & 1222; No. 1221 in the original list is NOT Angus MacDonell but Alexander Grant - a mistake of someone.
3. No. 1254 - "alias McD" - does this mean McDonell ?
4. Page 25 continues.

File 3 Page 25 cont'd

NUMBER	N°	NAMES	TOWNSHIP	REMARKS
2378	1209	McDonell Isabella alias Graham	Lancaster	Ent.[d] as Graham
2379	1264	McNeal Mary alias Fraser	ditto	Ent.[d] as Fraser
2380	(blank)	McLean John	Elisabethtown	
2381	(blank)	McLean Robert	ditto	
2382	(blank)	Myers John	ditto	
		carried to folio 37		
2383	(blank)[f]	Mitchel Jehiab	Bastard	
2384	(blank)	McLean Duncan	Augusta	
2385	(blank)	More Sylvester		
2386	(blank)	Morrison David		
2387	(blank)	McGloghlin* Robert	Cornwall	
2388	(blank)	McGloghlin* David	ditto	
2389	(blank)	Myers Michael		
2390	(blank)	Mandeville Richard Sen.[r]	Entered before see	No. 702
2391	(blank)	McCredy* David		
2392	(blank)	Monson* David		

NOTES:
1. The 4th blank entry, "JEHIAB", could be "JEHIAL".
2. The last ten names were carried over to the end of the journal - obviously as some added names not in the original list.

File 3 Page 26

26

N

NUMBER	N°	NAMES	TOWNSHIP	REMARKS
2393	62	Naughton Andrew	Grand River	
2394	63	Naughton Philander		
2395	69	Nicholson Robert	Augusta	
2396	1011f	Nudale* Adam	Williamsburg	
2397	1112	Naulton Thomas	Elisabethtown	
2398	1132	Nettleton Nathaniel	Augusta	Entd. Daniel
2399	1138	Nettleton Amos		
2400	1226	Noble William	Lancaster	
		O		
2401	(blank)	Otto Gottleeb*		
		P		
2402	10	Patton Philip	Matilda	
2403	41	Pottier John		
2404	61	Peterson Conradt		
2405	120	Pitman Cary		
2406	165	Pannal Abraham		
2407	199	Pattison Daniel	Yonge	
2408	254	Peeble Charles	Edwardsburg	
2409	272f	Peters Thomas		
2410	312f	Pennick Samuel	Elisabeth.	
2411	335	Pennock* Philimon		
2412	359f	Peebles Charles		before
2413	414f	Peterson Conradt*		
2414	419	Peet David		
2415	490	Putman Ephraim		
2416	502	Pescod John Senr.	Cornwall	
2417	503f	Pescod John Junr.		
2418	564	Parks Nathan Jun.		
2419	565f	Parks Robert		
2420	566	Parks Nathan Senr.		
2421	687	Peek Caleb		
2422	779f	Papst Rudolph	Osnabruck	omitted
2423	806	Platt John Lower Canada Blacksmith	Grand River Montreal	
2424	810	Perrigor James		

NOTES: 1. No. 1011 - otherwise NUDDAL/NUDAL. 2. Compare Nos.312 & 335.
3. No. 414 - at No. 414 spelled COONRADT. 4. No. 419 - 2nd choice PEEK. (Compare with 687). 5. Nos. 564 & 566 reversed here as to Junr. & Senr. compared to original list.
6. No. 806 - this proves the meaning of Grand River; it is not the Grand River in Brant County - but the Ottawa River. John Platt was a Revolutionary War notable who founded a very successful hardware business in Montreal. See Cdn. Genealogist 5:30 (Mar. 1983).

File 3 Page 27

27

P

NUMBER	N°	NAMES	TOWNSHIP	REMARKS
2425	823	Painting Timothy	Augusta	
2426	838	Prentis* Daniel	Charlottenburg	
2427	978	Parlow John	Matilda	
2428	979	Prunner Peter Jun.r		
2429	980 f	Prunner Peter Sen.r		
2430	1009	Piller Michael	Williamsburg	
2431	1078	Pearse John		
2432	1148	Proctor Joseph	Yonge	
2433	1155	Parish Ezekiel		
2434	1163	Pine Chese*		
2435	1206	Powell John	Lancaster	
2436	1269	Parker Robert	Edwardsburg	
2437	(blank)	Papts Adam by order of	Council	
2438	1193	Picard Margaret alias Curry	Lancaster	
2439	(blank)	Parish William	Yonge	
2440	(blank)	Papts Adam		before
		Q		
2441	116	Quinn Christopher	Augusta	
2442	533	Quin* John	Cornwall	
2443	534	Quin Michael		

NOTES: 1. No. 980 - Judge J.F. Pringle in his book, "Lunenburgh or the Old Eastern District" fails to show a land allottment for PETER PRUNNER; however, McNiff's 1786 map shows the allocation as Lot 15W/II of Osnabruck Twsp. - and this listing suggests Matilda Twsp. McNiff's map is preferred.

File 3 Page 28

		R		28
NUMBER	N°	NAMES	TOWNSHIP	REMARKS
2444	211	Robertson William	Edwardsburg	
2445	213f	Robertson Joseph		
2446	226f	Rudderback* John		
2447	227	Rudderback Simon		
2448	236	Robertson Joseph		
2449	250	Rose Samuel		
2450	251	Rose Aaron		son of Samuel
2451	259	Rose David		
2452	278	Rose Samuel		
2453	284	Rose Ezekiel		
2454	314	Reid Moses	Elisabethtown	
2455	321	Rood William	Augusta	
2456	358	Rorrison Basil	Elisabethtown	
2457	427	Rofs (Ross) Finlay	Charlottenburg	
2458	447	Robins William		
2459	451	Rose Charles		
2460	452	Rose William		omitted
2461	453	Rose Alexander		
2462	457	Runion Henry	Cornwall	
2463	459	Robertson Thomas		
2464	510	Robertson Daniel		
2465	536	Rofs (Ross) Thomas		
2466	635	Roise Evan Senior		
2467	636	Roise Evan Junior		
2468	662	Robertson Neil (Lieut)		
2469	672 f	Rofs (Ross) Alexander	Lancaster	
2470	673 f	Rofs (Ross) Thomas		
2471	674 f	Rofs (Ross) George		
2472	681 f	Rofs (Ross) Donald		
2473	682 f	Rofs (Ross) Thomas Ben		
2474	734 f	Redick John	Osnabruck	
2475	744 f	Ruport Padar (Peter)		
2476	754 f	Rofs (Ross) Jacob		
2477	769	Rambough Jacob		
2478	770	Rambough Amos		
2479	771	Rambough John		
2480	772	Rambough David		

NOTES:

1. Nos. 226 & 227 - at original listings spelling is RUDERBACK.
2. All the ROFS entries spelled that way as the old way of doubling an "S"; the interpretation "(ROSS)" is offered by the transcriber.
3. No. 744 - note the interpretation of "PADAR" offered by the original scribe.
4. No. 734 - a CHRISTOPHER REDDICK allotted Lot 28E/I Osnabruck per McNiff's 1786 map.
5. Page 28 continues.

File 3 Page 28 cont'd

NUMBER	N°	NAMES	TOWNSHIP	REMARKS
2481	918	Rofs (Ross) Donald	Lancaster	
2482	919 f	Rofs (Ross) John		
2483	946 f	Reddick George	Williamsburg	
2484	947	Reddick Christopher		
2485	948	Reddick Adam		
2486	1030	Russell William	Matilda	
2487	1054	Rose Alexander	Williamsburg	
2488	1068	Ridman Nicholas	Matilda	
2489	1071	Russell Michael		
2490	1095	Randolph Benjamin	Yonge	
2491	1116	Rose Moses	Bastard	
2492	1137	Reid William	Yonge	
2493	1160	Rose Samuel		

NOTES:

1. No. 946 - a GEORGE REDDICK allotted Lot 24E/II Williamsburg per McNiff's 1786 map.
2. No. 947 - see Note 4. Page 28.

File 3 Page 29

		R		29
NUMBER	N[o]	NAMES	TOWNSHIP	REMARKS
2494	1179	Rofs (Ross) Donald	Lancaster	
2495	1246	Rofs (Ross) Philip	Charlottenburg	
2496	1247	Rofs (Ross) Alexander		
2497	1270	Rofs (Ross) Thomas Taylor	Lancaster	
2498	1277	Russell Roswell	Charlottenburg	
2499	1024 f	Rosenbarger Jacob	Williamsburg	
		(The lower half of Page 29 continues with the letter "S")		
		S		
2500	1	Smith Richard	Osnabruck	
2501	74	Spicer Ezekiel	Augusta	
2502	75	Sherwood Justus* Esquire		
2503	81	Sparam Doctor		not ent[d] not UE
2504	92	Sweet Oliver		
2505	101	Smith Benoni		
2506	108	Sealey Justus		
2507	110	Sealey Joseph		
2508	118	Shibbarn Charles		
2509	119	Stratford Moses		
2510	121	Shoults* John		
2511	128	Smades* Joel		
2512	130	Spicer Daniel		
2513	135	Smith Dennis		
2514	138 f	Sheet Samuel		
2515	146	Scotte Francis		
2516	151 f	Stratford Thomas		
2517	152	Sweet Charles		
2518	153	Stamp Guillies		not entered not UE
2519	172	Shue Ezekiel junior		
2520	176	Sherwood Samuel		

NOTES:
1. No. 1024 - did the anglicization of this German name produce ROSE ?
2. No. 138 - otherwise SCHEIK/SHEEK. There was a Scheik's Island off Cornwall prior to the seaway flooding.
3. No. 151 - see footnote next page, ie, Nos. 180 & 345.

File 3 Page 30

		S		30
NUMBER	N[o]	NAMES	TOWNSHIP	REMARKS
2521	180[f]	Stratford Thomas	Augusta	before
2522	196	Shipman David	Elisabethtown	omitted Ent[d]. David
2523	215	Sharp John	Edwardsburg	
2524	217	Saunders Abraham		
2525	218	Saunders William		
2526	255	Smith Dennis		
2527	256	Silk Daily*		
2528	310	Servos Philip	Matilda	
2529	318	Stone Joel	Leeds	omitted
2530	319	Stephens Elishu*		
2531	345[f]	Stratford Thomas 3[d]	Augusta	
2532	349	Smith John		
2533	350	Stephens Roger		(see Page 31 contd)
2534	379	Snyder William Sen[r].	Elisabethtown	
2535	380	Snyder William Jun[r].		
2536	381	Smith Robert		
2537	382	Smith Stephen		
2538	383	Smith Encrease*		
2539	384	Smith James		
2540	389	Sealey Joseph		omitted
2541	390	Sealey Justus		
2542	409	Smith Thomas Esq[r].	Yonge	
2543	410	Smith George	Elisabethtown	
2544	411[f]	Smith ~~Florence~~ Terence		
2545	428	Summers Andrew	Charlottenburg	
2546	432[f]	Summers Jacob		
2547	464[f]	Sheets Jacob Sen[r].	Cornwall	
2548	465[f]	Sheets George		
2549	466[f]	Sheets William		
2550	468[f]	Sheek Christain		
2551	498	Smith John Sen[r].		
2552	499	Smith John Jun[r].		
2553	500	Smith Jacob		
2554	501	Smith Daniel		

NOTES:
1. No. 345 - the "3[d]" likely means the third time this name has been entered on the list; see No. 180 & 151.
2. No. 432 - the town of SUMMERSTOWN in Charlottenburg Twsp. named for this family.
3. Nos. 464, 465, 466 & 468 - see Note 2. on Page 29. CHRISTIAN SHEET, f/o CATHERINE who was w/o Sgt. JOHN W. EMPEY, was allotted Lot 25W/V Concession, Cornwall Twsp.
4. Page 30 continues. 5. No. 411 - FLORENCE lined through.

File 3 Page 30 cont'd

NUMBER	N^o	NAMES	TOWNSHIP	REMARKS
2555	531_f	Snetsinger Mathias		
2556	598_f	Selmser* Martin		
2557	599	Selmser* Nicholas		
2558	647^f	Stoneburner Jacob		omitted
2559	679	Snyder Jeremiah	Lancaster	
2560	683	Snyder Jacob		
2561	684	Snyder John		
2562	708	Snyder Adam	Cornwall	
2563	709_f	Snyder Conradt		
2564	713	Shevertfeger* Jno. a	Williamsburg	(The meaning of "a" unknown)
2565	731^f	Servos Chris^n.	Osnabruck	
2566	737	Stuart James		
2567	738	Stuart George		
2568	739	Stuart Henry		
2569	740	Stuart Gilbert		
2570	747	Stata Philip		
2571	749^f	Stoneburner Joseph		
2572	750^f	Stoneburner Leonard	Fifer Sir John's	Reg. K.R.N.Y.
2573	1091	Stevens Abel		

NOTES:
1. Nos. 598 & 599 - in original spelled SELMESER.
2. Nos. 647, 749 & 750 - otherwise spelled STEINBURNER, a German Palatine.
3. No. 713 - otherwise spelled SHWERDFEGER. A SAMUEL S(C)HWERDFEGER was the Lutheran Pastor at Williamsburg Lutheran/Anglican Church.
4. No. 731 - a CHRISTOPHER SERVOS (this entry could be of that name due to use of the abbreviation) was allotted Lot 4W/I Osnabruck. The name SERVOS is otherwise SERVISS/SERVICE et var and is believed to have originated in the 1600s from present day Czechoslovakia.

File 3 Page 31

S — 31

NUMBER	N°	NAMES	TOWNSHIP	REMARKS
2574	751	Stoneburner John		
2575	756	Summers David		
2576	891	Smith Peter Sen.[r]	Charlottenburg	
2577	892	Smith Peter Jun.[r]		
2578	893	Smith James		
2579	928	Sowils William Sen.[r]	Matilda	
2580	929	Sowils* William Jun.[r]		
2581	930	Sowils* John		
2582	935[f]	Stata Henry	Williamsburg	
2583	937	Strader Henry		
2584	938	Stamp Giles		
2585	952	Shaver John		
2586	959	Strader Simon	Matilda	
2587	960	Strader William		
2588	961	Strader John		
2589	963	Shaver John		
2590	964	Shaver Adam		
2591	983	Shaver Philip Jun.[r]		
2592	984	Stanford William		
2593	985	Stealey Martin		
2594	990	Shaver Philip Sen.[r]		
2595	991	Shaver Adam		2[f]
2596	992	Shaver Jacob		
2597	1001	Storin George	Williamsburg	
2598	1002[f]	Saver John	Matilda	
2599	1003	Service John		
2600	1040[f]	Sipes Andrew		
2601	1046	Shell John	Williamsburg	
2602	1047	Shell Benjamin	Matilda	
2603	1048	Shell Daniel	Williamsburg	
2604	1065	Shaver John	Matilda	2[f]
2605	1066	Shaver Conradt		
2606	1093	Slack Joseph	Bastard	
2607	1097	Scovils Samuel		
2608	1105	Stephens Pennuel*		
2609	1106	Stark James	Elisabethtown	
2610	1113	Simmond Caleb		
2611	1118	Snyder Mathew		
2612	1128	Storey Simon		omitted ent.[d] Solomon

NOTES:

1. No. 935 - 2nd choice STABA/STATIA; the name STATA/STATE is UEL.
2. No. 1002 - a JOHN SAVER allotted Lot 35W/I Matilda.
3. No. 1040 - an ANDREW SYPES allotted Lot 33E/III Matilda.
4. Matilda Twsp. had allocations to STRADERs, SHAVERs & SERVOS.
5. Page 31 continues.
6. The figures "2" in the Remarks column likely mean the 2nd time these names have appeared.

File 3 Page 31 cont'd

NUMBER	N^o	NAMES	TOWNSHIP	REMARKS
2613	1150	Starrs George	Yonge	
2614	1151	Sanders Henry		
2615	1165	Scott John Senr.		
2616	1174	Sutherland Walter Esqr.	Lancaster	
2617	1175	Sutherland John Johnson		
2618	1176	Sutherland Thomas		
2619	1177	Sutherland Alexander		
2620	1178	Sutherland George		
2621	1253	Sealye*Augustas		
2622	1271	Sealey James		
2623	1273	Sutherland John Stuart	Charlottenburg	
2624	1274	Sutherland Walter		
2625	1275	Scaret John		
2626	686	Swan Thomas Esqr.	Cornwall	
		carried to folio 35 under letter Y		
		(from page 35 under "Y")		
2627	(blank)	Salvester Levy	Elisabethtown	
2628	(blank)	Stevens Roger f	Augusta	
2629	(blank)	Snyder John	ditto	
2630	(blank)	Schaffer Nicholas f		
2631	(blank)	Sheek David f	Cornwall	
2632	(blank)	Sherwood Thomas		
2633	(blank)	Sherwood Reuben		son of Justiss* Error! (full ?) son of Thomas

NOTES:
1. No. 350 - seems to be duplication of (blank) ROGER STEVENS above.
2. (blank) SCHAFFER is an original spelling of SHAVER/SHAFFER in German.
3. (blank) SHEEK - David Sheek became a Justice of the Peace in Cornwall in the early 1800s.

File 3 Page 32

32

T

NUMBER	N°	NAMES	TOWNSHIP	REMARKS
2634	8	Terry Paul	Elisabethtown	
2635	36	Throop Dan	Augusta	
2636	136	Thompkins Israel		
2637	305	Thomas Peter	Elisabethtown	
2638	348	Thompson Daniel	Augusta	
2639	415	Thomas Jacob	Elisabethtown	
2640	712	Thomson George	Matilda	
2641	811	Tipple John should be (Teeple)	Osnabruck	
2642	971	Tetterley Peter vide Fetterley	Williamsburg	
2643	1049	Tillebough Peter		
2644	1060	Tillebough Martin	Matilda	
2645	1108f	Tuttle Jonathan	Yonge	
2646	1125f	Trumble Peter	Augusta 26 years of age in Loyalist. P.R.	Being over just now 96 cannot be a U.E.
2647	1143	Tuttle Samuel		
2648	1145	Tuttle Peter		
2649	1152	Tuttle Nathan	Yonge	
2650	1156	Thompson John		
2651	1205	Teynick Samuel	Lancaster	
2652	1019	*Tillebough Christain Jun	Matilda	
2653	1021	*Tillebough Christain Jun	Williamsburg	
2654	508	Toosler William This name should be "Dusler"	Cornwall	Ent.d Samuel
2655	545f	Tuttle Solomon	ditto	Ent.d Solomon
		V*& U*		
2656	14	Valentine John	Yonge	
2657	307f	Vancamp* Jacob	Matilda	
2658	308f	Vancamp* John		
2659	311	Vancamp* Peter		
2660	325	Vanvolkenburg Chloe	Augusta	
2661	471	Van Koughnet Mickle*	Cornwall	
2662	519	Valentine C. Widow		
2663	523	Van Koughnet John		
2664	907f	Urquhart William	Lancaster	
2664A	908f	Urquhart Alexander		
2665	1037	Vanallen Jacob	Matilda	

NOTES:

1. No. 1125 - the note is correct as written, but one must take exception to it as many "boys" of 10-12 served as drummers during the war.
2. No. 308 - a JOHN VAN CAMP allotted Lot 29E/I Matilda.
3. No. 545 - a SOLOMON TUTTLE allotted Lot 29W/I Osnabruck.
4. No. 2664A - omitted in first typing; given letter "A" so as not to disturb many hundreds of following entries.

File 3 Page 33

W 33

NUMBER	N°	NAMES	TOWNSHIP	REMARKS
2666	17	Whitney Elijah	Elisabethtown	
2667	30	Wing Gersham		
2668	37	Wooly John		
2669	44	Wickwire Levius	Augusta	
2670	45f	Wickwire Jonathan		
2671	91	Wiltsy Benond		
2672	105	Watson Major		
2673	169	Wilcox Hagard senior		
2674	170f	Wilcox Hagard junior		
2675	171	Wilton William		
2676	178	Wickwire Jonathan		before
2677	181	Weatherhead Samuel		
2678	231	Welsh William	Edwardsburg	
2679	301	Whitley John	Elisabethtown	
2680	304	Whitley John		
2681	306	Wright James		
2682	329	White John		
2683	339	Wickwire Philip	Augusta	
2684	352	Wilcox Leberry		
2685	354	White Joseph Junr.		
2686	356f	White Joseph Senr.		
2687	376	Wiltsey Benoni Junior	Elisabethtown	
2688	385	Wright William		
2689	386	Wright Samuel Junr.		
2690	387	Wright Sylvester		
2691	397	Wood Thomas		
2692	407	Waicoff John		
2693	416	White Joseph Junior		before Augusta
2694	472	Wright Ebenezer	Cornwall	
2695	473	Wright David		
2696	538	Waite Joseph		
2697	537	Wait George		
2698	548 f	Wood John		
2699	553 f	Waggoner Jacob Senr.		
2700	557 f	Waggoner Jacob Junior son	of Jacob Senior	
2701	558	Waggoner Henry	ditto	

NOTES:
1. Nos. 91 & 376 - large ink blot obscures No. 91 here and in the original. See No. 376, which confirms name from other sources where it is spelled "WILTSIE/WILTSEY //BENONI/BENONIE." This is 1st time name found spelled "BENOND".
2. No. 171 - 2nd choice WILLON
3. No. 553/7/8 - a common German Palatine name from Mohawk Valley.
4. Page 33 continues.

File 3 Page 33 cont'd

NUMBER	N°	NAMES	TOWNSHIP	REMARKS
2702	569	Wood Josiah		
2703	638	Warner Godfrey		
2704	640	Warner Michael Sen.[r]		
2705	643	Warner Michael Jun.[r]		
2706	648	Wood William		
2707	689	Willard Levi		
2708	704	Weaver Frederick		
2709	710	Weaver Peter		
2710	711	Weaver John		

NOTES:

File 3 Page 34

W

34

NUMBER	N°	NAMES	TOWNSHIP	REMARKS
2711	715	Weeger Jacob	Williamsburg	
2712	733 f	Wert Andrew	Osnabruck	
2713	765 f	Wert John jun.r		
2714	766 f	Weart Conradt		
2715	777	Winter Henry		
2716	778	Winter Peter		
2717	796	Warner George son of	Michael	
2718	797	Warner Conradt		
2719	799	Wright Asel		
2720	800	Wright Amos	Augusta	
2721	804	Wragg John	Grand River f	
2722	819	Wilkinson Richard Norton Capt.n	Charlottenburg	
2723	820 f	Wilkinson Walter son of ditto	Williamsburg	(lately of age 1803)
2724	934 f	Weart George		
2725	943	Wellery Henry		omitted
2726	962	Walliser Anthony	Matilda	
2727	966	Walliser John		
2728	967	Walliser Anthony Jun.r		
2729	988	Walter Martin		
2730	1008	Walter Philip		
2731	1029	Walliser Martin		
2732	1042	Wright Jesse		
2733	1070	Waggoner Henry		
2734	1134	Wilsie James	Yonge	
2735	1146	Ward Charles	Augusta	
2736	1147	Walker James		
2737	1161	Wickoff John	Yonge	
2738	1260	Whealer* David	Charlottenburg	
2739	1272	Whalen Michael		

NOTES:

1. Nos. 733, 765, 766 & 934 seem to be the same name in varients.
2. WALLISER is a German Palatine name anglicized to WALLACE.
3. No. 820 - considered in 1803 to be UEL as he is now of age. Compare with PETER TRUMBLE (No. 1125 on page 32). Inconsistency ?
4. This Grand River is the Ottawa River in Lower Canada.
5. Page 34 continues.

File 3 Page 34 cont'd

NUMBER	N°	NAMES	TOWNSHIP	REMARKS
2740	(blank)	Wiltsie John	Yonge	
2741	(blank)	Wood William	Cornwall	before
2742	(blank)	Wood John	ditto	before
2743	(blank)	Wood Benjamin	Charlottenburg	
2744	(blank)	Wood Roger	Cornwall	
2745	(blank)	Wood Stephen	ditto	
2746	(blank)	Wood Jonah Junior	ditto	
2747	(blank)	Wood Nathaniel	ditto	
2748	(blank)	Wragg Richard		
2749	(blank)	Wragg Thomas		
2750	1069	Wood Jonah Senior) (vide Jonah Wood)	Williamsburg now of Cornwall	
		carried over (to bottom page 35)		
2751	(blank)	Welch Margaret alias) Armstrong)	Edwardsburg	Ent.[d] as Armstrong
		(Page (Folio) 35 has only two "Y"s on it.)		
2752	924	Young James	Lancaster	
2753	1100	Yates John	Bastard	

NOTES:

File 3 Page 36

An additional List of U.E.[s] in the Eastern District

	Persons Names	
2754	Jonathan Millschurch	before
2755	Levy Silvester[f]	
2756	Ebenezer King	before
2757	Abijah Haly (Hawly)[f]	before
2758	John McLean	before
2759	William Campbell	before
2760	Edward Brown	before
2761	Roger Stephens	before
2762	Robert McLean	before
2763	Thadius Cartar* (as Thadeus Curtis ?)[f]	before
2764	John Snider	before
2765	John Myers	before
2766	Abraham Brown	before
2767	Ischial Mitchell	before
2768	Nicholas Hasking	before
2769	John Wiltsie	before
2770	Western Allan	before
2771	Duncan McLean	before
2772	Fred[k]. Johnson	before
2773	John Gardiner	before
2774	John Dauson	before
2775	Sylvester More[f]	
2776	David Haskins	before
2777	Cornelius Lozee	before
2778	William Parish	before
2779	Margaret Armstrong (alias Welch)	before
2780	Rebecca Deforrest	before
2781	William Wood	before
2782	John Wood	before
2783	Benjamin Wood	before
2784	Roger Wood	before
2785	Steven Wood	before
2786	Jonas Wood Jun[r].	before
2787	Nathaniel Wood	before
2788	David Monson[f]	
2789	Robert McLoghlin	before
2790	David McGloghlen	before
2791	Michael Myers	before
2792	Adam Papts	before
2793	Nicholas Schaffer	before
2794	Gottleib Otto	before
2795	William Baxter	before
2796	John Lang	before
2797	Peter Carpenter	before
2798	David Shak (Sheek)[f]	before
2799	William Bruce	before
2800	David Bruce	before
2801	Tunis Bender	before
2802	Margaret Bruce	before
2803	Richard Mandeville Sen	before

* * * * * * * *

Sent the Original List to David Burns Esq[r]. 13th April 1798 -------

July 26th 1798 in Council

2804 Daniel Livingston Deceased admitted to the Privileges of a U.E. Loyalist.

(Signed) Peter Russell

NOTES:

1. This is a true transcription of the original Folio 36. The only additions are the three names in brackets; HAWLY, CURTIS and SHEEK - as possible misspellings.
2. All these names appeared before on the list, even LEVY SILVESTER, SYLVESTER MORE and DAVID MONSON.
3. Folio 37 already copied as part of "M"s and "L"s.

File 3 Page 38

A list of names to be expunged from the U.E.
Lists Home District

2805[f] Capt George Dame
2806 John Warren Jun[r].
2807 Henry Warren
2808 Peter O Car*
2809 Timothy Murphy
2810 Peter Colerick
2811 Thomas Cooper
2812 James Cooper
2813 Sam[l]. Pew

Midland District

2814 Neil McLean Esq[r]. Ass[t]. Com[y]. General
2815 Lieut. Hector McLean
2816 Lieut. Arch[d]. Grant
2817 Lieut. John Connolly
2818 Lieut. Will[m]. McKay
2819 Will[m]. McDonell (late Storekeeper Kingston)
2820 Lieut. Allan McLean
2821 Commodore Bouchette
2822 John Kirby
2823 Robert Wilkins
2824 Tho[s]. Richardson
2825 Tho[s]. Winterbottom
2826 Lieut. Lewis Kotte

NOTES:
1. Page 39 is blank.
2. Capt. GEORGE DAME was a famous Company Commander in Butler's Rangers.

File 3 Page 40

	A list of Persons permitted to be Entered on the U.E. List	DISTRICT
2827	Peter Irish	Midland
2828	Lawrence Johnson	Home
2829	Anthony Hollingshead	do
2830	Nath[l]. Huson	do
2831	Thomas Sherwood	Eastern
2832	George Kintuer	do
2833	David Jacocks	do
2834	Capt[n]. Will[m]. Claus	Home
2835	Mihitable Buck	Eastern
2836	Thomas Hill	Home
2837	Peter Montrofs (Montross)	do
2838	Dan[l]. Louts	do
2839	John McLaney	do
2840	George Playter by Order of Lieut. Governor Simcoe[f]	
2841	Col. Shank	Home
2842	Col. Shaw	do
2843	Col. Smith	do
2844	Adam Papst	Eastern
2845	Levina Maybee	Home
2846	Dan[l]. Livingston deceased	Eastern
2847	Reuben Sherwood	do
2848	Widow Sarah Jones	Eastern

NOTE: 1. No District given for George Playter.

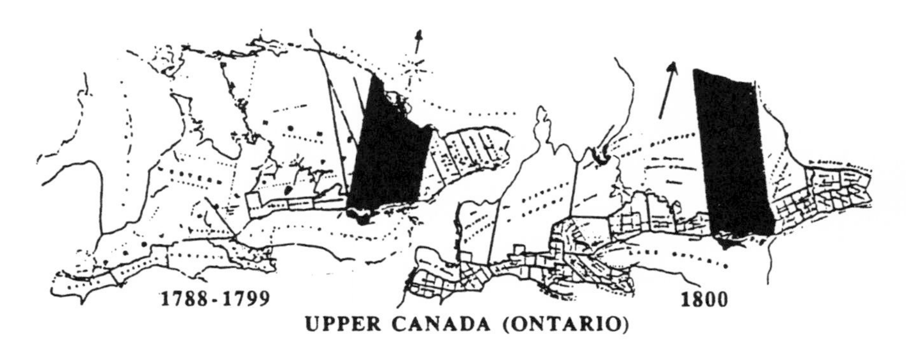

1788-1799 1800

UPPER CANADA (ONTARIO)

In 1796 the Midland District, earlier called the Mecklenburgh District, comprised Frontenac, Lennox and Addington, and Prince Edward Counties, and the southern part of Hastings County. In 1792 it also included a group of islands in Lake Ontario near the St. Lawrence River which were called Ontario County; this county was abolished in 1798 and is different from the Ontario County which was created from York County in 1851. The southern boundary of the Midland District was Lake Ontario; the Ottawa or Grand River was the northern boundary. In 1792 Kingston became the district town of the Midland District.

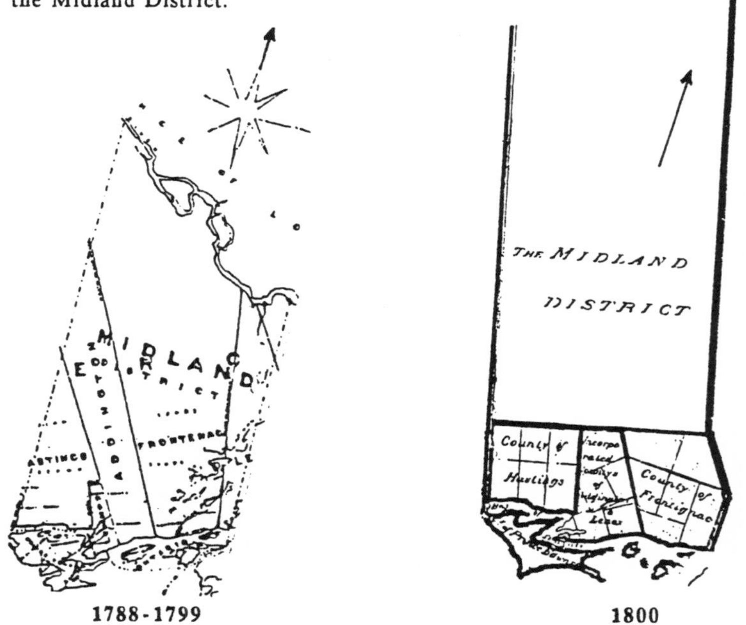

1788-1799 1800

THE MIDLAND DISTRICT

File 4

NATIONAL ARCHIVES OF CANADA (NAC)
UPPER CANADA (ONTARIO) DISTRICT LOYALIST ROLLS

Reference: NAC RG 1, L 7, vol. 52B(B as in Bravo) (FILES 1 to 15)

FILE 4

Archivist's Description

Not endorsed, but titled on first page "Upper Canada, Midland District" with a lengthy introduction similar to that on File 1. Contemporary copy, endorsed as from the original in the Crown Lands Office by David Burns, Clerk of that Office. On paper watermarked 1795 (identical to that of File 1), 32x19 cm, sewn. A list of some 1038 names, arranged by Township; 17 pages with a note of one name inserted.

Transcriber's Comments

The writing is generally quite easy to read with only a few letters in doubt; comparison with the File 5 entries (not all of which are exact copies of spellings/names) is a help. Each page is divided into two identical columns each without titles - but they allow a clerk's number (too faint to read) and a name followed with their status as to being judged to be worthy of U.E. designation or not. Each column requires one typewritten page; thus, two typewritten pages for each original page. There are not 1038 names as the archivist states (copied from the clerk's total) but only 1033 names including the single one added on page 34. The last 61 names do not have a Township of origin; indeed, the last 82 names are not identified as to Township.

There is little doubt that many are not "true" U.E.s, but sons/daughters of U.E.s; of course, this depends on one's definition of a U.E. The transcriber is heartened to not be able to identify some "late" Loyalists who came to this area of Upper Canada from the USA in response to another of Lt. Gov. Simcoe's Proclamations of 7 Feb 1792 offering free/cheap land for settlement. In later UCLPs, these people claimed to be "Loyalists". (See the transcriber's article in the NYG&B RECORD 113:161-164 (1982).

File 4 Page 1

NUMBER		
		(TITLE ON PAGE 1 OF FILE 4)
		UPPER CANADA MIDLAND DISTRICT
		Roll of the Inhabitants of the Midland District in the Province of Upper Canada who adhered to the Unity of the Empire and joined the Royal Standard in America before the Treaty of Separation in the year 1783.
		Taken in open Sefsions held at Kingston October 11th and at different adjournments to the 15th November 1796.
		Township of Kingston
3001	1	The Revd. John Stuart U.E.
3002	2	Richd. Cartwright Senr. U.E.
3003	3	Richd. Cartwright Junr. U.E.
3004	4 f	Jerh. Herkimer U.E.
3005	5 f	Neal McLean reduced afst. Commifsary General
3006	6	Hector McLean reduced Lieut.
3007	7	James McDonell U.E.
3008	8	Joseph Anderson U.E.
3009	9	Thomas Sparham U.E.
3010	10	Michael Grafs (GRASS) U.E.
3011	11 f	William Atkinson U.E.
3012	12 f	Lewis Kotte reduced German Officer
3013	13	Robert McAulay* U.E.
3014	14	Thomas Markland U.E.
3015	15 f	David Brafs (BRASS) U.E.
3016	16 f	Archd. Grant reduced Lieut.
3017	17 f	John Ferguson reduced Commy.
3018	18	John Conolly* reduced Lieut.
3019	19	Peter Smith U.E.
3020	20	Donald McDonell U.E.
3021	21	Christopher Robinson U.E.
		(end left column page 1)

NOTES:

1. Note the distinction made between a U.E. and a soldier.
2. No. 13 - in File 5 spelled "McCauley".
3. The margins of this page are in poor condition.
4. The original entry numbers are neither accurate or readable until approximately No. 150.
5. The right hand column of the cover page continues on page 2.
6. The pages are in two columns of names.

File 4 Page 1 cont'd

NUMBER			
3022	22	James Robins	U.E.
3023	23	William McKay reduced Lieut.[d]	
3024	24 f	William McDonell disch[d]. Soldier	
3025	25	Mary Brant	U.E.
3026	26	George Johnston	U.E.
3027	27	Elizabeth Johnston	U.E.
3028	28	Magdalen Johnston	U.E.
3029	29	Margaret Johnston	U.E.
3030	30 f	Joseph Franklin Sen[r].	U.E.
3031	31 f	Daniel McGuin	U.E.
3032	32 f	Nicholas Herkimer	U.E.
3033	33	Jacob Herkimer	U.E.
3034	34	Laurence Eldam discharged German Soldier	
3035	35	John Mosure*	U.E.
3036	36	John Brown disch[d]. Soldier	
3037	37	Emanuel Elderbeck	U.E.
3038	38	George Galloway	U.E.
3039	39	Thomas Moore	U.E.
3040	40 f	Michael Dederick	U.E.
3041	41	Lewis Grafs (GRASS)	U.E.
3042	42	Jacob Bastedo	U.E.
3043	43	Benjamin Valentine	U.E.

(end right hand column page 1)

NOTES:

1. No. 31 - 2nd choice McGuire (definitely McGU---).
2. No. 25 - the famous MOLLY BRANT, widow of SIR WILLIAM JOHNSON and sister of the renowned Indian Chief, JOSEPH BRANT.
3. Nos. 32 & 33 - sons of CAPTAIN JOHANN JOST HERKIMER, brother of the famous GENERAL NICHOLAS HERKIMER, the hero of the Battle of Driskany, 7 August 1777. GENERAL HERKIMER died as a result of this battle fought near present day Rome, New York.
4. No. 41 - originally a German name spelled "GRAS" meaning grass (as in a lawn).

File 4 Page 2

NUMBER			
		Township of Kingston contin[d].	2
3044	44	James Gale	U.E.
3045	45	Peter Wartman	U.E.
3046	46	Nich[s]. Whitsele disch[d]. German Soldier	
3047	47	Thomas Burnett	U.E.
3048	48	William Howe	U.E.
3049	49	John Everitt	U.E.
3050	50	Soloman Orser	U.E.
3051	51	Gilbert Orser	U.E.
3052	52	Barnabas Day	U.E.
3053	53	Alexander Simpson	U.E.
3054	54	John Marier	U.E.
3055	55	John Holmes	U.E.
3056	56	William Bell	U.E.
3057	57	John Most disch[d]. Soldier	
3058	58	William Wells	U.E.
3059	59	John Yorks	U.E.
3060	60	Richard Hall	U.E.
3061	61	Robert Graham	U.E.
3062	62	Elijah Grooms	U.E.
3063	63	Joseph Grooms	U.E.
3064	64	Matthew Burnett	U.E.
3065	65	James Brady	U.E.
3066	66	John Edgar	U.E.
3067	67	David Whiteman disch[d]. Soldier	
3068	68	Abraham Wartman	U.E.
3069	69	John Wartman	U.E.
3070	70	Barnabas Wartman	U.E.
3071	71	(blank) Myers reduced German Soldier	
3072	72	John Rowshorn D[o].	
3073	73	Amos Ainslie	U.E.
3074	74[f]	John Cannon	U.E.
3075	75	Barnabas Wemp	U.E.
3076	76	Richard Prentice	U.E.
3077	77	Charles McCullock* disch[d]. Artificer	
3078	78	James Harley D[o].	
3079	79	Jacob Powley	U.E.
		(end left column page 2)	

NOTES:

1. No. 74 - 2nd choice CARMAN - poor choice.
2. Fairly easy reading on this page.

File 4 Page 2 cont'd

NUMBER			
		Township of Kingston contin[d].	
3080	80	Francis Powley	U.E.
3081	81	Conrad Orval disch[d]. German Soldier	
3082	82	George Weston	U.E.
3083	83	Robert Tindall disch[d]. Soldier	
3084	84	John Warner D[o].	
3085	85	Mahalon* Knight	U.E.
3086	86	George Wesley	U.E.
3087	87	William Bower	U.E.
3088	88	Aaron Brewer	U.E.
3089	89	John Ferris	U.E.
3090	90	Lazarus Brewer	U.E.
3091	91	John Napping	U.E.
3092	92	Silas Palmer	U.E.
3093	93	Michael Taylor	U.E.
3094	94	Andrew Denyck	U.E.
3095	95	Arthur Orser	U.E.
3096	96	Isaac Orser	U.E.
3097	97	Britain Guinop	U.E.
3098	98	Michael Conlor disch[d]. Soldier	
3099	99	Arthur Yeomans	U.E.
3100	100	Jeremiah Lap	U.E.
3101	101	Terence Dunn disch[d]. Artificer	
3102	102	John Burnet*	U.E.
3103	103	Christopher Danby	U.E.
3104	104	Thomas Smith	U.E.
3105	105	John Smith	U.E.
3106	106	William Taylor	U.E.
3107	107	Bensley Peters	U.E.
3108	108	Nazarith Hill	U.E.
3109	109	George Harple	U.E.
3110	110	William Rancier	U.E.
3111	111	Peter Grafs (GRASS/GRAS)	U.E.
3112	112	Christo[r]. Furnier	U.E.
3113	113	Robert Williams disch[d]. Mariner	
3114	114	Christo[r]. Georgen disch[d]. Sold[r].	
3115	115	William Sheriff D[o].	
		(end right hand column page 2)	

NOTES:

File 4 Page 3

NUMBER		
		Township of Kingston 3
3116	116	John Lloyd disch[d] German Soldier
3117	117	Joseph Franklin Jun[r] U.E.
3118	118	Thomas Welkank* U.E.
3119	119	Widow Oneal* U.E.
3120	120	Samuel Ainslie U.E.
3121	121	James Dawson U.E.
3122	122	Antony* Dumell U.E.
3123	123	Philip Pember U.E.
3124	124	Thomas Cook disch[d] Soldier
3125	125	William Ashley D[o]
3126	126	John Grey disch[d] Artificer
3127	127	John Duncan D[o]
3128	128	Widow Wright U.E.
3129	129[f]	Widow Orser U.E.
3130	130	David Babcock U.E.
3131	131	Benjamin Babcock U.E.
3132	132	Matthew Van Order* U.E.
3133	133	Alex[r] Anderson disch[d] Soldier
3134	134	James Bayman disch[d] Mariner
3135	135	James Richardson D[o]
3136	136	Samuel Smith U.E.
3137	137[f]	Jean Baptiste Bouchette reduced Off[r] of the Marine
3138	138	Allan McLean reduced Officer
3139	139	Gilbert Purdy U.E.
3140	140	Arch[d] Fairfield U.E.
3141	141	Titus Fitz U.E.
3142	142	Stephen McLean disch[d] Artificer
3143	143	John Ferrier D[o]
3144	144	Hugh Campbell disch[d] Sold[r]
3145	145	Gaspe Strope* disch[d] German Sold[r]
3146	146	William Coffin U.E.
3147	147	William Taylor U.E.
		(end left hand column page 3)

NOTES:

1. No. 129 - ringed by a circle and underlined.
2. No. 137 - stroked through by three reverse obliques.

File 4 Page 3 cont'd

NUMEER			
		Township of Kingston	
3148	148	Allan McDonell	U.E.
3149	149	Lawrence* Herkimer	U.E.
3150	150	John Kirby	U.E.
3151	151	John Grant	U.E.
3152	152	Anthony McGuin	U.E.
3153	153	William Robins	U.E.
3154	154	Richard Robins	U.E.
3155	155[f]	Isaiah Van Order	U.E.
3156	156	Benjamin Babcock	U.E.
		Ernest Town	
3157	1	Will[m]. Johnston	U.E.
3158	2	Henry Simmonds	U.E.
3159	3	Gusbard Sharp	U.E.
3160	4	James Parrot	U.E.
3161	5	John Duzenberry*	U.E.
3162	6	Robert Clark	U.E.
3163	7[f]	Joshua Booth	U.E.
3164	8	Jephtha Hawley	U.E.
3165	9	Jacob Miller	U.E.
3166	10	Ichabod Hawley	U.E.
3167	11	Henry Finkle	U.E.
3168	12	John Thiele	U.E.
3169	13	John Garlock	U.E.
3170	14	John Shibley	U.E.
3171	15	Jacob Shibley	U.E.
3172	16	Daniel Carr Sen[r].	U.E.
3173	17	Daniel Carr Jun[r].	U.E.
3174	18	John Wist	U.E.
3175	19	David Wist	U.E.
3176	20	John Wist Jun[r].	U.E.
3177	21	Peter Thomas	U.E.
3178	22	Jacob Gordonier	U.E.
		(end right hand column page 3)	

NOTES:

1. No. 155 - first "a" of ISAIAH inserted with an inverted "v".
2. No. 7 - there is some faint, undecipherable writing beside name "BOOTH".

File 4 Page 4

NUMBER			
		Ernest Town contin[d].	4
3179	23	Henry Gordonier	U.E.
3180	24	Marcus Snyder	U.E.
3181	25	John Percy	U.E.
3182	26	James Cosway	U.E.
3183	27	John Davey	U.E.
3184	28	John Afselstine (ASSELSTINE)	U.E.
3185	29	John McKinny	U.E.
3186	30	David Hoffman	U.E.
3187	31	John Sharp Sen[r].	U.E.
3188	32	John Sharp Jun[r].	U.E.
3189	33	Daniel Walker Sen[r].	U.E.
3190	34	Daniel Walker Jun[r].	U.E.
3191	35[f]	John Maybe	U.E.
3192	36	Andrew Miller	U.E.
3193	37[f]	James McKim	U.E.
3194	38[f]	James McKim	U.E.
3195	39	William McKim	U.E.
3196	40	Colin McKenzie Sen[r].	U.E.
3197	41	Colin McKenzie Jun[r].	U.E.
3198	42	John Howard Sen[r].	U.E.
3199	43	John Howard Jun[r].	U.E.
3200	44	Thomas Howard	U.E.
3201	45	Edward Howard	U.E.
3202	46	John Ritchie	U.E.
3203	47	Thomas Jackson	U.E.
3204	48	George McGin	U.E.
3205	49	Michael Davey	U.E.
3206	50	Peter Davey	U.E.
3207	51	Henry Davey	U.E.
3208	52	Thomas Davey	U.E.
3209	53	Richard Robins	U.E.
3210	54	Matthias Rose	U.E.
3211	55	Matthias Rose Jun[r].	U.E.
3212	56	Freeman Burley	U.E.
3213	57	John Burley	U.E.
3214	58	Joseph Concklin	U.E.
3215	59	John Concklin	U.E.
		(end left hand column page 4)	

NOTES:

1. No. 35 - large ink blot at end of surname; does not obscure writing.
2. Nos. 37/38 - no distinction as to Junior/Senior here or in File 5.

File 4 Page 4 cont'd

NUMBER			
		Ernest Town contin[d]	
3216	60	James Jackson	U.E.
3217	61	David Jackson	U.E.
3218	62	Thomas Comber	U.E.
3219	63[f]	Jonas Amey	U.E.
3220	64	Martin Stover	U.E.
3221	65	John Stowood	U.E.
3222	66	Lewis Hicks	U.E.
3223	67	Simon Schneider	U.E.
3224	68[f]	Nicholas Amey	U.E.
3225	69	Daniel Frazer Sen[r]	U.E.
3226	70	Daniel Frazer Jun[r]	U.E.
3227	71	Davis Hawley	U.E.
3228	72	William Fairfield	U.E.
3229	73	Benjamin Fairfield	U.E.
3230	74	Jonathan Fairfield	U.E.
3231	75	Stephen Fairfield	U.E.
3232	76	Isaac Briscoe	U.E.
3233	77	Norris Briscoe	U.E.
3234	78	Nathan Briscoe	U.E.
3235	79	Andrew Miller	U.E.
3236	80	David Williams	U.E.
3237	81	Samuel Williams	U.E.
3238	82	Elijah Williams	U.E.
3239	83	David Williams Sen[r]	U.E.
3240	84	Jacob Hoffman	U.E.
3241	85[f]	John Scheider*	U.E.
3242	86[f]	Abraham Scheider*	U.E.
3243	87[f]	Isaac Schneider*	U.E.
3244	88	Peter Gilchrist	U.E.
3245	89	Neal Gilchrist	U.E.
3246	90	William Gilchrist	U.E.
3247	91	Francis Dickson	U.E.
3248	92	Barnabas Hough	U.E.
3249	93	Isaac Hough	U.E.
3250	94	John Van Ducar	U.E.
3251	95	Ralph Van Ducar	U.E.
3252	96	John Diamond	U.E.
		(end right hand column page 4)	

NOTES:

1. Nos. 63 & 68 - there is an interesting story here in the evolution of a name. As Palatine Germans, NICHOLAS EMICH fled to London, England in 1709; he eventually settled in Dutchess Co.,NYS. The name was spelled EMIG/ EIGHMIE et var in successive generations. In coming to Canada in 1783, and not being able to spell their name, the clerks etc. spelled it AMEY. The family is still extant in Dutchess Co. where the name is spelled EMIG et var.

2. Nos. 85/6/7 - note spelling errors with first two.

File 4 Page 5

NUMBER			
		Ernest Town	5
3253	97	Christopher Lake	U.E.
3254	98f	Bostain Hogle	U.E.
3255	99f	Andrew Shutler	U.E.
3256	100f	James Hogle	U.E.
3257	101	John Amey	U.E.
3258	102	Daniel Perry	U.E.
3259	103	William Fairfield	U.E.
3260	104	Benjamin Booth	U.E.
3261	105	Samuel Beach	U.E.
3262	106	Rufsel Hawley (RUSSEL HAWLEY)	U.E.
3263	107	John Cock	U.E.
3264	108	Adam Vanderheyder	U.E.
3265	109	William Amsbury	U.E.
3266	110	John Lindsey	U.E.
3267	111	Cornelius Putman	U.E.
3268	112	Bruen Hough	U.E.
3269	113	Frederick Baker	U.E.
3270	114	Peter Afselstine (ASSELSTINE)	U.E.
3271	115	Isaac Afselstine (ASSELSTINE)	U.E.
3272	116f	Thomas Frazer	U.E.
3273	117	Tunis Hagerman	U.E.
3274	118f	Magnus Shrawder	U.E.
3275	119	Philip Switzer	U.E.
3276	120f	Daniel Rose	U.E.
3277	121f	Hercules Kronkheit	U.E.
3278	122f	John Kronkheit	U.E.
3279	123	Stephen Boyce	U.E.
3280	124	Andrew Boyce	U.E.
3281	125	David Hartman	U.E.
3282	126	Philip Hartman	U.E.
3283	127	Ludovick* Hartman	U.E.
3284	128	Jacob Hartman	U.E.
3285	129	Jacob Hefs (HESS)	U.E.
3286	130	Peter Daly	U.E.
3287	131	Daniel Simmonds	U.E.
3288	132	John Simmonds	U.E.
		(end left hand column page 5)	

NOTES:

1. No. 99 - in File 5 , Nos. 99 & 100 are reversed.
2. No. 101 - see note 1 on page 8.
3. No. 117 - otherwise spelled HAEGAERMAN.
4. Nos. 121/2 - Walter Kronkheit, the TV News Announcer, traces his lineage back to this family in NYS as well.
5. No. 119 - SWITZER is an Irish Palatine name - from the German Palatines who fled to London, England in 1709 and were settled in Ireland (and NY State) in 1710 by Queen Anne. The name has defied anglicization over centuries.

File 4 Page 5 cont'd

NUMBER			
		Ernest Town	
3289	133	Nicholas Simmonds	U.E.
3290	134	James Beavins	U.E.
3291	135	Henry Clark	U.E.
3292	136	Adam Vent	U.E.
3293	137	Joseph Hoffman	U.E.
3294	138	Jacob Comber	U.E.
3295	139	Peter McPherson	U.E.
3296	140	John McPherson	U.E.
3297	141	Christian Abrahim*	U.E.
3298	142	John McDougall	U.E.
3299	143	Peter McDougall	U.E.
3300	144	Kenneth Frazer	U.E.
3301	145 f	David Frazer	U.E.
3302	146 f	Hermanus Sea	U.E.
3303	147	Peter Freelick	U.E.
3304	148	John Frazer	U.E.
3305	149	Robert Perry Sen.r	U.E.
3306	150	Robert Perry Jun.r	U.E.
3307	151	John Williams Sen.r	U.E.
3308	152	William Perry Sen.r	U.E.
3309	153	John Perry	U.E.
3310	154	William Perry Jun.r	U.E.
3311	155	James Johnston	U.E.
3312	156	Daniel Johnston	U.E.
3313	157	Andrew Johnston	U.E.
3314	158	David Shorey Sen.r	U.E.
3315	159	David Shorey Jun.r	U.E.
3316	160 f	Rufus Shorey	U.E.
3317	161 f	Gilbert Storms	U.E.
3318	162 f	Henry Storms	U.E.
3319	163	Jacob Storms	U.E.
3320	164	John Rogers	U.E.
3321	165	William Rogers	U.E.
3322	166	Armstrong Williams	U.E.
3323	167	Robert Williams	U.E.
3324	168	Joshua Williams	U.E.
		(end right hand column page 5)	

NOTES:

1. No. 146 - see NYG&B Record Vol. 114:163, The See Family. HARMANUS b. 5 July 1746; brothers JACOBUS & ABRAHAM all Loyalists. Of Huguenot origin, spelling varients include SEA/ZEH/CIE. Harmanus served in Jessup's Loyal Rangers.
2. Nos. 161/2/3 - poor, 2nd choice is STORINS.
3. No.147 - now FRALICK ?

File 4 Page 6

NUMBER			
		Ernest Town	6
3325	169	James Williams	U.E.
3326	170	John Williams Junr.	U.E.
3327	171	Elijah Hough	U.E.
3328	172	Samuel Hough	U.E.
3329	173	Sheldon Hawley	U.E.
3330	174	Martin Hawley	U.E.
3331	175	Samuel McKay	U.E.
3332	176	Matthew Clark	U.E.
3333	177	George Miller	U.E.
3334	178	Paul Comber	U.E.
3335	179	George Havens	U.E.
3336	180	John Ham	U.E.
3337	181	John Havens	U.E.
3338	182	Solomon Ball	U.E.
3339	183	Shadrach* Ball	U.E.
3340	184	Daniel Corban	U.E.
3341	185	William Walker	U.E.
3342	186	Weiden* Walker	U.E.
3343	187	John George	U.E.
3344	188	William Cottier	U.E.
3345	189	David Lockwood	U.E.
3346	190	Robert Havens	U.E.
3347	191 f	John Adam Friermut*	U.E.
3348	192	Donald McDonald	U.E.
3349	193	Andrew Rusk	U.E.
3350	194	William Cook	U.E.
3351	195	David Harris	U.E.
3352	196	Simon Swart	U.E.
3353	197	Michael Philips	U.E.
3354	198	David Purdy	U.E.
3355	199	Francis Redins	U.E.
3356	200	Thomas Freeman	U.E.
3357	201	Samuel Welch	U.E.
3358	202 f	Francois*Lerock Senr.	U.E.
3359	203 f	Francis Lerock Junr.	U.E.
3360	204	Peter Lerock	U.E.
		(end left hand column page 6)	

NOTES:

1. No. 191 - File 5 no help as there is a break in the paper. The above interpretation is believed correct.
2. No. 202/3 - note change in spelling; in File 5, both spelled FRANCOIS.

File 4 Page 6 cont'd

NUMBER			
		Ernest Town	
3361	205	James Work	U.E.
3362	206	John Lake Sen.[r]	U.E.
3363	207	John Lake Jun.[r]	U.E.
3364	208	Nicholas Lake	U.E.
3365	209	James Lake	U.E.
3366	210	Francis Hogle	U.E.
3367	211	John Leonard	U.E.
3368	212	John Clement	U.E.
3369	213	Henry Gickland	U.E.
3370	214	Adam Bower	U.E.
3371	215	John Chridsnager*	U.E.
		Township of Fredericksburg	
3372	1[f]	John Anderson	U.E.
3373	2	Charles Barnhart	U.E.
3374	3	Michael Bartley	U.E.
3375	4	William Bell	U.E.
3376	5[f]	Samuel Brunson	U.E.
3377	6	Duncan Bell	U.E.
3378	7	Isaak* Bartley	U.E.
3379	8	Aval Bradshaw	U.E.
3380	9	James Bradshaw Jun.[r]	U.E.
3381	10	James Bradshaw Sen.[r]	U.E.
3382	11	David Bradshaw	U.E.
3383	12	Gasper Bower	U.E.
3384	13	Adam Bower	U.E.
3385	14	Thomas Bell	U.E.
3386	15	Henry Brants	U.E.
3387	16	Samuel Brunson Sen.[r]	U.E.
3388	17	William Bowen	U.E.
3389	18	John Behn*	U.E.
3390	19[f]	Jacob Birch*	U.E.
3391	20	William Crawford	U.E.

(end right hand column page 6)

NOTES:

1. Because the numbering started afresh at No. 156 of Kingston, and the clerk's numbering was incorrect, the transcriber chose to start from number 1 again; this is being consistant in any case.
2. No. 5 - this name badly smeared; picked up from File 5 and from No. 16.
3. No. 19 - poor 2nd choice is BIREK; File 5 definitely BIRCH.

File 4 Page 7

NUMBER			
		Township of Fredericksburg	7
3392	21^{f}	Edward Carrscallen	U.E.
3393	22^{f}	John Carrscallen	U.E.
3394	23^{f}	Luke Carrscallen	U.E.
3395	24^{f}	James Carrscallen	U.E.
3396	25^{f}	George Carrscallen	U.E.
3397	26	Bryan* Crawford	U.E.
3398	27	Alex^{r}. Clark	U.E.
3399	28	James Cottier Senr.	U.E.
3400	29	Rich^{d}. Cottier	U.E.
3401	30	James Cottier Junr.	U.E.
3402	31	William Cadman	U.E.
3403	32	Alpheus Cadman	U.E.
3404	33	Asa Cadman	U.E.
3405	34	John Cornelius	U.E.
3406	35^{f}	Hugh Clark	U.E.
3407	36^{f}	Oliver Church	U.E.
3408	37	Oliver Church Junr.	U.E.
3409	38	Abraham Defoe	U.E.
3410	39	Jacob Diamond	U.E.
3411	40	Michael Defoe	U.E.
3412	41	John Diamond	U.E.
3413	42	John Defoe	U.E.
3414	43	Daniel Defoe	U.E.
3415	44	Peter Detlor	U.E.
3416	45	James Demorest	U.E.
3417	46	Valentine Detlor	U.E.
3418	47	Jacob Detlor	U.E.
3419	48	Samuel Detlor	U.E.
3420	49	John Detlor	U.E.
3421	50	George Detlor	U.E.
3422	51	Florence Dunovan	U.E.
3423	52	Matt^{w}. Dies Senr.	U.E.
3424	53	John Dies	U.E.
3425	54	Matthew Dies Junr.	U.E.
3426	55	Garret Dingman	U.E.
3427	56^{f}	Samuel Pattingall	U.E.
3428	57^{f}	Timothy Prindle*	U.E.
		(end of left hand column page 7)	

NOTES:

1. No. 57 - believed to otherwise be spelled PRINGLE.
2. No. 36 - large ink blot over 1st "C" of CHURCH.
3. Nos. 21 to 25 - there is an ink-over correction on all these names; in some it looks like a double "R" - in others a single "R". File 4 definitely a single "R".

File 4 Page 7 cont'd

NUMBER			
		Township of Fredericksburg	
3429	58	Joel Prindle*	U.E.
3430	59 f	Andrew Rickley	U.E.
3431	60	William Rambouch	U.E.
3432	61	Zenus Rofs (ROSS)	U.E.
3433	62	Asa Richardson	U.E.
3434	63	Thomas Richardson	U.E.
3435	64	William Richardson	U.E.
3436	65	Henry Richardson	U.E.
3437	66	William Shoeman	U.E.
3438	67	John Sills	U.E.
3439	68	James Simpson	U.E.
3440	69	John Smith	U.E.
3441	70	Peter Smith	U.E.
3442	71	Conrad Sills	U.E.
3443	72	William Shaw	U.E.
3444	73	Job Stains	U.E.
3445	74	Lawrence Sills	U.E.
3446	75	George Sills	U.E.
3447	76	George Schriver	U.E.
3448	77	Michael Smith	U.E.
3449	78	Jacob Smith Sen[r].	U.E.
3450	79	Jacob Smith Jun[r].	U.E.
3451	80	Daniel Smith	U.E.
3452	81	Comfort Smith	U.E.
3453	82	William Smith	U.E.
3454	83	Hazleton Spencer	U.E.
3455	84	Henry Seerman	U.E.
3456	85	Tobias Steely	U.E.
3457	86	William Schermerhorn	U.E.
3458	87	William Thomson	U.E.
3459	88	Gerrard Tyler	U.E.
3460	89	Timothy Thompson	U.E.
3461	90	Francis Vander Bogart	U.E.
3462	91	Thomas Wager	U.E.
3463	92	Everard Wager	U.E.
3464	93	William Wager	U.E.
3465	94 f	Samuel Walsh	U.E.
		(end of right hand column page 7)	

NOTES:

1. No. 60 - a name similar to this occurs in Eastern District - spelled RAMBOUGH in many records.
2. No. 94 - spelled WALSK in File 5.

File 4 Page 8

NUMBER			
		Township of Fredericksburg	8
3466	95	John Woodcock	U.E.
3467	96	Abraham Woodcock	U.E.
3468	97	Ebenezer Washburn	U.E.
3469	98	Albert Williams	U.E.
3470	99	Peter Young Sen[r].	U.E.
3471	100	Stephen Young	U.E.
3472	101	Henry Young Sen[r].	U.E.
3473	102	Henry Young Jun[r].	U.E.
3474	103	Peter Young Jun[r].	U.E.
3475	104	Andrew Huffnail	U.E.
3476	105	Rufsel Pitman (RUSSEL PITMAN)	U.E.
3477	106[f]	Peter Bowen	U.E.
3478	107[f]	Victor Bowen	U.E.
3479	108	Jacob Diamond Jun[r].	U.E.
3480	109	John Diamond	U.E.
3481	110	Andrew Embrie	U.E.
3482	111	Adam Earhart	U.E.
3483	112	David Embrie Jun[r].	U.E.
3484	113	John Embrie	U.E.
3485	114	Peter Frederick	U.E.
3486	115	Peter Fykes	U.E.
3487	116	James Fitchet	U.E.
3488	117	William Frazer	U.E.
3489	118	Richard Fitchet	U.E.
3490	119	Moses Foster	U.E.
3491	120	George Finkle	U.E.
3492	121	John Finkle	U.E.
3493	122	Jacob Finkle	U.E.
3494	123	Aara Ferguson	U.E.
3495	124	Warren Howell	U.E.
3496	125	Jacob Hoffman	U.E.
3497	126	John Hough	U.E.
3498	127	Philip Hoffman	U.E.
3499	128	Felix Harson	U.E.
3500	129	Elias Hoffman	U.E.
3501	130[f]	Johnston Harns	U.E.
		(end left hand column page 8)	

NOTES:

1. Nos. 106/7 - the name BOUEN was recorded in Fort Hunter Indian Chapel (west of Schenectady, NY) in their church register 1740/60s. See also FAMILIES 21:50.
2. No. 130 (et seq) - one could make HARRIS out of this name quite easily; but, when seen and compared in all four versions, it is definitely HARNS.

File 4 Page 8 cont'd

NUMBER			
		Township of Fredericksburg	
3502	131[f]	Gilbert Harns	U.E.
3503	132[f]	Isaiah Harns	U.E.
3504	133[f]	Thomas Harns	U.E.
3505	134	Adam Hedler	U.E.
3506	135	William Harlowe	U.E.
3507	136	Andrew Heron	U.E.
3508	137[f]	Gilbert Harns	U.E.
3509	138	Asa Huff	U.E.
3510	139	William Kitcheson	U.E.
3511	140	John Keller	U.E.
3512	141	Frederick Keller	U.E.
3513	142	James Kemp	U.E.
3514	143	Joseph Kemp	U.E.
3515	144	John Kemp	U.E.
3516	145	John Kemp Jun[r].	U.E.
3517	146[f]	William Koughnet	U.E.
3518	147	Charles Keller	U.E.
3519	148	David Lambert	U.E.
3520	149	William Lawer*	U.E.
3521	150	Harman* Laroway	U.E.
3522	151[f]	Henry Loukes*	U.E.
3523	152	James Lindsey*	U.E.
3524	153	Andrew Lyst	U.E.
3525	154	Richard Loyd*	U.E.
3526	155	Peter Laroway	U.E.
3527	156	Isaac Laroway Sen[r].	U.E.
3528	157	Isaac Laroway Jun[r].	U.E.
3529	158	Abraham Laroway	U.E.
3530	159	Jonas Laroway	U.E.
3531	160	Daniel Loyd*	U.E.
3532	161	Jacob Loukes	U.E.
3533	162	Abraham Loukes	U.E.
3534	163	George Loukes	U.E.
3535	164	Henry Lyst	U.E.
3536	165	James McTaggett	U.E.
3537	166[f]	John Milts	U.E.
		(end right hand column page 8)	

NOTES:

1. Nos. 131 & 137 - no junior or senior here; is this a duplication ? See footnote No. 2, Page 15.
2. No. 146 - usually spelled VAN KOUGHNET. The ancestor of a 1985 Federal Member of Parliament.
3. No. 151 - usually spelled LOUCK(S); original German LAUXS.
4. No. 166 et seq - the "T" is definitely crossed in both places; in File 5 spelling just as definitely MITTS. This is a poor 2nd choice. Definitely not MILLS.

File 4 Page 9

NUMBER			
		Township of Fredericksburg	9
3538	167[f]	Henry Milts	U.E.
3539	168	Daniel McMullen	U.E.
3540	169	Jonathan Miller	U.E.
3541	170	George Murdoff Sen[r].	U.E.
3542	171[f]	George Murdoff Jun[r].	U.E.
3543	172	James Murdoff	U.E.
3544	173	John Murdoff	U.E.
3545	174	Thomas Murdoff	U.E.
3546	175	Hugh McConnell	U.E.
3547	176	Owen McGrath	U.E.
3548	177	Alex[r]. Nicholson	U.E.
3549	178	John Neher	U.E.
3550	179	Elisha Philips	U.E.
3551	180	Cyrenus Parks	U.E.
3552	181	Nathaniel Parks	U.E.
3553	182	James Parks	U.E.
3554	183	Frederick Post	U.E.
3555	184[f]	Doctor Prindle*	U.E.
3556	185	Peter Philips	U.E.
3557	186	Daniel Lobedell	U.E.
3558	187	Richard Albertson	U.E.
3559	188	John Pickle Sen[r].	U.E.
3560	189	John Pickle Jun[r].	U.E.
3561	190	Archib[d]. Nicholson	U.E.
3562	191	James Johnston	U.E.
3563	192	James McNut	U.E.
3564	193	Thomas Saunderson	U.E.
3565	194	Matthew Benson	U.E.
3566	195	Paul Peterson	U.E.
3567	196	Christian Peterson	U.E.
3568	197	John Schermerhorn	U.E.
3569	198	Cornelius Benson	U.E.
3570	199	Henry Evans	U.E.
3571	200[f]	Peter Bower*	U.E.
3572	201	Martin Shoeman	U.E.
3573	202	Baultis Shoeman	U.E.
		(end left hand column page 9)	

NOTES:

1. No. 171 - there is a large ink blot in the form of "X C." after Junior. Meaning ?
2. No. 184 - see Note 1. page 13; this name spelled PRINGLE (Doctor) in other lists. The "D" is quite clear.
3. No. 200 - in File 5 written PETER BOWEN with a faint note above "a BOWEN Niagara Roll". Spelling BOWER & BOWEN quite distinct both places. Some confusion due to writing by original clerks and reviewers. See footnote No. 1, Page 15.

File 4 Page 9 cont'd

NUMBER			
		Township of Fredericksburg cont.	
3574	203	William Redford Crawford	U.E.
3575	204	Jacob Ferguson	U.E.
3576	205	Jacob Pattingall	U.E.
3577	206	John George Smith	U.E.
3578	207 f	John Bowen	U.E.
3579	208 f	Abraham Bowen	U.E.
3580	209	Nicholas Smith	U.E.
3581	210	Joseph Marsh	U.E.
3582	211	Zadock* Hawley	U.E.
3583	212	Josiah Cain	U.E.
		Township of Adolphus	
3584	1	John German	U.E.
3585	2	Abert* Benson	U.E.
3586	3 f	John Vanskiver	U.E.
3587	4	John Fitzgerald	U.E.
3588	5	Henry Redner	U.E.
3589	6	Henry Davis	U.E.
3590	7	Peter Rattan Jun.[r]	U.E.
3591	8	Michael Sloot	U.E.
3592	9	Philip Darland	U.E.
3593	10	Henry Hover	U.E.
3594	11	Abraham Maybe	U.E.
3595	12	John McMasters	U.E.
3596	13	Joseph Allison	U.E.
3597	14	William Moore	U.E.
3598	15	Christopher German	U.E.
3599	16	Abraham Bogart	U.E.
3600	17	Garret Benson	U.E.
3601	18	Peter Duylay*	U.E.
3602	19	Albert Cornell	U.E.
3603	20	William Clark	U.E.
		(end right hand column page 9)	

NOTES:

1. No. 207/8 - the problem is the closeness of the terminal "r" and "n" on a word; the "r" is like an inverted "j" without the dot - it terminates in the air on an up stroke. The "n" has two "humps" and terminates on the line. These are definitely BOWEN. See footnotes, p 15.
2. No. 4 - no known relationship to the transcriber. This JOHN FITZGERALD was a corporal in Jessup's Rangers and a clerk; he was born in Ireland.

File 4 Page 10

NUMBER			
		Township of Adolphus cont[d]	10
3604	21	Cornelius Van Horn	U.E.
3605	22	John Huyck	U.E.
3606	23	Paul Huff	U.E.
3607	24f	Gilbert Bogart	U.E.
3608	25	Owen Roblin Sen[r]	U.E.
3609	26f	George Rutler Sen[r]	U.E.
3610	27	John Roblin	U.E.
3611	28	Owen P. Roblin	U.E.
3612	29	John Cuniff	U.E.
3613	30	Jacob German	U.E.
3614	31	Norris Carr	U.E.
3615	32	Cornelius Sharp	U.E.
3616	33	Nicholas Peterson	U.E.
3617	34	Conrad Van Dusen	U.E.
3618	35	Peter Van Alstine	U.E.
3619	36	Alex[r] Fisher	U.E.
3620	37	William Casey	U.E.
3621	38f	Nicholas Haggerman*	U.E.
3622	39f	Barent Servis	U.E.
3623	40	William Rattan	U.E.
3624	41	Daniel Cole	U.E.
3625	42	Alex[r] Campbell	U.E.
3626	43	Peter Rattan Sen[r]	U.E.
3627	44	Thomas Dorland	U.E.
3628	45	Paul Trompeau	U.E.
3629	46	Cornelius Slouter	U.E.
3630	47	Peter Wanamaker	U.E.
3631	48	Joseph Cornell	U.E.
3632	49	Obadiah Simpson	U.E.
3633	50	Arch[d] Campbell	U.E.
3634	51	Peter Duylea*Jun[r]	U.E.
3635	52	Samuel Duylea	U.E.
		(end left hand column page 10)	

NOTES:

1. No. 25 - there is a large tick mark beside Senior.
2. No. 39 - otherwise spelled SERVOS/SERVICE et var.
3. No. 38 - another varient of HAEGAERMAN/HAGERMAN.
4. No. 27 - there is a large "X" beside the name corresponding to one beside PHILIP ROBLIN in next column.

File 4 Page 10 cont'd

NUMEER			
		Township of Adolphus cont.[d]	
3636	53	Joseph Duylea	U.E.
3637	54	Joseph Clark	U.E.
3638	55	Soloman* Huff Jun.[r]	U.E.
3639	56 f	Alex.[r] Van Alstine	U.E.
3640	57	Owen Roblin Jun.[r]	U.E.
3641	58	Cosfiares* Van Dusen	U.E.
3642	59	Cornelius Van Alstine	U.E.
3643	60	John Beneger	U.E.
3644	61	Henry Redner Jun.[r]	U.E.
3645	62	Augustus Shorts	U.E.
3646	63	Michael Marbet	U.E.
3647	64	Mary Fisher (Widow)	U.E.
3648	65 f	Peter Brunner	U.E.
3649	66	Philip Roblin	U.E.
3650	67	Casper Hover	U.E.
3651	68	Jacob Hover	U.E.
3652	69 f	John Ryckman	U.E.
3653	70	Jepts Huffnail	U.E.
3654	71	Michael Van Devart	U.E.
3655	72	William Griffiths	U.E.
3656	73	James Cuniff	U.E.
3657	74	Oliver Campbell	U.E.
3658	75	William Campbell	U.E.
		(end right hand column page 10)	
3652A	69A	Nicholas Peterson (omitted from proper sequence between Nos. 69 & 70)	U.E.

NOTES:

1. No. 57 - large tick mark beside junior.
2. No. 66 - large "X" beside surname.
3. No. 70 - in File 5, spelled GEPTS; here, it is definitely as written above. For "JEPHTHA" ?

File 4 Page 11

NUMBER			
		Part of Marysburg	11
3659	76	Arch[d]. McDonell	U.E.
3660	77	Peter Van Schiver	U.E.
3661	78	Joseph Hicks	U.E.
3662	79	Edward Hicks	U.E.
3663	80	Benjamin Hicks	U.E.
3664	81	David Embrie	U.E.
3665	82	Joshua Hicks	U.E.
3666	83	Mich[l]. Criderman	U.E.
3667	84	David Dulmadge	U.E.
3668	85	Stephen Farrington	U.E.
3669	86	Robert Farrington	U.E.
3670	87	Joseph Allen	U.E.
3671	88	John Allen	U.E.
3672	89	Jonathan Allen	U.E.
3673	90	James Hughs	U.E.
3674	91	Daniel Hicks	U.E.
3675	92	David Hicks	U.E.
3676	93 f	John Green 2	U.E.
3677	94	William Green 2	U.E.
3678	95 f	John Green	U.E.
3679	96	James Durolemy	U.E.
3680	97	Peter Frill	U.E.
3681	98	Samuel Farrington	U.E.
3682	99	Peter Dap*	U.E.
3683	100	Daniel Wright disch[d]. Brit[h]. Sold[r].	
3684	101	Henry Smith D[o].	
3685	102	James Edwards D[o].	
3686	103	Thomas Price D[o].	
3687	104	John Stewart D[o].	
3688	105	Lauchlin* McIntosh D[o].	
3689	106	Robert Thompson D[o].	
3690	107	Hugh Swiney D[o].	
3691	108	Robert Stewart D[o].	
3692	109	John McBean D[o].	
		(end left hand column page 11)	

NOTES:

1. No. 93 & 95 are squeezed in on either side of No. 94. The figure "2" beside these added entries likely is to count the number of JOHN GREENs & WILLIAM GREENs.

File 4 Page 11 cont'd

NUMBER		
		Part of Marysburg continued
3693	110 f	William Batty disch[d] Brit[h] Soldier
3694	111	Alex[r] McDonell D[o]
3695	112	John McDonell D[o]
3696	113	Michael McCarthy D[o]
3697	114	Reuben Hughes D[o]
3698	115	Henry Simmerman D[o]
3699	116	John Cummins D[o]
3700	117	William McKenzie D[o]
3701	118	Joseph Wright D[o]
3702	119	Conrad Vullicar D[o]
3703	120	Fred[k] Crammer D[o]
3704	121	Peter Collier D[o]
3705	122	John Moor D[o]
3706	123	John Vogley D[o]
3707	124	Thomas Roberts D[o]
3708	125	Robert Midleton* D[o]
3709	126	John Fearman D[o]
3710	127	Thomas McGowen D[o]
3711	128	Fred[k] Fisher D[o]
3712	129	Andrew Ellis D[o]
3713	130	John Simpson D[o]
3714	131	Nathan[l] Heald* D[o]
3715	132	Edward Powis D[o]
3716	133	John Lovell D[o]
3717	134	John OBrien* D[o]
3718	135	Fred[k] Phifer D[o]
3719	136	John Kenard D[o]
3720	137 f	John Byrns* D[o]
3721	138	Jacob Starts D[o]
3722	139	Henry Bird D[o]
3723	140	Henry Saunders D[o]
3724	141 f	Bart[w] Sleaphy D[o]
		(end right hand column page 11)

NOTES:

1. At No. 111 one can have no doubt of the 700 reading in the numbers column in the original. When one adds up the sub-totals of each Township, the total is 694 - the clerk was out six in his count.
2. No. 137 - same in File 5.
3. No. 141 - in File 5, written above in faint writing is the word "HIFFY". The correct spelling of the name ?

File 4 Page 12

NUMBER		
		Part of Marysburg continued 12
3725	142	John Heford disch^d Brit^h Soldier
3726	143	Richd Campbell D^o
3727	144	Robert Potten D^o
3728	145	Hugh Gallagher* D^o
3729	146	John Hancock D^o
3730	147	Thomas Loyd* D^o
3731	148	John Anderson D^o
3732	149	James Chavasey* D^o
3733	150	Thomas Roberts D^o
3734	151	William Rofs (ROSS) D^o
3735	152	John Segus* D^o
3736	153 f	Edward Bedford D^o
3737	154	Stephen Pilchard* D^o
3738	155	Richard Bibby D^o
3739	156	William Mulloy D^o
3740	157	Joseph McCarger D^o
3741	158	John Husley D^o
3742	159	Charles McDuff D^o
3743	160	Alexander McDonald D^o
3744	161	James Grant D^o
3745	162 f	William Binker* D^o
3746	163	Peter Strentts* D^o
3747	164	Andrew Hefse (HESSE) D^o
3748	165	James North D^o
3749	166	Ernest Nebling D^o
3750	167	Tobias Snider D^o
3751	168	Imanuel*Kief* D^o
3752	169	William Carson D^o
3753	170	Donald McCrimmon D^o
3754	171	James Wright D^o
3755	172	William Wright D^o
3756	173	Alex^r Rofs (ROSS) D^o
3757	174	William Rofs (ROSS) D^o
3758	175	Walter Rofs (ROSS) D^o
3759	176	Donald McIntosh D^o
		(end left hand column page 12)

NOTES:

1. No. 154 - 2nd choice PITCHARD, though the "T" is not crossed here or in File 5.
2. No. 162 - in File 5, spelled BINCKER; quite definite as written above.

File 4 Page 12 cont'd

NUMBER		
		Part of Marysburg continued
3760	177	William Harrison Sen.[r] disch.[d] Brit.[h] Soldier
3761	178	William Harrison Jun.[r] D.[o]
3762	179	Elisha Crane D.[o]
3763	180	Jeremiah Storm D.[o]
3764	181	David Hogan D.[o]
3765	182	Daniel Wilders D.[o]
3766	183	John Forner* D.[o]
3767	184	Christ.[n] Sirwall* D.[o]
3768	185	Samuel Higgins D.[o]
3769	186	Gasper Etzell D.[o]
3770	187	William Bridge D.[o]
3771	188	Ferdinand Shaffer D.[o]
3772	189[f]	John Dalhunly* D.[o]
3773	190	Cornelius Downey D.[o]
3774	191	Thomas Margerson D.[o]
3775	192	Thomas Harrison D.[o]
3776	193	Mich.[l] Clancey D.[o]
3777	194	G.J. Hudson D.[o]
3778	195	Michael Badderly D.[o]
3779	196	William Andrew D.[o]
3780	197	Patrick Peirce D.[o]
3781	198	Donald Grant D.[o]
3782	199	John Mills D.[o]
3783	200	Ludovick Hoffman D.[o]
3784	201	Colin Rofs (ROSS) D.[o]
3785	202	John McKay D.[o]
3786	203	James McCarthy D.[o]
3787	204[f]	John Lanecty* D.[o]
3788	205	William Hill D.[o]
3789	206	William Dennis D.[o]
3790	207	James McCurdy D.[o]
3791	208	William Blanchard D.[o]
3792	209	John Vallop D.[o]
3793	210	John Sutherland D.[o]
3794	211	Patrick Kelly D.[o]
		(end right hand column page 12)

NOTES: 1. No. 189 - in File 5 spelled DULHUNTY as the 2nd last letter has a cross there; here is hasn't. Compare with No. 204; LANECTY is correct both Files. Thus, DULHUNTY is a good second choice; even a good first choice.

File 4 Page 13

NUMBER		Part of Marysburg	13
3795	212[f]	James Alpin disch[d] Britt[h*] Soldier.	
3796	213	Frederick Lodwick Do.	
3797	214	John Dick Do.	
3798	215	Reeds* North Do.	
3799	216	Gustas* Paepper* Do.	
3800	217	John Grant Do.	
3801	218	Henry Cloudy Do.	
3802	219	Frederick Smith Do.	
3803	220	Henry Slusenburg Do.	
3804	221	John McDonell Do.	
3805	222	William Hartman Do.	
3806	223	Israel Simpson Do.	
3807	224	William Willekey Do.	
3808	225	Henry Buncker Do.	
3809	226	John Adcock Do.	
3810	227	Andrew Miller Disch[d] German Soldier	
3811	228	Bernard Inglehart Do.	
3812	229	James Denhart Do.	
3813	230	Martin Dreder Do.	
3814	231	John Kraigil Do.	
3815	232	Conrad Bungar Do.	
3816	233	Michael Kefsler (KESSLER) Do.	
3817	234	Philip Keller Do.	
3818	235	Frederick Newalt Do.	
3819	236	Frederick Myncher Do.	
3820	237	Henry David Do.	
3821	238	Christian Gants Do.	
3822	239	Gotlep* Hek* Do.	
3823	240	Jacob Metch Do.	
3824	241[f]	G.B. De Reitzenstine Do.	
3825	242	John Benth Do.	
3826	243	John Myneker* Do.	
3827	244	Daniel Abraham Do.	
3828	245	Nicholas Lehincter Do.	
3829	246	Sigismond Borman Do.	
		(end left hand column page 13)	

NOTES:

1. No. 212 - in File 5 misspelled as APLIN.
2. No. 241 - Baron von Reitzenstein, a Brunswick officer - see "Some Hessians of the U.E.L. Settlement in Marysburgh" by Alexander Smith in Ontario Historical Society Papers and Records, Volume 21 (1924), pages 259-261. He was in charge of the discharged German soldiers, mainly Brunswickers, who settled in Marysburg.

File 4 Page 13 cont'd

NUMBER		
		Part of Marysburg continued
3830	247	John Merckle Disch.[d] German Soldier
3831	248	William Gerberg D[o].
3832	249	Eveh.[t] Frike D[o].
3833	250	John Lotz D[o].
3834	251	John Damderf D[o].
3835	252	John Keaning D[o].
3836	253	Christian Imendol D[o].
3837	254	John Menuke D[o].
3838	255	Ernest Claprood* D[o].
3839	256	Gasper Mauk D[o].
3840	257	Gotlep Mauk D[o].
3841	258	Gasper Claus D[o].
3842	259	Henry Slieneman D[o].
3843	260	Gotlep Saupe D[o].
3844	261	Henry Rimmerman D[o].
3845	262	Gasper Vizer D[o].
		(end right hand column page 13)

NOTES: 1. Fairly easy to read for German names. The spellings are likely partially anglicized.

File 4 Page 14

NUMBER			
		Part of Marysburg & Sophiasburg	14
3846	1	Col. J. James Rogers	U.E.
3847	2	James Rogers	U.E.
3848	3	David M. Rogers	U.E.
3849	4	Henry Young	U.E.
3850	5	Daniel Young	U.E.
3851	6	Henry Young Junr.	U.E.
3852	7	John Stinson	U.E.
3853	8	John Stinson Junr.	U.E.
3854	9	John Richards	U.E.
3855	10	Owen Richards	U.E.
3856	11	John Richards Junr.	U.E.
3857	12	Daniel Richards	U.E.
3858	13	Moses Simmons	U.E.
3859	14	Jonathan Miller	U.E.
3860	15	John Miller	U.E.
3861	16	Cornelius Miller	U.E.
3862	17	Barret Dyer	U.E.
3863	18	William Dyer	U.E.
3864	19	Sampson Striker	U.E.
3865	20	James Blakely	U.E.
3866	21	Farrington Ferguson	U.E.
3867	22	Rozel Ferguson	U.E.
3868	23	Augustus Spencer	U.E.
3869	24	John Ogden	U.E.
3870	25	John Ogden Junr. [1]	U.E.
3871	26	Nathl. A. Gaffield	U.E.
3872	27	Daniel Pettit	U.E.
3873	28	William Smyth	U.E.
3874	29	John Peters	U.E.
3875	30	Jacob Corbman	U.E.
3876	31	Frederick Swartfeager*	U.E.
3877	32	Timothy Porter	U.E.
3878	33	Ferdinand Grout	U.E.
		(end left hand column page 14)	

NOTES:

1. The writing here is different than the preceding pages and is much larger with little chance of misinterpretation.

File 4 Page 14 cont'd

NUMBER			
		Part of Marysburg & Sophiasburg	
3879	34	Richard Ferguson	U.E.
3880	35	Richard Ferguson Jun[r].	U.E.
3881	36	Silas Dyer	U.E.
3882	37	David Simmon	U.E.
3883	38[f]	Daniel Kellen	U.E.
3884	39	Peter J. Smith	U.E.
3885	40	John Hurley	U.E.
3886	41	John Spencer	U.E.
3887	42	John Blaker	U.E.
3888	43	Thomas Goldsmith	U.E.
		Part of Sophiasburg & Ameliasburg	
3889	44	William Fox	U.E.
3890	45	John Weast	U.E.
3891	46	Henry Spencer	U.E.
3892	47	Benjamin Spencer	U.E.
3893	48	John Spencer	U.E.
3894	49	Andrew Spencer	U.E.
3895	50	John Spencer Jun[r].	U.E.
3896	51	James Morden	U.E.
3897	52	John Howell	U.E.
3898	53	Richard Morden	U.E.
3899	54	Trueman Knappin	U.E.
3900	55	Simon J. Cole	U.E.
3901	56	John Trompeau*	U.E.
3902	57	Tobias Rikerman	U.E.
3903	58	Frederick Fox	U.E.
3904	59	Gadlep* Magel	U.E.
3905	60	Stephen Roblin	U.E.
		(end right hand column page 14)	

NOTES: 1. No. 38 - in File 5 this is spelled KILLEN - but quite definite here.

File 4 Page 15

NUMBER			
		Part of Sophiasburg & Ameliasburg continued	15
3906	61	Matthew Steele	U.E.
3907	62[f]	Edward Rikerman	U.E.
3908	63	John Law Campbell	U.E.
3909	64	Josiah Dean	U.E.
3910	65	Samuel Dean	U.E.
3911	66	Abraham Peterson	U.E.
3912	67	Nicholas Peterson	U.E.
3913	68	Samuel Wright	U.E.
3914	69	James Peak	U.E.
3915	70	Rudolph Slauser	U.E.
3916	71	John Brooks	U.E.
3917	72	George Angle*	U.E.
3918	73	Peter Cole	U.E.
3919	74	Isaac De Mills	U.E.
3920	75	Bernard Cole	U.E.
3921	76	Henry Williams	U.E.
		(end left hand column page 15)	

NOTES: 1. No. 62 - someone tried spelling it RICKERMAN with a faint "C" stuck in place; File 5 does not use a "C" either.

File 4 Page 15 cont'd

NUMBER			
		Towship* of Thurlow	
3922	1	William Bell	U.E.
3923	2	Archibald Chisholm	U.E.
3924	3	Samuel Sherwood	U.E.
3925	4	John Lott Senr.	U.E.
3926	5	Henry Simons	U.E.
3927	6	John Taylor	U.E.
3928	7	Philip Swick	U.E.
3929	8	John Fairman Senr.	U.E.
3930	9	John McIntosh	U.E.
3931 f	10	Alexander Chisholm	U.E.
3932	11	John Cryselen*	U.E.
3933	12	George Singleton	U.E.
3934	13	Israel Ferguson	U.E.
3935 f	14	John Frederick	U.E.
3936	15	John McArthur	U.E.
		Township of Richmond	
3937	1	William R. Bowen	U.E.
3938	2	Isaac Van Alstine	U.E.
3939	3	Jonas Van Alstine	U.E.
3940 f	4	Isaac Van Alstine Junr.	U.E.
3941	5	Henry Bowen	U.E.
3942	6	Frederick Oliver	U.E.
3943	7	John Oliver	U.E.
3944	8	Cornelius Oliver	U.E.
3945	9	Aaron Oliver	U.E.
3946	10	Samuel Laws	U.E.
3947	11	Garret Van de Barrick	U.E.
3948	12	Andrew Kimmerly	U.E.
3949	13	Adam Segar	U.E.
3950	14	Staatz Segar	U.E.
3951 f	15	Lamber* Van Alstine	U.E.
		(end right hand column page 15)	

NOTES:

1. No. 3932 - checked to try CRYSLER; both File 4 & 5 same.
2. No. 3936 - pleasant to see McArthur spelled correctly for a change.
3. No. 3941 - no doubt as to spelling both Files.
4. No. 3951 - in File 5 spelled LAMBERT; neither a "T" nor space for one nere.

File 4 Page 16

NUMBER			
		Additional Names from different Townships	16
3952	1	Batties Harris	U.E.
3953	2	William Lofsie (LOSSIE)	U.E.
3954	3	James Bradshaw Jun[r].	U.E.
3955	4	Ladock* Threfser (THRESSER)	U.E.
3956	5	William Johnston	U.E.
3957	6	Conrad Frederick	U.E.
3958	7	William Sherrard	U.E.
3959	8	Martin Rush	U.E.
3960	9	Robert Wright	U.E.
3961	10	Richard Smith	U.E.
3962	11 f	Martin Dunyas not UE German Soldier	U.E.
3963	12	William Dougall	U.E.
3964	13	William Marsh	U.E.
3965	14	Matthias Marsh	U.E.
3966	15	George W. Myers	U.E.
3967	16	Tobias Myers	U.E.
3968	17	John W. Myers	U.E.
3969	18	Moore W. Hovendar	U.E.
3970	19 f	Nicholas Simmonds	U.E.
3971	20	James Smith	U.E.
3972	21	Daniel Fisher	U.E.

Signed (Rich[d]. Cartwright J.P. Chairman — Seal
(Thomas Markland J.P. — Seal
(William Atkinson J.P. — Seal
(Poole England Act[g]. Clerk of the Peace

(end left hand column page 16)

NOTES:

1. No. 11 - written to the left of "Martin" is the "German Soldier"; to the right of the surname is "not UE". The surname has been corrected to the above with a line through the last four letters originally written - DUYNES.

2. No. 19 - in File 5 spelled as SIMMONS.

File 4 Page 16 cont'd

NUMBER		
		Additions made to the List of U.E. Loyalists at the General Quarter Sefsions of the Peace for the Midland District held at Kingston the 10th Day of October Instant and continued by adjournment to the 20th Day of the same Month.
3973	1	Charles T. Peters
3974	2	Lieut. William Johnston
3975	3	Philip Reddie
3976	4	Martin Frelleigh
3977	5	Christina Taylor
3978	6	Bolton Evans
3979	7	Waite Wright
3980	8	Garret Miller
3981	9	Serjt. Robert Wilkin disch^{d}. from the Dragoons
3982	10	Julius Bush
3983	11	John Fisher
3984	12	Joseph Morden
3985	13	Daniel Lobdel
3986	14	John Griffiths
3987	15	John Crawford
3988	16	Gilbert Miller
3989	17	John McPherson
3990	18	Ann McCawley
3991	19	Elizabeth Kirby
3992	20	Alexander Dunbar
3993	21	Thomas Richardson disch^{d}. o Priv^{te}. Artillery
3994	22	Samuel Winterbottom D^{o}.
3995	23	Amos Lucas
		(end right hand column page 16)

NOTES:

1. Note that the designation "U.E." is missing from this list opposite each name. Note also that this list is not in File 5. This confirms archivist opinion that File 4, this File, was made from File 5, with the additions added afterwards.
2. The explanation of the clerk's errors in the numbering is now quite apparent - he numbered the book before entering the names. Thus, when an entry took up more than one line - as some did - he fell behind in his count.
3. See File 6; many on this List not U.E.s.

File 4 Page 17

NUMBER		
		Additions continued (this page not numbered - 17)
3996	24	George Lucas
3997	25	James Rankin
3998	26	Brian Bull
3999	27	Gabriel Orser
4000	28	John Dunahow
4001	29	Henry Bush
4002	30	Mary Phillips* now Merrils
4003	31 f	George OKill Stuart
4004	32	John Grafs (GRASS/GRAS)
4005	33	Peter Grafs
4006	34	Daniel Grafs
4007	35	Mary Grafs
4008	36	Eve Grafs now Wartman
4009	37	Bemsher Peters Junr.
4010	38 f	Catherine Herkimer now Markland
4011	39 f	Jane Herkimer now Anderson
4012	40 f	Mary Herkimer now Hamilton
4013	41	Mary Vent
4014	42	Ann McGuin now Vanorcle
4015	43	Mary Badgely now Atkinson
4016	44	Joseph Carnahan
4017	45	Daniel Lightheart
4018	46	Minard Harris
4019	47	Joseph Harris
4020	48	Peter Harris
4021	49	Mattias Marsh
4022	50	Samuel Marsh
4023	51	Benjamin Marsh
4024	52	Jeremiah Marsh
4025	53	William Marsh Senr.
		(end left hand column page 17)

NOTES:

1. Some interesting genealogical information on this page. There is a strong suggestion that some of these people are not U.E.s - but are actually sons/daughters of U.E.s.
2. No. 31 - a famous City of Kingston name.
3. Nos. 38/9/40 - see Note 3. on Page 2. Daughters of CAPTAIN JOHANN JOST HERKIMER.

File 4 Page 17 cont'd

NUMBER		
4026	54	Additions continued
4026	54	David Palmer
4027	55	David Palmer Jun[r].
4028	56	Caleb Palmer
4029	57	John Palmer
4030	58	Martin Rush
4031	59	Josiah Cafs (CASS)
4032	60[f] (1037)	William Marsh Jun[r].
		Signed (Richard Cartwright J.P. Chairman (of the Quarter Sefsions (William Atkinson J.P. ((Thomas Markland J.P.
		A Copy from the Originals in the Crown Office David Burns Clk. of the Crown &c
4033	61	Peter Valleau permitted on the 22nd June to be put on this List.

NOTES:

1. At No. 60 is the clerk's total - 1037 - names on this List. There are 1033 including No. 61.
2. One can not help but note that the leaders of the community were quick to get their names on this List, eg, see Page 1; a not too noble a trait of true leaders but indicative of the Officer class of the times that led to some strife. In contrast, in the Eastern District, the J.P.s found a way of burying their names in the mass. It was the leaders who seemed to also add their children's names here - as they controlled it ?

File 5

NATIONAL ARCHIVES OF CANADA (NAC)

UPPER CANADA (ONTARIO) DISTRICT LOYALIST ROLLS 1796-1803

Reference: NAC RG 1, L 7, vol. 52B (B as in Bravo) (Files 1 to 15)

FILE 5

Archivist's Description

Endorsed "U E Roll - Midland Dis^{t} 1796". Original District Roll (from which File 4 was copied), on paper watermarked similarily to File 2; 165x47 cm (several sheets pasted into roll form), broken on some folds. The names are entered in six columns, arranged by township and are noted as totalling 972 names.

Transcriber's Comments

The writing is generally much finer and less sophisticated than that of File 4. Some names lost on broken folds and assumed here from File 4. There are some spelling variations between the two Files; one might assume that File 4 contains corrections of File 5's misspellings - but that is not necessarily so. Some are transcription errors in File 4. There is very little doubt that parents included names of sons as UEs when they probably were too young to have fought during the war. This is particularily evident when four, six or even eight surnames follow one another with seniors and juniors used to distinguish duplicated names. This observation is also considered valid when one considers the much smaller lists of names in 1783/4 at Montreal; these military units were just not as large as these Rolls in File 4 & 5 would indicate.

There are 156 British Soldiers etc. and 43 discharged German Soldiers in this File. This total of 199 non-Loyalist people when subtracted from the total of 972 names leaves 773 "Loyalists". The existence of these non-Loyalists in this list indicates that the "true" Loyalists considered them worthy of recording in the context of Loyalists.

File 5

FILE 5

There is a heading across the width of File 5 which reads as follows:

(UPPER)CANADA
(MIDLAND)DISTRICT

A Roll of the Inhabitants of the Midland Dis(tric)t In the Province of Upper Canada who adhered to the Unity of the/
Empire and joined the Royal Standard in America before the Treaty of Separation in the Year 1783 -/
Taken in Open Sefsions held at Kingston October the 11th.. and at different Adjournments to the 15th.. of November 179(6)/

NOTES:

1. The margins of this folio are broken; hence some letters in brackets - indicating presumed letters.
2. The heading is on three lines; hence the oblique strokes to indicate the end of each line.
3. File 5 is a large sheet pasted together in the form of a roll; there are six equal sized columns. For purposes of identification they are lettered "A", "B", "C", "D", "E" and "F".
4. The double lines enclose the original manuscript material.
5. The asterix, "*" means Sic= as written= a likely error.

File 5

NUMBER	(Column "A")	NUMBER	(Column "A" continued)
	Township of Kingston	4083	Jacob Herkimer U.E.
4051	The Rev[d]. Jn[o]. Stuart U.E.	4084	Laurence Eldam discharged German Soldier
4052	Rich[d]. Cartwright Sen[r]. U.E.		
4053	Rich[d]. Cartwright Jun[r]. U.E.	4085	John Mosure U.E.
4054	Jer[t]. Herkimer U.E.	4086	John Brown discharged Sol[r].
4055	Neal McLean reduced asst. Commissary General		
		4087	Emanuel Elderback U.E.
4056	Hector McLean reduced Lieu[t].	4088	George Galloway U.E.
		4089[f]	(Thomas Moore) (U.E.)
4057	James McDonell U.E.	4090	Michael Dederick U.E.
4058	Joseph Anderson U.E.	4091	Lewis Grass U.E.
4059	Thomas Sparham U.E.	4092[f]	Jacob Bistedo* U.E.
4060	Michael Grass U.E.	4093	Benjamin Valentine U.E.
4061	William Atkinson U.E.	4094	James Gale U.E.
4062	Lewis Kotte reduced German Officer	4095	Peter Wartman U.E.
		4096	Nicholas Whitsele discharged German Soldier
4063	Robert McCauley U.E.		
4064	Thomas Markland U.E.	4097	Thomas Burnett U.E.
4065	David Brass U.E.	4098	William Howe U.E.
4066	Arch[d]. Grant reduced Lieu[t].	4099	John Everitt U.E.
4067	John Ferguson reduced Comm[y].	4100	Soloman* Orser U.E.
		4101	Gilbert Orser U.E.
4068	John Conolly reduced Lieu[t].	4102	Barnabas Day U.E.
		4103	Alexander Simpson U.E.
4069	Peter Smith U.E.	4104	John Marier U.E.
4070	Donald McDonell U.E.	4105	John Holmes U.E.
4071	Christopher Robinson U.E.	4106	William Bell U.E.
4072	James Robins U.E.	4107	John Most discharged Soldier
4073	William McKay reduced L[t].		
		4108	William(s) Wells U.E.
4074	Will[m]. McDonell discharged Sol[d].	4109	John Yerks* U.E.
		4110	Richard Hale U.E.
4075	Mary Brant U.E.	4111	Robert Graham U.E.
4076	George Johnston U.E.	4112	Elijah Grooms U.E.
4077	Elizabeth Johnston U.E.	4113	Joseph Grooms U.E.
4078	Magdalen Johnston U.E.	4114	Matthew Burnett U.E.
4079	Margaret Johnston U.E.	4115	James Brady U.E.
4080	Joseph Franklin Sen[r]. U.E.	4116	John Edgar U.E.
4081	Daniel McGuin U.E.	4117	David Whiteman dis[d]. Sol[r].
4082	Nicholas Herkimer U.E.	4118	Abraham Wartman U.E.

NOTES:

1. No discrepency here with File 4.
2. No. 4089 - on broken fold; thus, assumed as written.
3. No. 4092 - "BASTEDO" in File 4.
4. Column "A" continued on Page 2.
5. The asterix, "*" means Sic= as written= a likely error.

File 5

NUMBER	(Column "A" continued)	NUMBER	(Column "A" continued)
4119	John Wartman U.E.	4156	William Taylor U.E.
4120	Barnabas Wartman U.E.	4157	Bensley Peters U.E.
4121	(blank) Myers reduced German Soldier	4158	Nazarith Hill U.E.
4122 [f]	John Roushorn* Ditto	4159	George Harple U.E.
4123	Amos Ainslie U.E.	4160	William Rancier U.E.
4124	John Cannon U.E.	4161	Peter Grass U.E.
4125	Barnabas Wemp U.E.	4162	Christopher Furnier U.E.
4126	Richard Prentice U.E.	4163	Rob[t]. Williams dis[d]. Mariner
4127	Charles McCullock discharg-ed Artificer	4164	Chris[r]. Georgen dis[d]. Sol[r].
4128	James Harley Ditto	4165	William Sheriff Ditto
4129	Jacob Powley U.E.	4166	John Loyd* discharged German Soldier
4130	Francis Powley U.E.	4167	Joseph Franklin Jun[r]. U.E.
4131	Conrad Orval discharged German Soldier	4168 [f]	Thomas Welkank* Sn[r]. U.E.
4132	George Weston U.E.	4169	Widow Oneal U.E.
4133 [f]	Robert Tindal* dis[d]. Sol[r].	4170	Samuel Ainslie U.E.
4134 [f]	(John Warner) (Ditto)	4171	James Dawson U.E.
4135	Mahalon Knight U.E.	4172 [f]	Anthony* Dumell U.E.
4136	George Wesley U.E.	4173	Philip Pember U.E.
4137 [f]	William Bower U.E.	4174	Thomas Cook dis[d]. Soldier
4138 [f]	Aaron Brewer U.E.	4175	William Ashley Ditto
4139	John Ferris U.E.	4176	John Grey dis[d]. Artificer
4140	Lazarus Brewer U.E.	4177	John Duncan Ditto
4141	John Napping U.E.	4178	Widow Wright U.E.
4142	Silas Palmer U.E.	4179	Widow Orser U.E.
4143	Michael Taylor U.E.	4180	David Babcock U.E.
4144	Andrew Denyck U.E.	4181	Benjamin Babcock U.E.
4145	Arthur Orser U.E.	4182	Matthew Van Order U.E.
4146	Isaac Orser U.E.	4183	Alex[r]. Anderson Dis[d]. Soldier
4147	Britain Guinop U.E.	4184	James Bayman Dis[d]. Mariner
4148	Michael Conlor dis[d]. Soldier	4185	James Richardson Ditto
4149	Arthur Yoemans U.E.	4186	Samuel Smith U.E.
4150	Jeremiah Lap U.E.	4187 [f]	Jean Baptiste Bouchette reduced Offr of the Marine
4151	Terence Dunn dis[d]. Artificer	4188	Allan McLean reduced Off[r].
4152 [f]	John Burnet U.E.	4189	Gilbert Purdy U.E.
4153	Christopher Danby U.E.	4190	Archibald Fairfield U.E.
4154	Thomas Smith U.E.	4191	Titus Fitz U.E.
4155	John Smith U.E.	4192	Stephen McLean discharged Artificer

NOTES:
1. No. 4122 - ROWSHORN in File 4.
2. No. 4133 - TINDALL in File 4.
3. No. 4134 - on broken fold; thus, assumed as written.
4. Nos. 4137/8 - as written - quite definite.
5. No. 4152 - two "T"s at No. 4114; only one here.
6. No. 4168 - the Senior designation missing in File 4.
7. No. 4172 - ANTHONY here; ANTONY in File 4.
8. No. 4187 - stroked out as in File 4.
9. Column "A" continues on Page 3.

File 5

NUMBER	(Column "A" continued)	
4193	John Ferrier discharged Artificer	
4194	Hugh Campbell Dis[d]. Sol[r].	
4195	Gaspe Strope Discharged German Soldier	
4196	William Coffin	U.E.
4197	William Taylor Jun[r].	U.E.
4198	Allan McDonell	U.E.
4199	Laurence* Herkimer	U.E.
4200	John Kirby	U.E.
4201	John Grant	U.E.
4202	Anthony McGuin	U.E.
4203	William Robins	U.E.
4204	Richard Robins	U.E.
4205	Isaiah Van Order	U.E.
4206	Benjamin Babcock	U.E.
	(Column "A" ends about 5½ inches from the bottom of the page)	
	(Column "B")	
	Ernest Town	
4207	William Johnston	U.E.
4208	Henry Simmonds	U.E.
4209	Gusbard Sharp	U.E.
4210	James Parrot	U.E.
4211	John Duzenberry	U.E.
4212	Robert Clark	U.E.
4213	Joshua Booth	U.E.
4214	Jephtha Hawley	U.E.
4215	Jacob Miller	U.E.
4216	Ichabod Hawley	U.E.
4217	Henry Finkle	U.E.
4218	John Thiele	U.E.
4219[f]	John Garloch*	U.E.
4220	John Shibley	U.E.
4221	Jacob Shibley	U.E.

NUMBER	(Column "B" continued)	
4222	Daniel Carr Sen[r].	U.E.
4223	Daniel Carr Jun[r].	U.E.
4224	John Wist	U.E.
4225	David Wist	U.E.
4226	John Wist Jun[r].	U.E.
4227	Peter Thomas	U.E.
4228	Jacob Gordonier	U.E.
4229	Henry Gordonier	U.E.
4230	Marcus Snyder	U.E.
4231	John Percy	U.E.
4232	James Cosway	U.E.
4233	John Davey	U.E.
4234[f]	John Afselstine	U.E.
4235	John McKinney	U.E.
4236	David Hoffman	U.E.
4237	John Sharp Sen[r].	U.E.
4238	John Sharp Jun[r].	U.E.
4239	Daniel Walker Sen[r].	U.E.
4240	Daniel Walker Jun[r].	U.E.
4241	John Maybe	U.E.
4242	Andrew Miller	U.E.
4243[f]	James McKim	U.E.
4244[f]	James McKim	U.E.
4245	William McKim	U.E.
4246	Colin McKenzie Sen[r].	U.E.
4247	Colin McKenzie Jun[r].	U.E.
4248	John Howard Sen[r].	U.E.
4249	John Howard Jun[r].	U.E.
4250	Thomas Howard	U.E.
4251	Edward Howard	U.E.
4252	John Ritchie	U.E.
4253	Thomas Jackson	U.E.
4254	George McGin	U.E.
4255	Michael Davey	U.E.
4256	Peter Davey	U.E.
4257	Henry Davey	U.E.
4258	Thomas Davey	U.E.
4259	Richard Robins	U.E.
4260	Matthias Rose	U.E.
4261	Matthias Rose Jun[r].	U.E.

NOTES:

1. No. 4219 - GARLOCH quite definite here; File 4 definitely GARLOCK.

2. Nos. 4243/4 - as in File 4, no distinction between the two; one Junior and the other Senior assumed.

3. No. 4234 - old writing for double "s"; ASSELSTINE.

File 5

NUMBER	(Column "B" continued)		NUMBER	(Column "B" continued)	
4262	Freeman Burley	U.E.	4301	Ralph Van Ducar	U.E.
4263f	John Burley	U.E.	4302	John Diamond	U.E.
4264f	Joseph Concklin*	U.E.	4303f	Christopher Lake	U.E.
4265	John Conklin*	U.E.	4304f	Bostian*Hogle	U.E.
4266	James Jackson	U.E.	4305f	James Hogle	U.E.
4267	David Jackson	U.E.	4306	Andrew Shutler	U.E.
4268	Thomas Comber	U.E.	4307	John Amey	U.E.
4269	Jonas Amey	U.E.	4308	Daniel Perry	U.E.
4270	Martin Stover	U.E.	4309	William Fairfield	U.E.
4271	John Stowood	U.E.	4310	Benjamin Booth	U.E.
4272	Lewis Hicks	U.E.	4311	Samuel Beach	U.E.
4273	Simon Schneider	U.E.	4312	Russel Hawley	U.E.
4274	Nicholas Amey	U.E.	4313	John Cock	U.E.
4275	Daniel Frazer Senr.	U.E.	4314	Adam Vanderheyder	U.E.
4276	Daniel Frazer Junr.	U.E.	4315	William Amsbury	U.E.
4277	Davis Hawley	U.E.	4316	John Lindsey	U.E.
4278	William Fairfield	U.E.	4317	Cornelius Putman	U.E.
4279	Benjamin Fairfield	U.E.	4318	Bruen Hough	U.E.
4280	Jonathan Fairfield	U.E.	4319	Frederick Baker	U.E.
4281	Stephen Fairfield	U.E.	4320	Peter Afselstine	U.E.
4282	Isaac Briscoe	U.E.	4321	Isaac Afselstine	U.E.
4283	Norris Briscoe	U.E.	4322	Thomas Frazer	U.E.
4284	Nathan Briscoe	U.E.	4323	Tunis Hagerman	U.E.
4285	Andrew Miller	U.E.	4324	Magnes* Shrawder	U.E.
4286	David Williams	U.E.	4325	Philip Switzer	U.E.
4287	Samuel Williams	U.E.	4326	Daniel Rose	U.E.
4288	Elijah Williams	U.E.	4327	Hercules Kronkheit	U.E.
4289	David Williams Senr.	U.E.	4328	John Kronkheit	U.E.
4290	Jacob Hoffman	U.E.	4329	Stephen Boyce	U.E.
4291	John Schneider	U.E.	4330	Andrew Boyce	U.E.
4292	Abraham Schneider	U.E.	4331	David Hartman	U.E.
4293	Isaac Schneider	U.E.	4332	Philip Hartman	U.E.
4294	Peter Gilchrist	U.E.	4333	Ludovick* Hartman	U.E.
4295	Neal Gilchrist	U.E.	4334	Jacob Hartman	U.E.
4296	William Gilchrist	U.E.	4335	Jacob Hefs (HESS)	U.E.
4297	Francis Dickson	U.E.	4336	Peter Daly	U.E.
4298	Barnabas Hough	U.E.	4337	Daniel Simmonds	U.E.
4299	Isaac Hough	U.E.	4338	John Simmonds	U.E.
4300	John Van Ducar	U.E.	4339	Nicholas Simmonds	U.E.

NOTES:

1. Nos. 4264/5 - see the error or change in spelling between the two entries; in File 4 both spelled CONCKLIN.
2. No. 4304 - spelled as written, though 2nd choice is BOSTIEN; in File 4, BOSTAIN.
3. Nos. 4305/6 - this is as written with the order reversed from that of FILE 4.

File 5

NUMBER	(Column "B" continued)		NUMBER	(Column "C")	
				Ernest Town continued	
4340[f]	(J)ames B(eavins)	U.E.	4377	Elijah Hough	U.E.
4341	Henry Clark	U.E.	4378	Samuel Hough	U.E.
4342	Adam Vent	U.E.	4379	Sheldon Hawley	U.E.
4343	Joseph Hoffman	U.E.	4380	Martin Hawley	U.E.
4344	Jacob Comber	U.E.	4381	Samuel McKay	U.E.
4345	Peter McPherson	U.E.	4382	Matthew Clark	U.E.
4346	John McPherson	U.E.	4383	George Miller	U.E.
4347[f]	Christian Abrahim*	U.E.	4384	Paul Comber	U.E.
4348	John McDougall	U.E.	4385	George Havens	U.E.
4349	Peter McDougall	U.E.	4386	John Ham	U.E.
4350	Kenneth Frazer	U.E.	4387	John Havens	U.E.
4351	David Frazer	U.E.	4388	Solomon Ball	U.E.
4352[f]	Hermanas*Sea	U.E.	4389	Shadrack Ball	U.E.
4353	Peter Freelick*	U.E.	4390	Daniel Corban	U.E.
4354	John Frazer	U.E.	4391	William Walker	U.E.
4355	Robert Perry Sen[r].	U.E.	4392	Weiden* Walker	U.E.
4356	Robert Perry Jun[r].	U.E.	4393	John George	U.E.
4357	John Williams Sen[r].	U.E.	4394	William Cottier	U.E.
4358	William Perry Sen[r].	U.E.	4395	David Lockwood	U.E.
4359	John Perry	U.E.	4396	Robert Havens	U.E.
4360	William Perry Jun[r].	U.E.	4397[f]	John Adam Frier(mu)t	U.E.
4361	James Johnston	U.E.	4398[f]	Donald McDonal(d)	U.E.
4362	Daniel Johnston	U.E.	4399	Andrew Rusk	U.E.
4363	Andrew Johnston	U.E.	4400	William Cook	U.E.
4364	David Shorey Sen[r].	U.E.	4401	David Harris	U.E.
4365	David Shorey Jun[r].	U.E.	4402	Simon Swart	U.E.
4366	Rufus Shorey	U.E.	4403	Michael Phili(ps)	U.E.
4367	Gilbert Storms	U.E.	4404	David Purdy	U.E.
4368	Henry Storms	U.E.	4405	Francis Redins	U.E.
4369	Jacob Storms	U.E.	4406	Thomas Freeman	U.E.
4370	John Rogers	U.E.	4407	Samuel Welch	U.E.
4371	William Rogers	U.E.	4408	Francois* Lerock S(en)[r].	U.E.
4372	Armstrong Williams	U.E.	4409	Francois* Lerock J(un)[r].	U.E.
4373	Robert Williams	U.E.	4410	Peter Lerock	U.E.
4374	Joshua Williams	U.E.	4411	James Work	U.E.
4375	James Williams	U.E.	4412	John Lake Sen[r].	U.E.
4376	John Williams Jun[r].	U.E.	4413	John Lake Jun[r].	U.E.
	(end Column "B")				

NOTES:

1. No. 4340 - a broken fold here; letters in brackets assumed.
2. No. 4347 - this misspelling carried over to File 4.
3. No. 4352 - this misspelling corrected in File 4 to HERMANUS.
4. No. 4397/8 et seq - the letters missing because of broken folds in the paper are in brackets and are assumed from File 4.

File 5

NUMBER	(Column "C" continued)
	Ernest Town continued
4414	Nicholas Lake U.E.
4415	James Lake U.E.
4416[f]	F(rancis Hogle U.E.)
4417[f]	John (Leonard U.E.)
4418	John Clement U.E.
4419[f]	Henry Gichland* U.E.
4420	Adam Bower U.E.
4421[f]	John Chridsnoger* U.E.
	Township of Fredericksburg
4422	John Anderson U.E.
4423	Charles Barnhart U.E.
4424	Michael Bartley U.E.
4425	William Bell U.E.
4426	Samuel Brunson U.E.
4427	Duncan Bell U.E.
4428	Isaak* Bartley U.E.
4429	Aval Bradshaw U.E.
4430	James Bradshaw Jun[r]. U.E.
4431	James Bradshaw (Sen)[r]. U.E.
4432	David Bradsha(w) U.E.
4433	Gasper Bower U.E.
4434	Adam Bower U.E.
4435	Thomas Bell U.E.
4436	Henry Brants U.E.
4437	Samuel Brunson (S)en[r]. U.E.
4438	William Bowen U.E.
4439	John Behn U.E.
4440	Jacob Birch U.E.
4441	William Crawf(or)d U.E.
4442	Edward Carscallen U.E.
4443	John Carscallen U.E.
4444	Luke Carscallen U.E.
4445	James Carscallen U.E.
4446	George Carscallen U.E.
4447	Bryan Crawford U.E.
4448	Alexander Clark U.E.
4449	James Cottier Sen(io)rU.E.

NUMBER	(Column "C" continued)
4450	Richard Cottier U.E.
4451	James Cottier Jun[r]. U.E.
4452	William Cadma(n) U.E.
4453	Alpheus Cadma(n) U.E.
4454	Asa Cadman U.E.
4455	John Cornelius U.E.
4456	Hugh Clark U.E.
4457	Oliver Church U.E.
4458	Oliver Church Ju(n[r].) U.E.
4459	Abraham Defoe U.E.
4460	Jacob Diamond U.E.
4461	Michael Defoe U.E.
4462	(John Diamond) (U.E.)
4463	John Defoe U.E.
4464	Daniel Defoe U.E.
4465	Peter Detlor U.E.
4466	James Demorest U.E.
4467	Valentine Detlor U.E.
4468	Jacob Detlor U.E.
4469	Samuel Detlor U.E.
4470	John Detlor U.E.
4471	George Detlor U.E.
4472	Florence Dunovan U.E.
4473	Matthew Dies Sen[r]. U.E.
4474	John Dies U.E.
4475	Matthew Dies Jun[r]. U.E.
4476	Garret Dingman U.E.
4477	Samuel Pattingall U.E.
4478[f]	Timothy Prindle U.E.
4479[f]	Joel Prindle U.E.
4480	Andrew Rickley U.E.
4481	William Rambouch U.E.
4482	Zenus Ross U.E.
4483	Asa Richardson U.E.
4484	Thomas Richardson U.E.
4485	William Richardson U.E.
4486	Henry Richardson U.E.
4487	William Shoeman* U.E.
4488	John Sills U.E.

NOTES:

1. Nos. 4416/7 and others too numerous to mention, suffer from a large break on the fold with many letters lost - in brackets.
2. No. 4419 - correct as written; File 4 spelled GICKLAND.
3. No. 4421 - correct as written; File 4 spelled CHRIDSNAGER.
4. Nos. 4478/9 - one authority on this district, and ancestor, spells this name as PRINGLE; one was a Doctor.

File 5

NUMBER	(Column "C" continued)	
4489	James Simpson	U.E.
4490	John Smith	U.E.
4491	Philip Smith	U.E.
4492	Conrad Sills	U.E.
4493	William Shaw	U.E.
4494	Job Stains	U.E.
4495	Laurence* Sills	U.E.
4496	George Sills	U.E.
4497	George Schriver	U.E.
4498	Michael Smith	U.E.
4499	Jacob Smith Sen[r].	U.E.
4500	Jacob Smith Jun[r].	U.E.
4501	Daniel Smith	U.E.
4502	Comfort Smith	U.E.
4503	William Smith	U.E.
4504[f]	Hazleton Sp(encer)	U.E.
4505	Henry Seerm(an)	(U.)E.
4506	Tobias Steely	U.E.
4507	William Scherm(erhorn)	U.E.
4508	William Thoms(on)	(U.E.)
4509	Gerrard Tyler	U.E.
4510	Timothy Thom(pson)	U.E.
4511	Francis Vander Bogart	U.E.
4512	Thomas Wager	U.E.
4513	Everard Wager	U.E.
4514	William Wager	U.E.
4515[ff]	Samuel Walsk*	U.E.
4516	John Woodcock	U.E.
4517	Abraham Wood(cock)	U.E.
4518	Ebenezer Washbu(rn)	U.E.
4519	Albert William(s)	U.E.
4520	Peter Young Se(n[r].)	U.E.
4521	Stephen Young	U.E.
4522	Henry Young Se(n[r].)	U.E.
4523	Henry Young Ju(n[r].)	U.E.
4524	Peter Young J(un[r].)	U.E.
4525	Andrew Huffna(il)	U.E.
4526[f]	Russell* Pitma(n)	U.E.
4527	Peter Bowen	U.E.
4528	Victor Bowen	U.E.

NUMBER	(Column "C" continued)	
4529	Jacob Diamond Jun[r].	U.E.
4530[f]	John Diamond	U.E.
4531	Andrew Embrie	U.E.
4532	Adam Earhar(t)	U.E.
4533	David Embrie Jun[r].	U.E.
4534	John Embrie	U.E.
4535	Peter Frederick	U.E.
4536	Peter Fykes	U.E.
4537	James Fitchet	U.E.
4538	William Frazer	U.E.
4539	Richard Fitchet	U.E.
4540	Moses Foster	U.E.
4541	George Finkle	U.E.

(end Column "C")

(COLUMN "D")

Fredericksburg Continued

NUMBER	Name	
4542	John Finkle	U.E.
4543	Jacob Finkle	U.E.
4544	Aara Ferguson	U.E.
4545	Warren Howell	U.E.
4546	Jacob Hoffman	U.E.
4547	John Hough	U.E.
4548	Philip Hoffman	U.E.
4549	Felix Harson	U.E.
4550	Elias Hoffman	U.E.
4551	Johnston Harns	U.E.
4552[f]	Gilbert Harns	U.E.
4553	Isaiah Harns	U.E.
4554	Thomas Harns	U.E.
4555	Adam Hedler	U.E.
4556	William Harlowe	U.E.
4557	Andrew Heron	U.E.
4558[f]	Gilbert Harns	U.E.
4559[f]	Assa* Huff	U.E.
4560	William Kitcheson	U.E.
4561	John Keller	U.E.

NOTES:

1. No. 4504 et seq - much of this column is affected by a fold.
2. No. 4515 - quite definite as above; File 4 just as definite.
3. No. 4526 - note two "L"s in RUSSELL here; only one in File 4.
4. No. 4530 - something written above this name with a bracket beside it. Looks like "not entered".
5. No. 4515 - something written above name - not readable.
6. Nos. 4552/4558 - no distinction given between the two.
7. No. 4559 - quite definitely "ASSA"; File 4 also definite "ASA".

File 5

NUMBER	(Column "D" continued)		NUMBER	(Column "D" continued)	
	(Fredericksburg continued)		4601	Cyrenus Parks	U.E.
4562	Frederick Keller	U.E.	4602	Nathaniel Parks	U.E.
4563	James Kemp	U.E.	4603	James Parks	U.E.
4564	Joseph Kemp	U.E.	4604	Frederick Post	U.E.
4565	John Kemp	U.E.	4605	Doctor Prindle*	U.E.
4566	John Kemp Junr.	U.E.	4606	Peter Philips	U.E.
4567	William Koughnet	U.E.	4607 f	Daniel Lobedell	U.E.
4568	Charles Keller	U.E.	4608	Richard Albertson	U.E.
4569	David Lambert	U.E.	4609	John Pickle Senr.	U.E.
4570	William Lawer*	U.E.	4610	John Pickle Junr.	U.E.
4571	Harman* Laroway	U.E.	4611	Archibald Nicholson	U.E.
4572 f	Henry Loukes*	U.E.	4612	James Johnston	U.E.
4573	James Lindsey	U.E.	4613	James McNut	U.E.
4574	Andrew Lyst	U.E.	4614	Thomas Saunderson	U.E.
4575	Richard Loyd*	U.E.	4615	Matthew Benson	U.E.
4576	Peter Laroway	U.E.	4616	Paul Peterson	U.E.
4577	Isaac Laroway Senr.	U.E.	4617	Christian Peterson	U.E.
4578	Isaac Laroway Junr.	U.E.	4618	John Schermerhorn	U.E.
4579	Abraham Laroway	U.E.	4619	Cornelius Benson	U.E.
4580 f	(Jonas Laroway)	U.E.	4620	Henry Evans	U.E.
4581	Daniel Loyd*	U.E.	4621 f	Peter Bowen	U.E.
4582 f	Jacob Loukes	U.E.	4622	Martin Shoeman	U.E.
4583 f	Abraham Loukes	U.E.	4623	Baultis Shoeman	U.E.
4584 f	George Loukes	U.E.	4624 f	William Redford Crawford	
4585	Henry Lyst	U.E.	4625	Jacob Ferguson	U.E.
4586	James McTaggett	U.E.	4626	Jacob Pattingall	U.E.
4587 f	John Mitts*	U.E.	4627	John George Smith	U.E.
4588 f	Henry Mitts*	U.E.	4628	John Bowen	U.E.
4589	Daniel McMullen	U.E.	4629	Abraham Bowen	U.E.
4590	Jonathan Miller	U.E.	4630	Nicholas Smith	U.E.
4591	George Murdoff Senr.	U.E.	4631	Joseph Marsh	U.E.
4592	George Murdoff Junr.	U.E.	4632 f	Zadock* Hawley	U.E.
4593	James Murdoff	U.E.	4633	Josiah Cain	U.E.
4594	John Murdoff	U.E.			
4595	Thomas Murdoff	U.E.		Township of Adolphus	
4596	Hugh McConnell	U.E.			
4597	Owen McGrath	U.E.	4634	John German	U.E.
4598	Alexander Nicholson	U.E.	4635	Abert* Benson	U.E.
4599	John Neher	U.E.	4636	John Vanskiver	U.E.
4600	Elisha Philips	U.E.			

NOTES:

1. Nos. 4572/4582/3/4 - otherwise spelled LOUCHS/LOUCKS; from the German LAUXS.
2. No. 4580 - completely missing; lost on broken fold.
3. No. 4587/8 - quite definitely MITTS; File 4 MILTS.
4. No. 4607 - faint writing above - possibly reads "before as in Kingston".
5. No. 4621 - faint writing above - possibly "a Bowen Niagara Roll."
6. No. 4624 - the original very crowded; no room for "U.E."
7. No. 4632 - checked with other "Z"s; this is quite definite.

File 5

NUMBER	(Column "D" continued)	
4637	John Fitzgerald	U.E.
4638	Henry Redner	U.E.
4639	Henry Davis	U.E.
4640	Peter Rattan Jun[r].	U.E.
4641	Michael Sloot	U.E.
4642	Philip Darland	U.E.
4643	Henry Hover	U.E.
4644	Abraham Maybe	U.E.
4645	James McMasters	U.E.
4646	Joseph Allison	U.E.
4647[f]	William More*	U.E.
4648	Christopher German	U.E.
4649	Abraham Bogart	U.E.
4650	Garret Benson	U.E.
4651	Peter Duylay*	U.E.
4652	Albert Cornell	U.E.
4653	William Clark	U.E.
4654	Cornelius Van Horn	U.E.
4655	John Huyck	U.E.
4656	Paul Huff	U.E.
4657	Gilbert Bogart	U.E.
4658	Owen Roblin Sen[r].	U.E.
4659	George Rutler Sen[r].	U.E.
4660	John Roblin	U.E.
4661	Owen P. Roblin	U.E.
4662	John Cuniff	U.E.
4663	Jacob German	U.E.
4664	Norris Carr	U.E.
4665	Cornelius Sharp	U.E.
4666	Nicholas Peterson	U.E.
4667	Conrad Van Dusen	U.E.
4668	Peter Van Alstine	U.E.
4669	Alexander Fisher	U.E.
4670	William Casey	U.E.
4671[f]	Nicholas Hagerman*	U.E.
4672	Barent Lewis	U.E.
4673	William Rattan	U.E.
4674	Daniel Cole	U.E.
4675	Alexander Campbell	U.E.

NUMBER	(Column "D" continued)	
	(Adolphus continued)	
4676	Peter Rattan Sen[r].	U.E.
4677	Thomas Dorland	U.E.
4678	Paul Trompeau	U.E.
4679	Cornelius Slouter	U.E.
4680	Peter Wanamaker	U.E.
4681	Joseph Cornell	U.E.
4682	Obadiah Simpson	U.E.
4683	Archibald Campbell	U.E.
4684	Peter Duylea Jun[r].	U.E.
4685	Samuel Duylea	U.E.
4686	Joseph Duylea	U.E.
4687	Joseph Clark	U.E.
4688	Soloman* Huff Jun[r].	U.E.
4689	Alexander Van Alstine	U.E.
4690	Owen Roblin Jun[r].	U.E.
4691	Cosfiares* Van Dusen	U.E.
4692	Cornelius Van Alstine	U.E.
4693	John Beneger	U.E.
4694	Henry Redner Jun[r].	U.E.
4695	Augustus Shorts	U.E.
4696[f]	Michael Marbit*	U.E.
4697	Mary Fisher (Widow)	U.E.
4698	Peter Brunner	U.E.
4699	Philip Roblin	U.E.
4700	Casper Hover	U.E.
4701	Jacob Hover	U.E.
4702	John Ryckman	U.E.
4703	Nicholas Peterson	U.E.
4704	Jepts Huffnail	U.E.
	(end Column "D")	
	(Column "E")	
	Adolphus Continued	
4705	Michael Van Devart	U.E.
4706	William Griffiths	U.E.
4707	James Cuniff	U.E.
4708	Oliver Campbell	U.E.
4709	William Campbell	U.E.

NOTES:

1. No. 4647 - spelled MOORE in File 4.
2. No. 4671 - spelled HAGGERMAN in File 4.
3. No. 4696 - spelled MARBET in File 4.

File 5

NUMBER	(Column "E" continued)		NUMBER	(Column "E" continued)	
	Part of Marysburg		4746	Michael McCarthy	Do
4710	Archibald McDonell	U.E.	4747	Reuben Hughs*	Do
4711[f]	Peter Vanschiver*	U.E.	4748	Henry Simmerman	Do
4712	Joseph Hicks	U.E.	4749	John Cummins	Do
4713	Edward Hicks	U.E.	4750	William McKenzie	Do
4714	Benjamin Hicks	U.E.	4751	Joseph Wright	Do
4715[f]	David Embrie	U.E.	4752	Conrad Vullicar	Do
4716	Joshua Hicks	U.E.	4753	Frederick Crammer	Do
4717	Michael Criderman	U.E.	4754	Peter Collier	Do
4718	David Dulmadge	U.E.	4755	John Moor	Do
4719	Stephen Farrington	U.E.	4756	John Vogley	Do
4720	Robert Farrington	U.E.	4757	Thomas Roberts	Do
4721	Joseph Allen	U.E.	4758	Robert Midleton*	Do
4722	John Allen	U.E.	4759	John Fearman	Do
4723	Jonathan Allen	U.E.	4760	Thomas McGowen	Do
4724	James Hughs	U.E.	4761	Frederick Fisher	Do
4725	Daniel Hicks	U.E.	4762	Andrew Ellis	Do
4726	David Hicks	U.E.	4763	John Simpson	Do
4727[f]	William Green	U.E.	4764	Nathaniel Heald	Do
4728	John Green	U.E.	4765	Edward Powis	Do
4729	James Durolemy	U.E.	4766	John Lovell	Do
4730	Peter Frill	U.E.	4767	John OBrien*	Do
4731	Samuel Farrington	U.E.	4768	Frederick Phifer	Do
4732	Peter Dap*	U.E.	4769[f]	John (Kenar)d	Do
4733	Daniel Wright discharged British Soldier		4770	John Byrns	Do
4734	Henry Smith	Ditto	4771	Jacob Starts	Do
4735	James Edwards	Do	4772	Henry Bird	Do
4736	Thomas Price	Do	4773	Henry Saunders	Do
4737	John Stewart	Do	4774[f]	Bartholomew Steaphy	Do
4738	Lauchlin McIntosh	Do	4775	John Heford	Do
4739	Robert Thompson	Do	4776	Richard Campbell	Do
4740	Hugh Swiney	Do	4777	Robert Potten	Do
4741	John McBean	Do	4778	Hugh Gallagher	Do
4742	Robert Stewart	Do	4779	John Hancock	Do
4743[f]	William (Batty)	Do	4780	Thomas Loyd*	Do
4744[f]	Alexander (McDonell)	Do	4781	John Anderson	Do
4745	John McDonell	Do	4782	James Chavasey	Do
			4783[f]	Thomas Roberts	Do
			4784	William Ross	Do
			4785	John Segus	Do

NOTES:

1. No. 4711 - surname not broken in two here; see File 4.
2. No. 4715 - some faint, indecipherable writing supra.
3. No. 4727 - in File 4 there is a JOHN GREEN above and below WILLIAM GREEN; not so here - only below.
4. No. 4743/4 - a broken fold destroyed some writing.
5. No. 4747 - in File 4 spelled HUGHES.
6. No. 4774 - supra is written "HIFFY".
7. No. 4783 - supra is written "before". Likely means entered before.
8. No. 4769 - broken fold again; assumed missing letters bracket.[d]

File 5

NUMBER	(Column "E" continued)		NUMBER	(Column "E" continued)	
	Part of Marysburg contin.[d]			Part of Marysburg cont.[d]	
4786	Edward Bedford(discharged British Soldier)		4823	Cornelius Downey	Do
4787	Stephen Pilchard	Do	4824	Thomas Margerson	Do
4788	Richard Bibby	Do	4825	Thomas Harrison	Do
4789	William Mulloy	Do	4826	Michael Clancey	Do
4790	Joseph McCarger	Do	4827	G.J. Hudson	Do
4791	John Husley	Do	4828	Michael Badderly	Do
4792	Charles McDuff	Do	4829	William Andrew	Do
4793	Alexander McDonell	Do	4830	Patrick Peirce	Do
4794	James Grant	Do	4831	Donald Grant	Do
4795[f]	William Bincker*	Do	4832	John Mills	Do
4796	Peter Strentts	Do	4833	Ludovick Hoffman	Do
4797	Andrew Hesse	Do	4834	Colin Ross	Do
4798	James North	Do	4835	John McKay	Do
4799	Ernest Nebling	Do	4836	James McCarthy	Do
4800	Tobias Snider	Do	4837	John Lanecty	Do
4801	Imanuel* Kief*	Do	4838	William Hill	Do
4802	William Carson	Do	4839	William Dennis	Do
4803	Donald McCrimmon	Do	4840	James McCurdy	Do
4804	James Wright	Do	4841	William Blanchard	Do
4805	William Wright	Do	4842	John Vallop	Do
4806	Alexander Ross	Do	4843	John Sutherland	Do
4807	William Ross	Do	4844	Patrick Kelly	Do
4808	Walter Ross	Do	4845	Jam(es) Alpin*	Do
4809	Donald McIntosh	Do	4846	Frederick Lodwick	Do
4810	William Harrison Sen.[r]	Do	4847	John Dick	Do
4811	William Harrison Jun.[r]	Do	4848	Reeds North	Do
4812	Elisha Crane	Do	4849	Gustas Paepper	Do
4813	Jeremiah Storm	Do	4850	John Grant	Do
4814	David Hogan	Do	4851	Henry Cloudy	Do
4815	Daniel Wilders	Do	4852	Frederick Smith	Do
4816	John Forner	Do	4853	Henry Slusenburg	Do
4817	Christian Sirwall	Do	4854	John McDonell	Do
4818	Samuel Higgins	Do	4855	Matthew Hartman	Do
4819	Gasper Etzell	Do	4856	Israel Simpson	Do
4820	William Bridge	Do	4857	William Willekey	Do
4821	Ferdinand Shaffer	Do	4858	Henry Buncker	Do
4822[f]	John Dalhunty*	Do	4859	John Adcock	Do

NOTES:

1. No. 4795 - spelled BINKER in File 4.
2. No. 4822 - spelled DALHUNLY in File 4; the "T" is definitely crossed here - not so in File 4.
3. One must suspect that some of these discharged British Soldiers were either German mercenaries, or that some of the discharged German Soldiers got mixed in this list. Some of the names are quite German sounding/spelled.

File 5

NUMBER	(Column "E" continued)	
	Part of Marysburg contd.	
4860	Andrew Miller discharged German Soldier	
4861	Bernard Inglehart	Ditto
4862	James Denhart	Do
4863	Martin Dreder	Do
4864	John Kraigil	Do
4865	Conrad Bunger	Do
4866	Michael Kessler	Do
4867	Philip Keller	Do
4868	Frederick Newalt	Do
4869[f]	Frederick Myncker	Do
4870	Henry David	Do
4871	Christain* Gants	Do
4872	Gotlep Hek	Do
4873	Jacob Metch	Do
4874[f]	G.B. De Reitzenstine	Do
	(end Column "E")	
	(Column "F")	
	Marysburg continued	
4875	John Benth discharged German Soldier	
4876	John Myneker	Ditto
4877	Daniel Abraham	Do
4878	Nicholas Lehincter	Do
4879[f]	Sigismund* Borman	Do
4880	John Merckle	Do
4881	William Gerberg	Do
4882	Eveht. Frike	Do
4883	John Lotz	Do
4884	John Damderf	Do
4885	John Keaning	Do
4886	Christian Imendol	Do
4887[f]	John Menuke	Do
4888	Ernest Claprood	Do
4889	Gasper Mauk	Do

NUMBER	(Column "F" continued)	
4890	Gotlep Mauk	Do
4891	Gasper Claus	Do
4892	Henry Slieneman	Do
4893	Gotlep Saupe	Do
4894[f]	Henry Rimmerman	Do
4895	Gasper Vizer	Do
	Part of Marysburg & Sophiasburg	
4896[f]	Coll. J. James Rogers	U.E.
4897	James Rogers	U.E.
4898	David M. Rogers	U.E.
4899	Henry Young	U.E.
4900	Daniel Young	U.E.
4901	Henry Young Junr.	U.E.
4902	John Stinson	U.E.
4903	John Stinson Junr.	U.E.
4904	John Richards	U.E.
4905	Owen Richards	U.E.
4906	John Richards Junr.	U.E.
4907	Daniel Richards	U.E.
4908	Moses Simmons	U.E.
4909	Jonathan Miller	U.E.
4910	John Miller	U.E.
4911	Cornelius Miller	U.E.
4912[f]	(Barret Dyer)	(U.E.)
4913	William Dyer	U.E.
4914	Sampson Striker	U.E.
4915	James Blakely	U.E.
4916	Farrington Ferguson	U.E.
4917	Rozel Ferguson	U.E.
4918	Augustus Spencer	U.E.
4919	John Ogden	U.E.
4920	John Ogden Junr.	U.E.
4921	Nathanl. A. Gaffield	U.E.
4922	Daniel Pettit	U.E.
4923	William Smyth	U.E.

NOTES:

1. No. 4869 - spelled MYNCHER in File 4; quite definite here.
2. No. 4874 - below this entry is faint writing - difficult to read, possibly "Gasper Vizer ... U.E. or Do". See No. 4895 for a complete entry of this name.
3. No. 4879 - clear as written; File 4 clearly SIGISMOND.
4. No. 4887 - 2nd choice MENSKE.
5. No. 4912 - complete entry lost on broken paper fold.
6. Ncs. 4896 et seq suggests these entries are not legitimate UEL qualified persons; seems to be many sons of Loyalists.

File 5

NUMBER	(Column "F" continued)	
	Part of Marysburg & Sophiasburg continued	
4924	John Peters	U.E.
4925	Jacob Corbman	U.E.
4926	Fred[k]. Swartfeager	U.E.
4927	Timothy Porter	U.E.
4928	Ferdinand Grout	U.E.
4929	Richard Ferguson	U.E.
4930	Rich[d]. Ferguson Jun[r].	U.E.
4931	Silas Dyer	U.E.
4932	David Simmon	U.E.
4933	Daniel Killen	U.E.
4934	Peter J. Smith	U.E.
4935	John Hurley	U.E.
4936	John Spencer	U.E.
4937	John Blaker	U.E.
4938	Thomas Goldsmith	U.E.
	Part of Sophiasburg and Ameliasburg	
4939	William Fox	U.E.
4940	John Weart	U.E.
4941	Henry Spencer	U.E.
4942	Benjamin Spencer	U.E.
4943	John Spencer	U.E.
4944	Andrew Spencer	U.E.
4945	John Spencer Jun[r].	U.E.
4946	James Morden	U.E.
4947	John Howell	U.E.
4948	Richard Morden	U.E.
4949	Trueman Knappin	U.E.
4950	Simon J. Cole	U.E.
4951	John Trompeau	U.E.
4952	Tobias Rikerman	U.E.
4953	Frederick Fox	U.E.
4954	Gadlep* Magel	U.E.
4955	Stephen Roblin	U.E.

NUMBER	(Column "F" continued)	
4956	Matthew Steele	U.E.
4957	Edward Rikerman	U.E.
4958	John Law Campbell	U.E.
4959	Josiah Dean	U.E.
4960	Samuel Dean	U.E.
4961	Abraham Peterson	U.E.
4962	Nicholas Peterson	U.E.
4963	Samuel Wright	U.E.
4964	James Peak	U.E.
4965	Rudolph Slauser	U.E.
4966	John Brooks	U.E.
4967	George Angle	U.E.
4968	Peter Cole	U.E.
4969	Isaac De Mills	U.E.
4970 [f]	Barnard* Cole	U.E.
4971 [f]	Henry Williams	(blank)
	Township of Thurlow	
4972	William Bell	U.E.
4973	Archibald Chisholm	U.E.
4974	Samuel Sherwood	U.E.
4975	John Lott Sen[r].	U.E.
4976	Henry Simons	U.E.
4977	John Taylor	U.E.
4978	Philip Swick	U.E.
4979	John Fairman Sen[r].	U.E.
4980	John McIntosh	U.E.
4981	Alexander Chisholm	U.E.
4982 [f]	John Cryselen*	U.E.
4983	George Singleton	U.E.
4984	Israel Ferguson	U.E.
4985	John Frederick	U.E.
4986	John McArthur	U.E.

NOTES:

1. No. 4970 - clearly B<u>A</u>RNARD here; File 4 B<u>E</u>RNARD just as clear.
2. No. 4971 - no "UE" shown; File 4 it is there.
3. No. 4982 - quite correct as written - in fact the ending "N" has been made meticulously.

File 5

NUMBER	(Column "F" continued)		NUMBER	(Column "F" continued)	
	Township of Richmond			Additional Names from different Townships	
4987	William R. Bowen	U.E.	5002	Batties Harris	U.E.
4988	Isaac Van Alstine	U.E.	5003 f	William Lossie	U.E.
4989	Jonas Van Alstine	U.E.	5004 f	James Bradshaw Jun.	U.E.
4990	Isaac Van Alstine Jun.[r]	U.E.	5005	Ladock* Thresser	U.E.
4991	Henry Bowen	U.E.	5006	William Johnston	U.E.
4992	Frederick Oliver	U.E.	5007	Conrad Frederick	U.E.
4993	John Oliver	U.E.	5008	William Sherrard	U.E.
4994	Cornelius Oliver	U.E.	5009	Martin Rush	U.E.
4995	Aaron Oliver	U.E.	5010	Robert Wright	U.E.
4996 f	Samuel Laws	U.E.	5011	Richard Smith	U.E.
4997	Garret VandeBarrick	U.E.	5012 f	Martin Dunyes*	U.E.
4998	Andrew Kimmerly	U.E.	5013	William Dougall	U.E.
4999	Adam Segar	U.E.	5014	William Marsh	U.E.
5000	Staatz Segar	U.E.	5015	Matthias Marsh	U.E.
5001	Lambert* Van Alstine	U.E.	5016	George W. Myers	U.E.
			5017	Tobias Myers	U.E.
			5018 f	John W. Myers	U.E.
			5019	Moore W. Hovenden*	U.E.
			5020	Nicholas Simmons	U.E.
			5021	James Smith	U.E.
			5022	Daniel Fisher	U.E.

(The endorsation is spread across the bottom of all six columns. Seals are beside each Justice of the Peace's signature).

N..B.. 972 Names

Poole England Act[g]. Rich[d]. Cartwright J.P. Thomas Markland J.P.
Clerk of the Peace Chairman

(This fourth signature is in line with the other three; in this transcription, there is not enough room to put all four on one line) (William Atkinson J.P.

NOTES:

1. No. 4997 - surname all one word here; File 4, three words.
2. No. 5004 - supra is written faintly "before in Fredericksburg".
3. No. 5005 - 2nd choice LODOCK. File 4 it is LADOCK.
4. No. 5012 - written faintly beside is "German". Spelling clear.
5. No. 5019 - spelling quite clear; File 4 also quite clear as HOVENDAR.
6. This transcription confirms the clerk's count of 972 names.
7. This File does not have the added names that File 4 has, as they were likely added to that final copy at/by order of the Legislative Council.

File 6

NATIONAL ARCHIVES OF CANADA (NAC)

UPPER CANADA (ONTARIO) DISTRICT LOYALIST ROLLS 1796-1803

Reference: NAC RG 1, L 7, vol. 52B (B as in Bravo) (Files 1 to 15)

FILE 6

Archivist's Description

Wrapper endorsed "Midland Dist. Additions to the U E List", with a longer title in the document itself. Original c. 1797, annotated in red ink; 40x12 cm. Broken on one fold. Paper watermarked 1795. The names correspond to entries on pages 16-17 of File 4.

Transcriber's Comments

Easily read because of large writing. Annotations not carried onto File 4 and they are quite important to genealogists. The original does not provide numbers as some other Files do.

File 6 Page 1

NUMBER		
		Additions made to the List of U.E. Loyalists at the General Quarter Sefsions of the Peace for the Midland District held at Kingston the Tenth day of October Instant and Continued by Adjournment to the 20th day of the same Month.
5401		Charles T. Peters not entitled not UE
5402		Lieut. William Johnson
5403		Philip Reddie
5404		Martin Freleigh
5405		Christina Taylor
5406		Bolton Evans
5407		Waite Wright
5408		Garret Miller
5409		Serjeant Robert Wilkin Discharged from the Dragoons
5410		Julius Bush
5411		John Fisher
5412 f		Joseph Morden
5413		Daniel Lobdel entered before under Ger(--?--)
5414		John Griffiths
5415		John Crawford
5416		Gilbert Miller
5417		John McPherson
5418		Ann McCaulay not UE
5419		Elizabeth Kirby not UE
5420		Alexander Dunbar
5421	not UE	Thomas Richardson Discharged Private Artillery
5422	not UE	Samuel Winterbottom Dº Dº
5423		Amos Lucas
5424		George Lucas
5425		James Rankin
5426		Brian Bull
5427		Gabriel Orser
5428		John Dunahow
5429		Henry Bush
5430	not UE	Mary Phillips now Merrils

NOTES:

1. The cover marked "Midland Dist. Additions to the U.E. List".
2. This File not dated anywhere - but assumed 1796 or 1797.
3. The notations on the left and after the names believed to be in red ink.
4. No.5413 - can not find a discharged German Soldier of this name; there is a Daniel Abraham No. 3827 in File 4.

File 6 Page 2

NUMBER		
5431	not UE	George OKill Stuart
5432	not UE	John Grafs (GRASS))
5433	not UE	Peter Grafs (GRASS)) Sons & Dau.[s]
5434	not UE	Daniel Grafs (GRASS)) of UEs
5435f	not UE	Mary Grafs (GRASS))
5436	not UE	Eve Grafs (GRASS)------)---- now Wartman
5437	not UE	Bemster Peters Jun.[r])
		(end first page of FILE 6)
5438	not	Catherine Herkimer now Markland)
5439	not	Jane Herkimer now Anderson) not UEs
5440	not	Mary Herkimer now Hamilton)
5441	not	Mary Vent) but
5442	not	Ann McGuin now Vanorder) Sons & Dau.[rs]
5443	not	Mary Badgely now Atkinson)
5444		Joseph Carnahan
5445		Daniel Lightheart
5446		Minard Harris
5447	not	Joseph Harris
5448	not	Peter Harris
5449		Mathias* Marsh
5450		Samuel Marsh
5451		Benjamin Marsh
5452		Jeremiah Marsh
5453		William Marsh Sen.[r]
5454		David Palmer
5455	not	David Palmer Jun.[r] son of David) sons of UE
5456	not	Caleb Palmer (--?--))
5457	not	John Palmer) not intitled*
5458		Martin Rush
5459		Josiah Cafs (CASS)
5460	not	William Marsh Jun.[r] not UE
		Richard Cartwright, J.P. Chairman of the Quarter Sefsions
		William Atkinson J.P.
		Thomas Markland J.P.
		(end second and final page File 6)

NOTES:

1. There was space on page 1 for "not UE" to left of those names affected; only space on page 2 for "not".
2. No. 5436 - the "now Wartman"actually inside the brackets.
3. This File/Roll of names is duplicated in File 4, pages 32, 33 & 34. The notations here are helpful though.

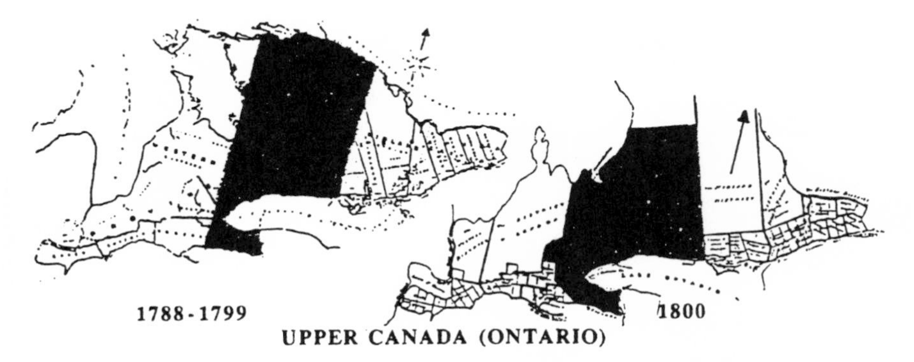

1788-1799 1800

UPPER CANADA (ONTARIO)

In 1796 the Home District, formerly called the Nassau District, consisted of the territory between lines drawn north from the mouth of the Trent River and the tip of Long Point on Lake Erie. This large district included Lincoln, York, Northumberland and Durham Counties and part of Oxford, and Norfolk Counties. The original district town was Niagara and it was replaced in 1801 by York. In 1800 the Niagara region was separated and formed the Niagara District, with Niagara as the district town; Niagara was earlier known as Newark and is now called Niagara-on-the-Lake.

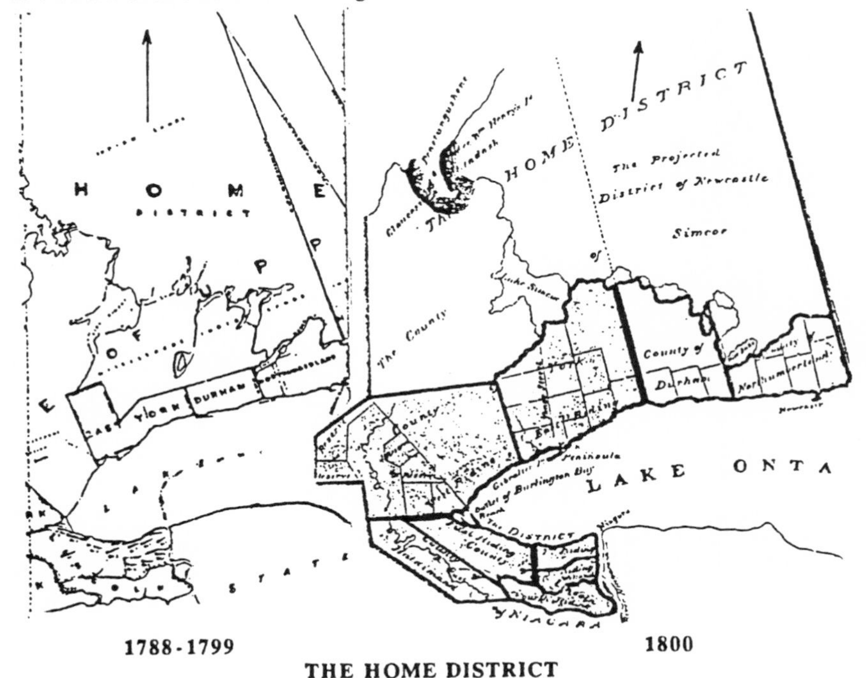

1788-1799 1800

THE HOME DISTRICT

File 7

NATIONAL ARCHIVES OF CANADA (NAC)

UPPER CANADA (ONTARIO) DISTRICT LOYALIST ROLLS

Reference: NAC RG 1, L 7, vol. 52B(B as in Bravo) (FILES 1 to 15)

FILE 7

Archivist's Description

HOME (or NIAGARA) DISTRICT

Endorsed "UE Roll -- Niagara District - 1797", with a longer title on the first page. Certified contempory copy, by Ralfe Clench, 39x25 cm, on paper with watermark of 1795; 12 numbered pages; evidence of sewing into book format. Alphabetically arranged listing of 679 entries.

Transcriber's Comments

The heading on Page 1 is as follows: "List of Persons who have satisfied the Justices of the Peace for the/ Home District, in Sessions assembled that they joined the Royal Standard/ in America before the year 1783. Newark (Niagara-on-the-Lake) 15th of October 1797./" Under the Heading are two faint notes: "(1796 --?-- additions)"; and, "679 Names".

The List is moderately easy to read; some letters are formed in different ways and this leads to confusion, but, the transcription is considered quite accurate. There is much good genealogical information here,eg, living or dead is recorded, widows re-marrying, some sons of fathers are listed, and a few new locations are given. There are obviously more than just Butler's Rangers on this list; many Officers and NCOs are not from that unit. These could be discharged British Soldiers/Officers. It is interesting that some women were accepted as UEs and others not - criteria ?.

The transcriber continues to use the asterix, "*", to indicate "SIC" or an apparent mistake or "as written". The clerk has used an "o" supra on the left margin to indicate the entry/person is not entitled to be on the list as a UE; all others have a tick/check mark to indicate they are approved. The reader is referred to FAMILIES (OGS Quarterly Publication) 20:21 (1981) for an up to date Nominal Roll of Butler's Rangers. It is noted that the clerk numbered each

..... / 2

File 7

- 2 -

page but the numbers for pages 1 and 2 can not be seen. Also, the clerk started on page 1 to total the entries by each letter and group of letters; he later settled down to doing his sums by letter only.

The list is in two columns per page and is likely only for persons in the Niagara area as there is at least one notation that someone is now at York (Toronto). All that is between the double lines is the transcription; outside the double lines are transcriber's notations and the index numbers that run from No. 5501 to 6179.

NOTE:

Nos. 5517/8/9 - Benedict received 13,400 acres in Upper Canada but made no permanent settlement here. His two sons, Richard and Henry did settle. Richard's son, Edward William Benedict Arnold, settled in Sarnia area where his descendants still live.

File 7 Page 1

NUMBER		NUMBER	
	A		B (1)
5501	Ayckler William	5527	Buckner Mathias
5502	Anguish Jacob Senr. (dead)	5528	Bowman Jacob
5503	Austin Solomon	5529	Bowman Henry
5504	Anker Frederick jun^{r}.*	5530	Brown Joseph
5505	Alexander Hugh	5531	Boyce John Senr.
5506	Aker Lambert (spelling variants include ACKER/AKER/ACRE/EKOR)	5532	Bowman Adam jun^{r}.
5507	Austin Joel	5533	Bowman Adam Senr.
5508	Anguish Henry	5534	Brown John
5509	Anker Frederick Senr.	5535	Bender Philip
5510	Anker Charles	5536	Bassey Robert
5511	Anker August	5537	Bradt Andrew Captain
5512	Adair John	5538	Bassey Jacob
5513$_{f}$	Ainsley Johanna	5539	Beebe* Eden Serjeant
5514	Anderson Simon	5540	Bell Derick
5515	Anderson Elias	5541	Bradt John Lieut.
5516$_{f}$	Anderson Alexander	5542	Barthol Keephart
5517	Arnold Benedict Brig^{r} General	5543	Buck Philip
5518^{f}	Arnold Richard Lieut.-	5544	Bower Peter Corporal
5519^{f}	Arnold Henry Lieut.-	5545	Bowen Cornelius
	19	5546	Beebe Joshua (dead)
	B	5547	Brown William
5520	Butler John L^{t}.Co^{l}. (dead)	5548	Butler Johnson Ensign
5521	Ball Jacob Senr. Lieut.	5549	Ball Jacob, son to Jacob Ball Senr.L^{t}.
5522	Butler Thomas Lieut.	5550	^{o}Ball Jacob, son to Peter Ball L^{t}.
5523	Butler Andrew Lieut.	5551	Burtch Charles
5524	Ball Peter Lieut.	5552	Burtch Edee
5525$_{f}$	Bowman Peter	5553	Bradt Arent (dead)
5526	Basteder* David	5554	Brundige* James
	26		28

NOTES:

1. No. 5514 et seq - the "S" is often written as "f" as it was at that time, eg, Anderfon; the double "ss" was "fs".
2. No. 5526 - correct as written; an error for BASTEDO ?
3. The page number is missing.
4. All between the double lines is what appears in the original double columned list.
5. Nos. 5517/8/9 - see note page 2 of introduction this File.

File 7 Page 2

NUMBER		NUMBER	
	(2) B		C
5555	Burns James	5589	Clench Ralfe Lieutenant
5556	Bennet James (dead)	5590	Campbell Robert Serjeant
5557	Banta Weeart* Cap[th] - (dead)	5591	Clows John Corporal
5558	Beasley Richard	5592	Crumb Benony
5559	Boss Elizabeth	5593	Clandenning Walter
5560	Bowman Abraham	5594	Conkling Robert
5561	Brown James	5595	Carle John
5562	Buckner Henry Serjt.	5596[f]	[o]Cassada Daniel
	(alias Buigner)	5597[f]	Cassada Luke
5563	Berdan Albert	5598	Cummings Thomas
5564[f]	Beech John	5599	Coghill George Sen[r].(dead)
5565	Barnum Nathaniel (dead)	5600	Casselman John
5566	Barnhart John	5601	Coghill John
5567	Boice John jun[r*].	5602	Clandenning Abraham
5568	Buigner John Sen[r]. (dead)	5603	Coon John Serjt.
5569	Backer John (Mulatto Man)	5604	Crantz Michael
5570	Betron* David	5605	Clandenning James Sen[r].
5571	Butler Philip		(dead)
5572	Bayeux Thomas	5606	Clement Joseph Lieut.
5573	Boesvoort* Elias	5607	Clement James
5574[f]	Beardslay C.B. Attorney	5608	Crumb William
5575	Beegraft Benjamin	5609[f]	Chrysler Adam Lieut.
5576	Bradt John (dead)		(dead)
5577	Burch John Esq[r]. (dead)	5610	Cox Samuel
5578	Bradt Minar	5611	Clement John Lieut.
5579	Bowen William	5612	Colrake Peter
5580	Bowlsby Richard	5613	Chisholm John
5581	Bowlsby Thomas	5614	Cain Barnabas
5582	Burch Martha Mrs.	5615	Clement Lewis Sen[r]. (dead)
5583	Baker Jack (Black Man)	5616	Collard John
5584	Buck Jonathan	5617	Cooper James
5585	Brakenridge Francis	5618	Cooper Thomas
5586	Boice John Sen[r].	5619	Coghill George jun[r*].
5587	Buckner Henry Sen[r].	5620	Caldwell John
5588	Birdsall Samuel (dead)	5621	Crawford James
	69		

NOTES:

1. No. 5574 - the only Attorney seen in any UE List.
2. No. 5596/7 - spelling variants include CASSADY/CASSIDY/CASHATY.
3. No. 5609 - in Eastern District this name usually CRYSLER.
4. No. 5564 - quite definite as copied; actually, the entry is over-written to emphasize it. In File 8 it could be BACH or BEECH. In File 10 it could be BUCK or BEECK only the "u" or "ee" being in doubt. The name is likely BUCK as that name appears elsewhere; BEECH does not.

File 7 Page 3

NUMBER	
	C
5622	Chisholm George
5623	Coghill Peter
5624	Clandenning John
5625 f	Carle Jonas
5626	Cosby George
5627	Cain John
5628	Coltman John Serjeant
5629	Chambers Ahijah*Serjeant
5630 f	Corus Cos
5631	Collins Alexander
5632	Clench V. Benjamin
5633	Cummings Jane Mrs.
5634	Coffin James (Commissary)
5635	Clement Joseph Serjeant
5636	Collins John
5637 f	Campbell George Serjeant
5638 f	Campbell James
5639	Carty Thomas Senr. (dead)
5640	Clarke Alexander
5641	Cole John
5642	Chrysler Peter
5643	Culver Timothy
5644	Cheu* Johnson W^{m}. Ensign
5645 f	o Clench Elizabeth Mrs.
5646	Claus Daniel Colonel(dead)
5647	Cesar John (Black Man)
	59
	D
5648	Dame George Captain
5649 f	Dachsteder Frederick Lieut. (dead)
5650	De Pew Charles
5651	Decker (no 2nd name - from other records, like-ly JACOB)

NUMBER	
	D 3
5652	Dagherty*Anthony
5653	De Pew John Junr.
5654	De Pew William (dead)
5655	Davis William
5656	Duforest* Abraham
5657	Denniston Robert
5658	Doan Aaron
5659	Davis Isaac
5660	Dennis John
5661	Doan Joseph
5662	Dill Henry
5663	De Pew John Senr.
5664	Dachsteder John Lieutenant
5665	De Cowe Jacob
5666	Duggan Cornelius
5667	Davis Benjamin
5668	Dachsteder John Junr. Corporal
5669	Dill Barsnet* Senr.
5670	Doyle Benjamin
5671	Davis Thomas
5672	Derby John
	25
	E
5673	Emmit Stephen
5674	Elsworth Francis
5675	English Andrew
5676	o Evertson John (dead)
5677	Eil alias Oil Nicholas
5678	Evringham James
	6
	F

NOTES:

1. No. 5625 - possibly more correctly CARROL.
2. No. 5630 - Caspar Corus died 24 Nov 1835 aged 96 years.
3. No. 5637/8 - JAMES & ROBERT Campbell listed as Sergeants; GEORGE as a Private in FAMILIES 20:21 (1981).
4. No. 5645 - the "o" supra was used by someone checking off this list to indicate not eligible to be on the UEL List; all others had a simple tick/check mark indicating eligibility.
5. No. 5649 - the above FAMILIES reference gives him as Sergeant.

File 7 Page 4

NUMBER		NUMBER	
	4 F		G
5679	Frelick John	5710	Garner John
5680	Forbush Nicholas	5711	Gahagan* Oliver
5681	Fields Gilbert	5712	Glover Jacob
5682	Frelick Benjamin Corporal	5713	Gilmore Benjamin
5683 f	Frey Bernard Captain		11 H
5684	Feero* Peter	5714	Hunt Edward
5685	Fields George Sen[r]. (dead)	5715	House James
5686	Fairchild Benjamin Corporal	5716 f	Hunter John
5687	Frost Edmund	5717	Hill Carney (or Carney Hill)
5688	Forsyth George	5718	Hardison Benjamin
5689	Forsith* James	5719 f	House Philip
5690	Fowler John	5720	Hainer John
5691	Force Philip	5721 f	Hagerman Arnold Serjeant
5692	Frey Philip Ensign	5722	Hainer Albert
5693	Flack Archibald	5723	House Daniel
5694	Francis W[m]. Q[r]. Mast[r].	5724	Hodgkinson William
5695	Francis Catherine	5725	Henry James
5696	Ferris Joshua	5726 f	Hoghtellin* James
5697	Fisher George	5727 f	Haslip James Corporal
5698	Fields Rebecka* formerly Mrs. Johnston	5728	Hainer Richard
5699	Freeman John	5729	Haines Nathaniel
5700	Forrest Laurania formerly Mrs. Morden	5730	Hare Peter Captain
5701	File John Corporal	5731	Hare John Lieut. (dead)
5702	Fulton James Captain	5732	Hare Peter (dead)
	24 G	5733	Hare William
5703	Greenlaw Jonathan (dead)	5734	Herkimer George Lieut. (dead)
5704	Gamble William	5735	House John
5705	Grigg John	5736	House George
5706	Green Benjamin	5737	House Harmanus
5707	Gilbert Josiah	5738 f	Haverland Harmanus Sen[r].
5708	Gould John	5739	Haverland Harmanus jun[r].
5709	Garner William	5740	Harris Henry
		5741	Harris John
		5742	Harris Thomas

NOTES:

1. No. 5684 - otherwise spelled FERRO.
2. No. 5717 - all in brackets are clerk's writings.
3. No. 5738 - HARMANUS stroked through; ANDREW substituted supra.
4. No. 5727 - spelling variants include HAYSLIP/HEASLIP.
5. Nos. 5720/2/8 - spelling variants include HANOR/HEANER.

File 7 Page 5

NUMBER		NUMBER	
	H		H 5
5743	Howey Robert	5775	Hill Solomon Corporal
5744	Hazen Daniel Serjeant	5776	Hallowell Benjamin
5745	Huffman Christopher	5777 f	Hewston Joshua (dead)
5746	Henn Michael	5778	Hopkins Silas Senr.
5747	Hendershote* Peter	5779	Hansen* Richard Lieut.
5748	Huffman Nicholas	5780	o Horton Isaac
5749	Huffman Jacob	5781	o Horton Edmund
5750	Hodgkinson John	5782	Hyndman Samuel
5751	Hunsinger John		69
5752	House Frederick		J
5753	Hosteter* John	5783	Johnson Brant Lieutenant
5754	Haggerty Hugh	5784	Johnston* William Lieutenant
5755	Hill John Senr.	5785	Johnston* John Captn. (dead)
5756	Hitchcock Miles	5786	Jones James (dead)
5757	o Holmes Asa	5787	Johnston Ralph
5758	o Hamilton Catherine Mrs. (dead)	5788	o Johnston Conrade*
5759	o House Joseph	5789	o Johnson Jemima Miss
5760	o House George junr.*	5790	o Johnson Sarah Miss
5761	o House John junr.*	5791	o Johnson Mary Miss
5762	Hanse Joseph Senr.	5792	Johnston John now in (Britain ?)
5763	o Hill John junr.	5793	Johnston Jonas
5764	o Hanse Joseph junr.	5794	Jones Jane Mrs.
5765	o Hanse John	5795	Jones Ebenezer
5766	o Hanse Philip	5796	Johnston John now in Stamford
5767	Hardy John Serjeant	5797	o Johnston Henry
5768	Henry Philip	5798	Johnson John Sir
5769	Hare John Captain (dead)	5799	Jarviss* William
5770	Hilts Joseph	5800	o Johnston Elizabeth (Widow)
5771	Hilton B. William Serjeant	5801	o Jarviss Samuel
5772	Hoff Henry	5802	Johns Solomon Lieut. (dead)
5773	Hoff John	5803	Jones John
5774	Hanshaw Mary now Mrs. Moody		21 K

NOTES:

1. The "o" supra indicates not eligible as a UE.
2. No. 5778 - 2nd choice is TITUS.

File 7 Page 6

NUMBER	
	6
	K
5804	Kemp Mathew
5805	Kern Mathias
5806	[o]Kerr Elizabeth Mrs. (dead)
5807	Kilman Jacob
5808	Kenny James
5809	Kilman John
5810	Keefer George Sen.[r] (dead)
5811	Kettle Jeremiah Sen.[r]
	8
	L
5812[f]	Larroway Peter
5813	Livingston Neil
5814	Livingston John (dead)
5815	Lemons Joseph Sen.[r] (dead)
5816	Lockwood Josiah
5817	London Bartholemy
5818	Lowe Elizabeth Mrs.
5819	Lambert Cornelius Corporal
5820[f]	Larroway Jonas
5821[f]	Larroway Abraham
5822	Laurance*George
5823[f]	Lutz Sampson
5824	Lymburner Mathew
5825[f]	Lampman Peter
5826	Lampman Frederick
5827	Land Abel
5828	Lockwood Benjamin
5829	Lippincott Richard
5830	Laurence* Richard
5831	[o]Lymburner Mathew (dead)
5832	Lyons Benjamin
5833[f]	Land Robert
	L
5834	Lymburner John
5835	Lotteridge Robert Capt.[n] (dead)
5836	[o]Lotteridge John
5837	[o]Lotteridge William
	26
	M
5838	Miller Henry
5839	Matlack Caleb
5840	McFall David Lieut.
5841	McFall Neil (dead)
5842	Mills John
5843	Mathews Jonathan
5844	Major John (dead)
5845	[o]Munroe Robert Sen.[r]
5846	Munroe John Lieut.
5847	McKay John
5848	Marcellis Baptist John
5849	McLaughlan James
5850	McDonell Miles Ensign
5851	McNeil John
5852	McRobert Mary Mrs.
5853	McLean Donald
5854	Martin Peter (Black Man)
5855	McDonell Helena Mrs. (dead)
5856	McIntire Daniel Sen.[r]
5857	[o]Muirhead Deborah Mrs.
5858	Moss John
5859	Moody Walter
5860	May William
5861	McDonald John Corporal
5862[f]	[o]McDonell Alexander Lieut.
5863	McDonald Christian
5864	Miller George
5865	McMicking Peter

NOTES:

1. No. 5812/20/21 - otherwise LARRAWAY.
2. No. 5823 - spelling variants include LUTES/LOUTS.
3. Nos. 5825/33 - a Mohawk Valley name.
4. No. 5862 - the non-eligibility as a UE could be that he is discharged British Officer.
5. The asterix means Sic = as written a likely mistake.
6. The "[o]" supra is some authority's indication of non-eligibility as UE.

File 7 Page 7

NUMBER	
	M
5866 f	McDonell Peter Serjeant
5867	Maby Lewis Serjeant
5868	McClellan William
5869	Marakle Frederick
5870	Marakle John Serjeant
5871	Marakle James
5872	o Marakle Henry
5873	Martha* John
5874	McDonald Ronald Serj[t]. (dead)
5875	Mattice Abraham
5876	Murray Duncan Lieut.(dead)
5877	Millard Dan Corporal
5878	Murray John Q[r]. Mas[r].
5879	McDonell Allan Capt[n].(dead)
5880	o McDonell Areas*
5881	Millard Jesse
5882	McMichael Isaac
5883	Magaw Patrick
5884	Millard Thomas (dead)
5885	Morden Moses
5886	Mathews James
5887	McCall* Daniel Sen[r].
5888	McNabb John (Commissary)
5889 f	McNabb Alexander
5890	Maby Frederick (dead)
5891	Marcellis Peter
5892	Morden John
5893	o Maby John
5894	Morden Ralph (dead)
5895	McNabb James Doctor (dead)
5896	Malcolm Finlay
5897	Miller Peter (dead)
5898	McLaughlan Edward
5899	McCool Archibald (dead)

NUMBER	
	M 8
5900	McCool William
5901	McDonald William
5902	Miller Andrew
5903	McQuin Alexander Sen[r].
5904	Muckle* John
5905 f	Miller Thomas
5906	Medaugh Stephen
5907	Meredith Charles
5908	Montross Silas
5909	Merritt Thomas Lieutenant
5910	McMichael Edward
5911	Medaugh James
5912	McMicking Thomas
5913	Murphy Timothy
5914	Morden Ralph
5915	o Morden James
	78
	N
5916 f	Nicholson Robert
5917	Newberry William Serjeant
5918	Newkirk James
5919	Neil George
5920	Nellis William
5921	Nellis Warner
5922	Nellis Abraham
5923	o Nellis John
5924	Nellis W[m]. Henry Capt[n]. (dead)
5925	Nellis Robert Lieutenant
5926	North Thomas
5927	o Newkirk John
5928	o Nellis Prissilla Mrs.
	13
	O

NOTES:

1. No. 5867/90 - spelling variants include MAYBEE/MAYBEY.
2. No. 5906 - variants include MIDDOUGH.
3. No. 5917 - Sgt. Newberry and Lieut. Henry Hare were hanged as spies at Canajoharie (35 miles west of Schenectady on the south bank of the Mohawk River) in July 1779. (See page 16 File 3). Lieut. Henry Hare does not appear on this list for some reason; maybe because his children are listed for the Eastern District where his widow and her second husband settled.

File 7 Page 8

NUMBER		NUMBER	
	8		
	O		P
5929	OConnelly* James	5965[f]	o Peters Samuel Reverend
5930	Osterhout William	5966[f]	o Peters Birdseye* W[m].
5931	OCarr* Peter	5967	Petty Margery formerly
5932	Outhouse* Nicholas		wife to Barhard Foster
5933	Overholt Abraham	5968	Palmer David
5934	Overholt Elizabeth Mrs.		33
5935	Overholt Stots*		Q
	7	5969	Quick Benjamin
	P	5970	Quick Solomon
5936	Pawling Benj[m]. Capt[n].	5971	Quin Michael
5937	Pawling Jesse Q[r]. Mast[r].	5972	Quant* Frederick
5938	Page Joseph		4
5939	Price Christian		R
5940	Pickard Benjamin	5973	Rodney Brydges George
5941	Pickard James		Serjeant
5942	Post Jacob	5974	Ramsay David
5943[f]	Parepoint* Richard	5975	Ryerse Samuel Captain
	(blackman)	5976	Ryerse J. Lieut.
5944	Phelps Elijah	5977	Reily* John Serjt.
5945	Plato Christian	5978	Reide* George
5946	Plato Peter	5979	Ransier George
5947	Petry Joseph Serj[t].	5980	Richards Christopher
5948	Putman Henry	5981	Ricely* Christian
5949	Pickard William	5982	Rowe Frederick Corporal
5950	Petry Jost John	5983	Rowe John Serjeant
5951	Prout Sheerman*	5984	Reynolds Caleb Lieut.
5952	Powell John Captain	5985	Robertson James (blackman
5953	Price David	5986	Robertson Prince(blackman
5954	Pettit John	5987	Rooreback Barent Captain
5955	Powell Dummer* W[m]. Hanb[l].	5988	Russell James
5956	Pell Joshua	5989	Reide William
5957	o Pew* Samuel	5990	o Robinson Anthony
5958	Plater George	5991	Rose Donald
5959	Pound Daniel	5992	o Ridoubt* Mary Mrs.
5960	Parker John	5993	Ryckman John Lieut.
5961[f]	Philips John		21
5962[f]	Pemberton James		
5963[f]	Pell Joseph		
5964[f]	Pell Jonathan		

NOTES:

1. Nos. 5961/2/3/4 - placed in left hand column from right hand column to ensure there was space for large number of names.
2. No. 5943 - otherwise spelled PIERPOINT.
3. No. 5965/6 - beside entries is faintlv written "OFF": this Reverend Samuel Peters did not come settle in Upper Canada; he was the father of Hannah, wife of William Jarvis, Secretary of Upper Canada.

File 7 Page 9

NUMBER	S
5994	Stacey John
5995	Smith Jacob Sen.[r]
5996	Stine John Serjeant (dead)
5997	Sacheverell Jane Mrs.
5998	Scott Archibald
5999	Stofle John
6000	Simons Titus Sen.[r]
6001	[o]Simons Titus Jun.[r] son of Titus
6002	Shank David Captain
6003	Stooks Hannah Mrs. formerly Widow Sipes
6004	Swayze Isaac
6005	Swayze Caleb
6006	Spurgin William
6007	Swayze Richard
6008	Smith Elias
6009	Seacord James Sen.[r] (dead)
6010	Slingerlandt* Anthony(dead
6011	Springer David (dead)
6012	Skinner Timothy
6013	Seacord Peter Sen.[r]
6014	[o]Seacord James Jun.[r] son of James
6015	[o]Seacord David Jun.[r] do
6016	Seacord Peter Jun.[r]
6017[f]	Street Samuel Jun.[r]
6018[f]	Smith John Sen.[r] (at Grand River)
6019	Stewart Thomas
6020[f]	[o]Slingerlandt Walter
6021	Stiles Silah*
6022	Stooks Edward
6023	Seacord Solomon Lieut.
6024	Schram Frederick Corporal

NUMBER	S (9)
6025	Spingsteen Stats
6026	Seacord John Sen.[r]
6027	Seacord John Jun.[r]
6028	Seacord Stephen Serjeant
6029	Spencer Robert
6030	Slingerlandt Richard
6031	Stevens John Sen.[r]
6032	Schram Valentine
6033	Showers Michael Sen.[r] (dead)
6034	Stuart George
6035	Smith Nicholas
6036	Smith John
6037	Seacord Silas Serjeant
6038	Stull Latham
6039	Snider John
6040	Seacord David Sen.[r]
6041	Shaw Michael
6042	Smith Henry
6043	Schram Jeremiah
6044	Schram John
6045	Springer Richard
6046	Sipes Jacob
6047	Sipes Jonas
6048	Sims Joseph Serjeant
6049	Soper Samuel (dead)
6050	Seagar Frederick
6051	Seagar Jacob
6052[f]	Snyther* Jacob Serjeant
6053	Stoner John
6054	Slingerlandt Gerrit
6055	[o]Slingerlandt Teunis*
6056	Stevens Aaron Commissary
6057	Servos Daniel Lieutenant
6058	Servos Jacob Lieutenant

65

NOTES:

1. No. 6017 - 2nd choice STRUT.
2. No. 6018 - Grand River is in Brant County.
3. No. 6020 - the "o" supra has a tick mark inside it; suspect that the circle is the correct version.
4. No. 6052 - in other Files, surname written the same way; however, the rank given is Corporal.

File 7 Page 10

NUMBER	
	10
	S
6059	Seacord Daniel
6060	o Springer Daniel son of David
6061	o Springer John do
6062	o Springer Benjamin
6063	Stone John
6064	Stewart Alexander Lieut.
6065	Steel William
6066	Slighter John
6067	Smith Hart
6068	Smith John (dead)
6069 f	o Seacord John son of --?--
6070	Sheehan Butler Walter
6071	o Smith Kennedy William
6072	Smith John
6073	Stevens John jun.r
	80
	T
6074	Tousack Casper (dead)
6075	Turnbull William
6076	Tredwell John
6077	Ten Broeck Peter Captain
6078	Terry Parshall
6079	Thompson Peter
6080	Thompson Andrew Cap.t (dead)
6081	Tederick* Lucas
6082	Tederick* Jacob Serjeant
6083	Tracey Timothy
6084	Thomas Jacob
6085	Teeple Peter Serjeant
6086	Thompson Samuel
6087	o Ten Brock* Jacob son of Peter
6088	Thacher John

NUMBER	
	T
6089	o Ten Broeck Nicholas son of Peter
6090	Trainer John
6091	o Ten Broeck John son of Major Peter
6092	Thompson Archibald (now at York)
6093	Thompson George
6094	Tice Gilbert Captain
6095	Thompson Archibald
6096	
	22
	V
6096	Van Every McGregor (dead)
6097	Van Dreser Peter
6098	Volick Isaac
6099	Vrooman Adam Serjeant
6100	Volick Storum*
6101	Van Every Samuel
6102	Van Petten* Arent
6103	Van Alstine Jacob
6104	Van Every William
6105	Van Every David Serjeant
6106	Van Derlip* Frederick (dead)
6107	Van Derlip Elizabeth Miss
6108	Van Derlip Mary Miss
6109	Van Derlip William
6110	o Van Derlip John
6111	o Van Derlip Edward son of Frederick
6112	Van Hoofen Richard
6113	Vincent Elijah Ensign
6114	o Van Every Peter (dead)
6115	o Van Every Henry son of McGregor
6116	o Van Every Andrew son of McGregor
6117 f	o Vohik* John

NOTES:

1. No. 6069 - the name is there but too faint to read on this photocopy.
2. No. 6117 - there is no room for the total 22.

File 7 Page 11

NUMBER	
	W
6118	Walker William
6119	Williams Samuel
6120	Williams Rachel
6121	Wilmot Allan
6122	Wall Edward (dead)
6123	o Warren Henry) sons of
6124	o Warren John junr.) John not UEs
6125	Wilson John
6126	Wilson Benjamin
6127f	Wilson John (Irish)
6128	o Wilson John (son of Serjt. John)
6129	o Wilson Thomas (son to Irish) John
6130	o Wilson Charles do
6131f	o Wilson Zilman do
6132	Wilson Crowell
6133	Woodley George
6134	Wilson Jacob
6135	Wilson Joseph
6136	Wardle Cornelius
6137	Whitsele Andrew
6138	Wardle Michael
6139	Westbrook Anthony
6140	o Westbrook Alexander son of Anthony
6141	o Westbrook John son of Anthony
6142	Wrong John
6143	o Westbrook Hagar
6144	o Westbrook Andrew son of Anthony
6145	Weaver Francis
6146	Whitner Henry
6147	Walker Jacob (dead)
6148	Warner Christian Serjeant
6149	Winney Cornelius Corporal

NUMBER	
	11
	W
6150	Windecker Henry
6151	Wintermute Peter Corporal
6152	Wintermute John Corporal
6153	Wintermute Abraham Corporal
6154	Wintermute Philip
6155	Wintermute Benjamin
6156f	Wilson John Serjeant
6157	Wormwood Mathew
6158	Wright Gabriel
6159	Welch Thomas Qr. Mastr.
6160	Williams Frederick
6161	Wintermute Mary Mrs.
6162	Wheeler Ephraim
6163	Wilkins Isaac
6164	Wilkins Martin
6165	Wilson Bathsheba (formerly Widow Soper)
6166	Whitmire* John
6167	Wychoff Peter
50	Y
6168	Young John Lieutenant
6169	Young Abraham
6170	Young John junr.
6171	o Young Joseph son of Lieut. John
6172	Young John Serjeant
6173	Young Henry
6174	Young Daniel Serjeant
6175	Younglove Ezekiel*
6176	Young Philip
6177	Young Adam Senr. (dead)
6178	Young George

NOTES:

1. No. 6128 - See Loyalist Lineages of Canada Volume II - Part 2 page 974.
2. No. 6132 - there is some indecipherible writing beside entry.
3. No. 6157 - this is a very English-sounding name; apparently it was a German name spelled WORMWÖD.

File 7 Page 12

NUMBER		NUMBER	
	U.E. Roll Niagara District 1797 Y		12 The above list* a true Copy/ from the Records of the Court of/ Q.r Sessions Home District of Upper/ Canada. Ralfe Clench Clerk of the Peace of H.D.
6179	Young Jacob Serjeant 12 Whole Amounting to 679f R. Hamilton Chairman P.J.f Jos.ph Edwards J.P. Geo. Forsyth J.P. Arch.d Cunninghame* J.P. J.s Ball J.P.f James Muirhead J.P. 1797		

NOTES:

1. The clerk's total agrees with the transcriber's.
2. The Chairman, R. Hamilton was the P.J. - Presiding Justice.
3. The fifth J.P. is likely JACOB Senior, ie, J.s Ball.
4. There are some faint vertical, formal printed remarks above Clerk's certification that appears to read: "Entered 1827 P.R. " plus some other even fainter remarks.

File 8

NATIONAL ARCHIVES OF CANADA (NAC)
UPPER CANADA (ONTARIO) DISTRICT LOYALIST ROLLS

Reference: NAC RG 1, L 7, vol. 52B(B as in Bravo) (FILES 1 to 15)

FILE 8

Archivist's Description

Home (or Niagara) District

Endorsed "UE Roll, Home District", with the date 11th Octr 1796 in a different hand, as well as the note "Ex Cl 8 Sept 1808 with New Book - J McG". (Ex Cl means Executive Council). Original, on paper not watermarked as to date; 114x54 cm, broken on folds into 16 pieces (although originally pasted into roll format). The list is arranged alphabetically and includes 470 names (actually 472 names); it was signed 12 January 1797 at Newark (Niagara-on-the-Lake).

Transcriber's Comments

The Heading, on two lines (indicated by oblique strokes), reads: "List of those Persons who attended at the General Quarter Sessions of the Peace holden* for the Home District (Michaelmas Term) in the Town (of)/ Newark. Province of Upper Canada on the 11th day of October 1796 and 36th Year of Our Lord King George the IIId of Great Britain, France & Ireland &c &c./

The writing is considerably easier to read than File 7 with the letters up to a quarter inch high; the writing is much more flowing and sophisticated. There are five columns in the format that run alphabetically down the first column about two thirds of the way - then switch to the second column. The bottoms of all five columns are used later in the alphabet. There are no addresses given like the Eastern and Midland Districts. There are 472 names/ entries as opposed to the clerk's claim of 470. Much shorter than File 7, this is no doubt the original of File 7 to which some added names where entered - some not accepted as UEs. Spelling of names was checked against both Files with considerable success.

The obviously extra names of military people is explained by the footnote on Page 7 about JOHN WRONG; they were former British Officers and Soldiers- but were they true UEs?

File 8

INDEX NUMBER	
	A
6201	Ayckler William
6202	Anguish Jacob (deceased)
6203	Austin Solomon
6204	Anker Frederick Junr.
6205	Alexander Hugh
6206	Aker Lambert
6207	Austin Joel
6208	Anguish Henry
6209	Anker Frederick Senr.
6210	Anker Charles
6211	Anker August
6212	Adair John
	12
	B
6213	Butler John Lt.Col.deceased
6214	Ball Jacob Senr. Lieutenant
6215	Butler Thomas Lieut.
6216	Butler Andrew Lieut.
6217	Ball Peter Lieut.
6218	Bowman Peter
6219	Bowman Jacob
6220	Bowman Henry
6221	Brown Joseph
6222	Boyce John Senr.
6223	Bowman Adam Junr.
6224	Bowman Adam Senr.
6225	Brown John
6226	Bender Philip
6227	Bassey Robert
6228	Bradt Andrew Captain
6229	Bassey Jacob
6230	Beebe Eden Serjeant
6231	Bell Derick*
6232	Bradt John Lieutenant
6233	Barthol Keephart
6234	Boice John Junr.
6235	Buck Philip
6235A	Buck John[f]
	B
6236	Bower Peter Corporal
6237[f]	Bowen Cornelius
6238[f]	(B)eeby Joshua (deceased)
6239	(Br)own William
6240	Butler Johnson Ensign
6241	Ball Jacob
6242	Burtch Charles
6243	Burtch Edee
6244	Bradt Arent
6245	Brundige James
6246	Burns James
6247	Bennet James (deceased)
6248	Banta Weeart Captn. (deceased)
6249[f]	Beasly* Richard
6250	Boss Elizabeth
6251	Bowman Abraham
6252	Brown James
6253	Buckner Henry Serjeant
6254	Berdan Albert
6255	Barnum Nathaniel (deceased)
6256	Barnhart John
6257[f]	Basteder David
	45
	C[f]
6258	Clench Ralfe Lieutenant
6259	Campbell Robert Serjeant
6260	Clows John Corporal
6261	Crumb Benony
6262	Clandenning Walter
6263	Conklin Robert
6264	Carle John
6265	Cassada Daniel
6266	Cummings Thomas
6267	Coghill George Senr. (deceased)
6268	Cassleman John

NOTES:

1. No. 6249 - correct as above; File 7 spelled BEASLEY.
2. No. 6257 - not present in File 7, there are two letters before this name here, which can not be read: eg, "De".
3. The "B" column is followed by the "R" column in this paste-up; we follow the alphabet and go to the "Cs" in second column at the top.
4. Nos. 6238/9 - the margin broken; a few letters lost.
5. JOHN BUCK left off transcription: see No. 7055.

File 8

INDEX NUMBER	(Column "C" continued)	INDEX NUMBER	
6269	Coghill John	6304	Dagherty* Anthony
6270	Clandenning Abraham	6305	De Pew John Junr.
6271 f	Coon John, Serjeant	6306	De Pew William
6272	Crantz Michael	6307	Davis William
6273	Clement Joseph Lieutenant	6308	Duforest*Abraham
6274	Clement James	6309	Denniston Robert
6275	Crumb William	6310	Doan Aaron
6276	Chrysler Adam Lieutenant (deceased)	6311	Davis Isaac
6277	Cox Samuel	6312	Dennis John
6278	Clement John Lieutenant	6313	Doan Joseph
6279	Colrake Peter	6314	De Pew John Senr.
6280	Chisholm John	6315	Dachsteder John Lieutenant
6281	Cain Barnabas	6316	De Cowe Jacob
6282	Clement Lewis Senr. (deceased)	6317	Duggan Cornelius
6283	Collard John	6318	Davis Benjamin
6284	Cooper James	6319	Dachsteder John Junr. Corporal
6285	Cooper Thomas	6320	Dill Henry
6286	Coghill George Junr.		21
6287	Caldwell John		E
6288	Crawford James	6321	Emmit Stephen
6289	Chisholm George	6322	Elsworth Francis
6290	Coghill Peter	6323	Evringham James
6291	Clandenning John		3
6292	Carle Jonas		F
6293	Cosby George	6324	Frelick John
6294	Cain John	6325	Forbush Nicholas
6295	Coltman John Serjeant	6326	Fields Gilbert
6296 f	Chambers Ahijah*Serjeant	6327	Frelick Benjm. Corporal
6297 f	Corus* Cos*	6328	Frey Bernard Captain
6298	Collins Alexander	6329	Feero* Peter
6299	Clench V. Benjamin	6330 f	Fields George (deceased)
	42	6331 f	Files John
	D	6332	Fairchild Benjamin Corporal
6300	Dame George Captain	6333	Frost Edmund
6301	De Pew Charles	6334	Forsyth George
6302	Dachsteder Frederick (Lieut.) deceased	6335 f	Forsyth James
6303 f	Decker Thomas		

NOTES:

1. No. 6271 - in german this name spelled KUHN.
2. No. 6296 - in File 7 and here name is spelled AHIJAH.
3. No. 6297 - spelling variants include CHOERUS; and CASTEL(1st).
4. No. 6303 - 2nd choice DEEKER; File 7 definitely DECKER. Spelling variants include DAKERS/DYKES/DYKER.
5. No. 6330 - the senior designation missed here; included File 7
6. No. 6331 - in File 7 spelled FILE_; Corporal's rank missed.
7. No. 6335 - in File 7 FORSYTH spelled FORSITH for James.
8. Many Toronto names here: Elsworth, Clandenning, Collard etc.

File 8

INDEX NUMBER	(Column "F" continued)	INDEX NUMBER	(Column "H" continued)
6336	Fowler John	6371	Harris Henry
6337	Force Philip	6372	Harris John
6338	Frey Philip Ensign	6373	Harris Thomas
6339	Fulton James Captain 16	6374	Howey Robert
	G	6375	Hazen Daniel Serjeant
		6376	Huffman Christopher
6340 f	Green Benjamin	6377	Henn Michael
6341	G(reen)law Jonathan (deceased)	6378	Hendershote* Peter
		6379	Huffman Nicholas
6342	Gilbert Josiah	6380	Huffman Jacob
6343	Gould John	6381	Hodgkinson John
6344	Garner William	6382	Hunsinger John
6345	Gardner John	6383	House Frederick
6346	Gahagan* Oliver	6384	Hosteter John
6347	Glover Jacob	6385	Haggerty Hugh
6348	Gilmore Benjamin 8 (9)	6386	Hitchcock Miles
	H	6387	Holmes Asa
		6388	Hamilton Catharine Mrs.
6349	House Philip	6389	House Joseph
6350	Hainer John	6390	Hanes Joseph Sen[r].
6351 f	Haggerman Arnold Serjeant	6391	Hill John Jun[r].
6352	Hill Carney	6392	Hardy John Serjeant
6353	Hainer Albert	6393	Henry Philip
6354	House Daniel	6394	Hare John Capt[n].(deceased)
6355	Hodgkinson William	6395	Hill John Sen[r].
6356	Henry James	6396	Hunt Edward
6357	Hoghtellin James	6397	House James
6358	Haslip James Corporal	6398	Hunter John
6359	Hainer Richard	6399	Hardison Benjamin 49 (51)
6360	Haines Nathaniel		J
6361	Hare Peter Captain		
6362	Hare John Lieut.(deceased)	6400	Johnson Brant Lieutenant
6363	Hare Peter (deceased)	6401	Johnston* William Lieut.
6364	Hare William	6402	Jones James (deceased)
6365	Herkimer George Lieutenant (deceased)	6403	Johnston Ralph
		6404	Johnston Conrade*
6366	House John	6405	Johnson Jemima Miss
6367	House George	6406	Johnson Sarah Miss
6368	House Harmanus	6407	Johnson Mary Miss
6369	Haverland Harmanus Sen[r].	6408	Johnston John Capt[n]. (deceased)
6370	Haverland Harmanus Jun[r].		

NOTES:

1. No. 6341 - this entry squeezed into column; clerk did not count it in his total either. Total is 9.
2. No. 6352 - same as No. 6341 - squeezed in and not counted - though the clerk made some other mistake in totalling as the "H" total should be 51.
3. The "G" & "H" columns are marred by a broken fold with some letters lost.

File 8

INDEX NUMBER	(Column "J" continued)	INDEX NUMBER	(Column "M" continued)
6409	Johnston John	6442	Maby Lewis Serjeant
6410	Johnston Jonas	6443	McClellan W^{m}.
6411	Jones Jane Mrs.	6444	Marakle Frederick
6412	Jones Ebenezer	6445	Marakle John Serjeant
	13	6446	Marakle James
	K	6447	Martha John
6413	Kilman Jacob	6448	McDonald Ronald Serjt. (deceased)
6414	Kenny James		
6415	Kilman John	6449	Mattice Abraham
6416	Keefer George Senr. (dec^{sd})	6450	Murray Duncan Lieut. (deceased)
6417	Kettle Jeremiah Senr.		
	5	6451	Murray John Q^{r}. Mast^{r}. (deceased)
	L		
6418	Larroway Jonas	6452	Millard Dan Corporal
6419	Lambert Cornelius Corporal	6453	McDonell Allan Captn. (deceased)
6420	Lampman Frederick		
6421 f	Land Abel	6454	Millard Jesse
6422 f	Lockwood Benjamin	6455	Magaw Patrick
6423	Lippincott Richard	6456	Millard Thomas
6424	Laurance Richard	6457	Morden Moses
6425	Lymburner Mathew (deceased)	6458	Mathews James
6426	Lyons Benjamin	6459	McNabb John
6427	Land Robert	6460	McNabb Alexander
6428	Lotteridge Robert Captn. (deceased)	6461 f	Maby Frederick (deceased)
		6462	McNabb James D^{r}. (deceased)
6429 f	Larroway Abr^{m}.	6463	Marcelles* Peter
6430 f	Laurance George	6464	Morden John
6431 f	Lutz Sampson	6465	Morden Ralph (deceased)
6432 f	Lampman Peter	6466	Malcolm Finlay
6433 f	Lymburner Mathew	6467	Miller Peter (deceased)
6434 f	Lymburner John	6468	McLauchlan Edward
	17	6469	McCool Archibald (deceas^{d}.)
	M	6470	McCool William
6435	May William	6471	McDonald William
6436	McDonald John Corporal	6472	Miller Andrew
6437	McDonald Christian	6473	Muckle John
6438	Miller George	6474	Miller Thomas
6439	McMicking Peter	6475	Medaugh Stephen
6440	McMichael Isaac	6476	Meridith Charles
6441	McDonald Peter Serjeant	6477	Montross Silas

NOTES:

1. From No. 6429 to No. 6434, the entries are doubled up and crowded/squeezed into space intended for the beginning of the "Ms".
2. No. 6462 - the abbreviation, "D^{r}.", is for Doctor.
3. No. 6423 - a Toronto name; as is the one above it.

File 8

INDEX NUMBER	(Column "M" continued)
6478	Merritt Thomas Lieutenant
6479	McMichael Edward
6480	Medaugh James
6481	McMicking Thomas
6482	Murphy Timothy
	48
	N
6483[f]	Newberry Wm. Serjt. (deceased)
6484	Newkirk James
6485	Neil George
6486	Nellis William
6487	Nellis Warner
6488	Nellis Abraham
6489	Nellis Wm. Henry Capt. (deceased)
6490	Nellis Robert Lieutenant
6491	North Thomas
	9
	O
6492	OConnelly James
6493	Osterhout William
6494	OCarr Peter
6495	Outhouse Nicholas
6496	Overholt Abraham
	5
	P
6497	Pawling Benjm. Captain
6498	Pawling Jesse Qr. Mastr.
6499	Page Joseph
6500	Price Christian
6501	Pickard Benjamin
6502	Pickard James
6503	Post Jacob
6504	Parepoint Richard (blackman)
6505	Phelps Elijah
6506	Plato Christian
6507	Petry Joseph Serjeant
6508	Putman Henry
6509	Pichard William

INDEX NUMBER	
6510[f]	Petry John Jost
6511	Prout Sheerman*
6512	Powell John Captain
6513	Price David
6514	Pettit John
6515	Powell D. Wm. Hambl.
6516	Pell Joshua
6517	Pew Samuel
6518	Plater George
6519	Pound Daniel
6520	Plato Peter
	24
	Q
6521	Quick Benjamin
6522	Quick Solomon
6523	Quarry Joseph[f] Negroe*
	3
	R
6524	Reily John Serjeant
6525	Reide George
6526	Ransier George
6527	Richards Christian
6528	Ricely Christian Corporal
6529	Rowe Frederick Corporal
6530	Rowe John Serjeant
6531	Reynolds Caleb Lieutenant
6532	Robertson James
6533	Robertson Prince
6534	Rooreback* Barent Captn.
6535	Russell James
6536	Reide William
6537[f]	Ridoubt* Mary Mrs.
6538	(R)ose Donald
6539	Ryckman John Lieut.
	16
	S
6540	Swayze Isaac
6541	Spurgin William
6542	Swayze Caleb
6543	Swayze Richard
6544	Smith Elias

NOTES:

1. No. 6483 - see footnote No. 3, page 7 of File 7.
2. Half the "Rs" finish off the fourth column; the last half are in the first column under the "Bs".
3. No. 6537 - another well known Toronto name spelled RIDOUT.
4. No. 6510 - spelling variants include PETERY/PETERS/PETRIE; the latter spelling is as it was in the Mohawk Valley.

File 8

INDEX NUMBER	(Column "S" continued	INDEX NUMBER	(Column "S" continued)
6545	Seacord James Sen.[r] (deceased)	6582	Soper Samuel
6546	Slingerlandt Anthony (deceased)	6583	Seagor Frederick
6547	Springer David (deceased)	6584	Seagor Jacob
6548	Skinner Timothy	6585	Snyther Jacob Corporal
6549	Seacord Peter Sen.[r]	6586	Stoner John
6550	Seacord Peter Jun.[r]	6587	Stevens Arent (Commissary)
6551[f f]	Street Samuel Sen.[r]	6588[f]	Servoss Daniel Lieutenant
6552	Smith John Sen.[r] (at Grand River)	6589[f]	Servoss Jacob Lieutenant
6553	Stewart Thomas	6590[f]	Seacord Daniel
6554	Stiles Selah*	6591	Smith John
6555[f]	Stooks Edward	6592	Stone John
6556	Seacord Solomon Lieut.	6593	Stewart Alexander Lieut.
6557[f]	Schram Frederick Corporal	6594	Steel William
6558[f]	Springsteen States*	6595	Slighter John
6559[f]	Seacord John Sen.[r]	6596	Smith Hart
6560	Seacord John Jun.[r]	6597	Sheehan B. Walter
6561	Seacord Stephen Serjt.		58
6562	Spencer Robert		T
6563	Slingerland* Richard	6598	Ten Broeck Peter Capt.[n]
6564	Stevens John Sen.[r]	6599	Terry Parshall
6565	Schram Valentine	6600	Thompson Peter
6566	Showers Michael Sen.[r] (deceased)	6601	Thompson And.[w] Capt.[n] (deceased)
6567	Stuart George	6602	Tedenick Lucas
6568	Smith Nicholas	6603	Tedenick Jacob Serjeant
6569	Smith John	6604	Tracey Timothy
6570	Seacord Silas Serjeant	6605	Thomas Jacob
6571	Stull Latham	6606	Teeple Peter
6572	Snider John	6607	Thompson Samuel
6573	Seacord David Sen.[r]	6608	Thacher John
6574	Shaw Michael	6609	Trainer John
6575	Smith Henry	6610[f]	Thompson Archibald
6576	Schram Jeremiah	6611	Thompson George
6577	Schram John	6612	Tice Gilbert Capt.[n] (deceased)
6578	Springer Richard	6613[f]	Thompson Archibald
6579	Sipes Jacob		16
6580	Sipes Jonas		(Nos. 6610/13 - no differentiation between the two. EKF)
6581	Sims John (Serjeant)		

NOTES:

1. No. 6551 - less chance here vs File 7 for this to be STRUT; the problem is the two "e"s fall together to form an open "a".
2. No. 6555 - no problem reading this; definitely STOOKS.
3. Nos. 6559 & 6590 ends each column; initials "R.H." appear at end of each column. "R.H." for R. Hamilton, presiding J.P.
4. Nos. 6588/9 - definitely SERVOSS; on checking File 7, Nos. 6057 and 6058, they also are both SERVOSS.
5. Nos. 6610/13 - see footnote No. 1, page 7.
6. No. 6551 - see page 7 for certification by SAMUEL STREET.

File 8

INDEX NUMBER		INDEX NUMBER	(Column "W" continued)
	V	6650	Windecker Henry
6614 f	Vollick* Isaac	6651	Wintermute Peter Corporal
6615 f	Vrooman Ada(m) Serjeant	6652	Wintermute John D^o
6616 f	Vollick* Stor(um)	6653	Wintermute Abraham D^o
6617 f	Van Every Sa(mu)el	6654	Wintermute Philip
6618	Van Alstine Jacob	6655	Wintermute Benjamin
6619	Van Every William	6656	Wilson John Serjeant
6620	Van Every David Serjt.	6657	Wormwood Mathew
6621	Van Derlip Frederick	6658	Wright Gabriel
	(deceased)	6659	Welch Thomas Q^r. Mast^r.
6622	Van Derlip Elizabeth Miss	6660	Williams Frederick
6623	Van Derlip Mary Miss	6661	Wardle Michael
6624	Van Derlip William		34
6625	Van Hoofen Richard		Y
6626	Vincent Elijah Ensign	6662	Young John Lieutenant
6627	Van Petten Arent	6663	Young Abraham
	14	6664	Young John, Serjeant
	W	6665	Young Henry
6628	Walker William	6666	Young Daniel Serjeant
6629	Williams Samuel	6667	Younglove* Ezekiel*
6630	Williams Rachel	6668	Young John Junr.
6631	Wilmot Allan	6669	Young Philip
6632	Wall Edward (deceased)	6670	Young Adam Senr. (deceased)
6633	Warren Henry	6671	Young George
6634	Warren John Junr.	6672	Young Jacob Serjt.
6635	Wilson Benjamin		(deceased)
6636	Wilson John Irish		11
6637	Wilson John		Newark Jany. 12th 1797
6638	Woodley George		R. Hamilton Chairman
6639	Wilson Jacob		
6640	Wilson Joseph	f	Saml. Street J.P.^{f}
6641	Wardle Cornelius		
6642	Whitsell Andrew		William Dickson J.P.
6643 f	Westbrook Anthony		(See No. 6551 - there can be no doubt as to the above certification; it is definitely SAMUEL STREET EKF)
6644	Wrong John		
6645	Weaver Francis		
6646	Whitner Henry		
6647	Walker Jacob (deceased)		
6648 f	Warner Christian Serjeant		
6649	Winney Cornelius Corporal		

NOTES:

1. Nos. 6615/6/7 - some letters lost on the broken fold.
2. Nos. 6618/6649 - initials "R.H." again at column bottom.
3. No. 6644 - Dr. NORMAN M. WRONG, a professor of the transcriber at the University of Toronto, wrote an article in the MEDICAL GRADUATE, Fall 1983, 28:1, describing his ancestor, JOHN WRONG, as a native of the Barbados who came to Quebec City 17 August, 1780 age 21; he joined the British Forces, served there and at Detroit. He settled in Stamford Twsp. outside Niagara Falls. Thus, some British soldiers were considered Loyalists in spite of today's definition.

File 9

NATIONAL ARCHIVES OF CANADA (NAC)

UPPER CANADA (ONTARIO) DISTRICT LOYALIST ROLLS

Reference: NAC RG 1, L 7, vol. 52B(B as in Bravo) (FILES 1 to 15)

FILE 9

ARCHIVIST'S DESCRIPTION

Endorsed "Roll continued of U E Loyalists - Home District - 31 Oct, 1797", with a long note by the Deputy Clerk of the Crown for Lincoln County. Original, signed by Justices of the Peace, on paper watermarked 1794; 76x33 cm, now breaking on folds. The list is arranged alphabetically and includes 145 names. There is an accompaning contemporary copy (34x21 cm, badly broken on folds and along margins); the copy is a single sheet covering the letters A-W on its two sides.

TRANSCRIBER'S COMMENTS

The cover has a title " Filed as Record in the Court of King's Bench the 20th November 1797. (Signed) William Dickson/Dy Clk of the Crown/ County of Lincoln/". Elsewhere on the cover is the title "Roll Continued/ of/ U E Loyalists,/ Home District/ 31 Oct 1797."

Above the list of names on page 1 is the heading "Roll Continued of U E Loyalists. Home District. 31st of October 1797". Above that heading, in quite faint writing is "All marked thus X are inserted in the U E List signed 15 Oct 1797 Q.U.G. (or S)". The contemporary copy bears the same heading.

The interest here is why these people were forgotten in the first list and why they qualified to be added later. There are slight variations in one File to another - spellings, added information etc. They are worthwhile to study in each case to see if there is a variation. The writing in the copy is superior to the original and leads to firmer interpretations of the writing.

File 9

INDEX NUMBER		INDEX NUMBER	(Column "C" continued)
	A	6733	Clarke Alexander
6701[f]	Arnold Benedict, Brigadier Gen[l].	6734	Cole John
6702[f]	Arnold Richard Lieut.	6735	Crumb William
6703[f]	Arnold Henry Lieut.	6736	Chrysler Peter
6704	Ainsley Johanna) In UE	6737	Culver Timothy
6705	Anderson Simon) List	6738	Chew Johnson W[m].
6706	Anderson Alexander) dated	6739	Clandenning James Sen[r]. (dead)
	6 October 15th 1797	6740	Cesar John (Black Man)
	B	6741	Claus Daniel Colonel (dead)
6707[f]	Buichner* John sen[r]. (dead)		17
6708	Backer John (Mulatto Man)		D
6709	Betron David	6742	Dill Barsnett*
6710	Butler Philip	6743	Doyle Benjamin
6711	Bayeux Thomas	6744	Davis Thomas
6712	Boervort* Elias	6745	Dachsteder, John jun[r]. Corp[l].
6713	Beardsley Crannel B.		
6714	Begraft Benjamin	6746	Darby John
6715	Bradt John (dead)		5
6716	Burch John Esq[r]. (dead)		E
6717	Bradt Minar	6747	English Andrew
6718	Bowen William	6748	Evertson John (dead)
6719	Bowlsby Richard		2
6720	Bowlsby Thomas		F
6721	Burch Martha Mrs.	6749	Flack Archibald
6722	Baker Jack (Black Man)	6750	Francis Catharine Mrs.
6723	Buck Jonathan	6751	Francis W[m]. Q[r]. Mast[r].
6724	Brakenridge Francis	6752	Ferris Joshua
	18	6753	Fisher George
	C	6754	Fields Rebecka* Mrs. formerly Mrs. Johnston
6725	Cummings Jane Mrs.		
6726	Clench Elizabeth Mrs.	6755	Freeman John
6727	Coffin James (Commissary)	6756	Forrest Laurania Mrs. formerly Mrs. Morden
6728	Clement Joseph Serjt.		
6729	Collins John	6757	File_ John Corporal
6730	Campbell George Serjt.		9
6731	Campbell James		
6732	Carty Thomas (dead)		

NOTES:

1. All entries on this page have large "X"s opposite the name or between first and second names, EXCEPT the first three, ie, Nos. 6701, 6702 & 6703.
2. No. 6707 - see File 7, Nos. 5562 & 5568; there seems to be confusion about the spelling. Quite definite as recorded above for File 9.
3. Most of the spellings correspond with Files 7 & 8; there are minor variations.

File 9

INDEX NUMBER	
	G
6758	Gamble William
6759	Grigg John
	2
	H
6760^{f}	Hilton B. W^{m}. Serjt.
6761	Hoff Henry
6762	Hoff John
6763	Hanshaw Mary (now Mrs. Moody)
6764	Hill Solomon
6765	Hazen Daniel Serjt.
6766	Hallowell Benjamin
6767	Hewston Joshua (dead)
6768	Hopkins Silas Senr.
6769	Hansen Richard Lieut.
6770	Horton Isaac
6771	Hyndman Samuel
6772	Hilts Joseph
	13
	J
6773	Johnson John Sir
6774	Johnston Henry
6775	Johnston John
6776	Jarviss* W^{m}. Esqr.
6777	Johnston Elizabeth Mrs.
6778	Jarviss* Samuel
6779	Johns Solomon Lieut.(dead)
	7
	K
6780	Kerr Elizabeth Mrs. (dead)
	1
	L
6781	Larroway Peter
6782	Livingston Neil
6783	Livingston John (dead)
6784	Lemons Joseph Senr. (dead)
6785	Lockwood Josiah
6786	London Bartholemy
6787	Lowe Elizabeth Mrs.
	M
6788	Martin Peter (black Man)
6789	McDonell Helena Mrs. (dead)
6790	McIntire Daniel Senr.
6791	Muirhead Deborah Mrs.
6792	Moss John
6793	Moody Walter
6794	Matlack Caleb
6795	McFall David Lieut.
6796	McFall Neil Lieut.
6797	Mills John
6798	Mathews Jonathan
6799	Major John (dead)
6800	Munroe Robert Senr.
6801	McKay John
6802	Marcellis Baptist John
6803	McLaughlan James
6804	McDonell Miles Ensign
6805	McNeil John
6806	MacRobert Mary Mrs.
6807	McLean Donald
	20
	N
6808	Nicholson Robert
	1
	O
6809	Overholt Elizabeth Miss
6810	Overholt Stots*
	2
	P
6811	Parker John
6812	Philips John
6813	Pemberton James
6814	Pell Joseph
6815	Pell Jonathan
6816	Peters Samuel Revnd.
6817	Peters B. W^{m}. Esqr.
6818	Petty Margery Mrs. formerly Widow Foster

NOTES: 1. No. 6760 - only entry on this page without an "X" beside it.

File 9

INDEX NUMBER	(Column "P" continued)	INDEX NUMBER	
6819	Palmer David	6845	Wilson Bathsheba formerly Widow Soper
	9		
	Q		
6820	Quin Michael	Personal(	R. Hamilton Chairman
6821	Quant Frederick	Signa- (	Jos^{ph}. Edwards J.P.
	2	tures (	Geo. Forsyth J.P.
	R		
6822	Rodney Brydges George Serj^{t}.		
6823	Ramsay David		
6824	Ryerse Samuel Captain		
6825	Ryerse J. Lieutenant		
	4		
	S		
6826	Smith Jacob Senr.		
6827	Stine John Serjt. (dead)		
6828	Sachevervell Jane Mrs.		
6829	Scott Archibald		
6830	Stofle John		
6831	Simons Titus Senr.		
6832	Shank David Capt.		
6833	Stooks Hannah Mrs. formerly Widow Sipes		
6834	Stacey John		
	9		
	T		
6835^{f}	Tousack Casper (dead)		
6836	Turnbull William		
6837	Tredwell John		
	3		
	V		
6838^{f}	Van Dresen*		
	1		
	W		
6839	Wintermute Mary Mrs.		
6840	Wheeler Ephraim*		
6841	Wilkins Isaac		
6842	Wilkins Martin		
6843	Wychoff Peter		
6844	Whitmire John		

NOTES:

1. No. 6835 - poor 2nd choice is TORSACK.
2. No. 6838 - 2nd choice VAN DRESER.
3. All entries on this page have a large "X" opposite the name.
4. File 9 continues with a contemporary copy as described by the archivist.

File 9

INDEX NUMBER	
6846	Arnold Benedict Brigadier General
6847	Arnold Richard Lieut.
6848	Arnold Henry Lieut.
6849	Ainsley Johanna
6850	Anderson Simon
6851	Anderson Alexander
	B
6852	Buickner John Senr. (dead)
6853	Backer John (Mulatto man)
6854	Betron David
6855	Butler Philip
6856	Bayeux Thomas
6857[f]	Brewort* Elias
6858[f]	Beardsley Crannel B.
6859	Begraft Benjamin
6860	Bradt John (dead)
6861	Bradt Minar
6862	Bowen William
6863	Bowlsby Richard
6864	Bowlsby Thomas
6865	Burch John Esqr. (dead)
6866	Burch Martha Mrs.
6867	Baker Jack (black man)
6868	Buck Jonathan
6869	Brakenridge Francis
	C
6870	Cummings Jane Mrs.
6871[f]	Clench Elizabeth Mrs.
6872	Coffin James (Commissary)
6873	Clement Joseph Serjt.
6874	Collins John
6875	Campbell George Serjt.
6876	Campbell James
6877	Carty Thomas (dead)
6878	Clarke Alexander
6879	Cole John
6880	Crumb William
6881	Chrysler Peter

INDEX NUMBER	(Column "C" continued)
6882	Culver Timothy
6883	Chew Johnson W^{m}.
6884	Clandenning James sen^{r*}.
6885	Cesar John (black man)
6886	Claus Daniel Colonel (dead)
	D
6887[f]	Dill Barsnett sen^{r*}.
6888	Doyle Benjamin
6889	Davis Thomas
6890[f]	Dochsteder[1] John jun^{r}. Corp.
6891	Darby John
	E
6892	English Andrew
6893	Evertson John (dead)
	F
6894	Flack Archibald
6895	Francis W^{m}. Q^{r}. Mas^{r}.
6896	Francis Catharine Mrs.
6897	Ferris Joshua
6898	Fisher George
6899	Field Rebecka Mrs. formerly Mrs. Johnston
6900[f]	Freeman John
6901	Forrest Laurania Mrs. formerly Mrs. Morden
6902	File_ John Corporal
	G
6903	Gamble William
6904	Grigg John
	H
6905	Hilton B. W^{m}. Serjt.
6906	Hoff Henry
6907	Hoff John

NOTES:

1. No. 6857 - quite definite as written; other Files BOESVOORT.
2. Nos. 6858/6887/6900 are all underlined for some reason.
3. No. 6871 - one wonders why the clerk of the Crown entered a relative on this additions list. (Note 1, page 5 applies).
4. No. 6890 - one of the many spelling variants of this German-Palatine name from the Mohawk Valley. There has been an extensive family genealogy written by Doris Dockstader Rooney 1918 La Mesa Drive, Dodge City, USA 67801.

File 9

INDEX NUMBER	(Column "H" continued)
6908	Hanshaw Mary (now Mrs. Moody)
6909	Hill Solomon
6910	Hazen Daniel Serjt.
6911	Hallowell Benjamin
6912	Hewston Joshua (dead)
6913	Hopkins Silas senr.
6914	Hansen Richard Lieut.
6915	Horton Isaac
6916	Hyndman Samuel
6917	Hilts Joseph
	J
6918	Johnson John Sir
6919	Johnston John
6920	Jonston Henry
6921	Jarviss Wm. Esqr.
6922	Johnston Elizabeth Mrs.
6923[f]	Jarviss Samuel
6924	Johns Solomon Lieut.(dead)
	K
6925	Kerr Elizabeth Mrs. (dead)
	L
6926	Larroway Peter
6927	Livingston Neil
6928	Livingston John (dead)
6929	Lemons Joseph senr. (dead)
6930	Lockwood Josiah
6931	London Bartholemy
6932	Lowe Elizabeth Mrs.
	M
6933	Martin Peter (black man)
6934	McDonell Helena Mrs. (dead)
6935	McIntire Daniel senr.
6936[f]	Muirhead Deborah Mrs.
6937	Moss John

INDEX NUMBER	(Column "M" continued)
6938	Moody Walter
6939	Matlack Caleb
6940	McFall David Lieut.
6941	McFall Neil Lieut.
6942	Mills John
6943	Mathews Jonathan
6944	Major John (dead)
6945	Munroe Robert senr.
6946	McKay John
6947	Marcellis Baptist John
6948	McLaughlan James
6949[f]	McDonell Miles Ensign
6950	McNeil John
6951[f]	McRobert Mary Mrs.
6952	McLean Donald
	N
6953[f]	Nicholson Robert
	(THIS COPY ENDS HERE EKF)

NOTES:

1. Nos. 6923/6936/6949 - all have the note after the entry that reads "Ex ' "; this is interpreted to mean placed on the list by order of the Executive Council. They were likely important personages and favoured.
2. No.6951 - elsewhere spelled Mac ROBERT - the only one in list.
3. No. 6953 - beside entry is note - "2 -?- not back from Scotland".

File 10

NATIONAL ARCHIVES OF CANADA (NAC)

UPPER CANADA (ONTARIO) DISTRICT LOYALIST ROLLS 1796-1803

Reference: NAC RG 1, L 7, vol. 52B (B as in Bravo) (Files 1 to 15)

FILE 10

Archivist's Description

Endorsed "U E Roll, Home Dist[t]" and "U E Roll, Home District". Contemporary, certified copy, on paper assembled into a large sheet, 75x54 cm and haphazardly mended in the past; broken on folds. A list of some 484 names (actually 485 names), essentially duplicating the list in File 8, likewise arranged in alphabetical order.

Transcriber's Comments

The heading over the top of this large sheet reads: "A List of those Persons who have been Admitted (in ?) the General Quarter Sessions of the Peace holden* for/ the Home District/ As U E Loyalists, Having adhered to the Unity of the Empire during the American War/" (on three lines).

The writing starts early as being quite easy to read; as it progresses, difficulty arises. It is quite apparent that the clerk, in making the copy, attempts - usually with good results - to correct the spelling errors; he is not always successful. Some names are modernized. The sheet is divided into six columns and are used in succession. The clerk's attempt to keep a running total of names is successful up to No. 7346, when the crowded sheet makes him miscount; his final total is out by one.

Because there are so many spelling changes on some sheets, the reader is reminded that the asterix is used to denote "Sic", ie, as written, a possible error. Everything between the double lines is a true transcription of the original.

File 10

INDEX NUMBER		INDEX NUMBER	(Column "B" continued)
	A		
7001	Ayckler William	7036	Bowen* Peter Corporal
7002	Anguish Jacob Deceased	7037	Bowen Cornelius Corporal
7003	Austin Solomon	7038	Beebe Joshua Deceased
7004	Anker Frederick Jun[r].	7039	Brown William
7005	5 Alexander Hugh	7040	40 Butler Johnson Ensign
7006	Aker Lambert	7041	Ball Jacob
7007	Austin Joel	7042	Burtch Charles
7008	Anguish Henry	7043	Burtch Edee
7009	Anker Frederick Lieut.	7044	Bradt Arent
7010	10 Anker Charles	7045	45 Brundige James
7011	Anker August	7046	Burns James
7012	Adair John	7047	Bennet James deceased
	B	7048	Banta Weeart Captain Deceased
7013	Butler John, Lieut. Col. deceased	7049	Beasley* Richard
7014	Ball Jacob Sen[r]. Lieut.	7050	50 Boss Elizabeth
7015	15 Butler Thomas Lieut.	7051	Bowman Abraham
7016	Butler Andrew Lieut.	7052	Brown James
7017	Ball Peter Lieut.	7053	Buckner Henry Serjt.
7018	Bowman Peter	7054	Berdan Albert
7019	Bowman Jacob	7055[f]	55 Buck John
7020	20 Bowman Henry	7056	Barnum Nathaniel Deceased
7021	Brown Joseph	7057	Barnhart John
7022[f]	Boice John Senior	7058	Basteder David
7023	Bowman Adam Junior	7059[f]	Buckner Mathias
7024	Bowman Adam Sen[r].	7060[f]	60 Buckner Henry
7025	25 Brown John		C
7026	Bender Philip	7061	Clench Ralfe Lieut.
7027	Bassey Robert	7062	Campbell Robert Serjt.
7028	Bradt Andrew Captain	7063[f]	Claws*John Corporal
7029	Bassey Jacob	7064[f]	Crumb Bennony*
7030	30 Beebe Eden Serjt.	7065[f]	65 Clendenning* Walter
7031	Bell Dorick*	7066	Conklin Robert
7032	Bradt John Lieut.	7067	Carle John
7033	Barthol Keephart	7068[f]	Cassady*Daniel
7034[f]	Boice John Jun[r].	7069	Cummings Thomas
7035	35 Buck Philip	7070	70 Coghill George Sen[r]. deceased

NOTES:

1. The clerk has added numbers - at every fifth name.
2. Nos. 7022/34 - in faint writing, to the left, is "omitted".
3. No. 7055 - left off File 8 transcription; not added/corrected as its insertion would be too difficult.
4. Nos. 7059/60 - these do not appear in File 8; there is no explanation why they have been added here.
5. Nos. 7063/4/5/8 - note the clerk has changed spellings here compared to File 8. It is suspected that these above are more correct.

File 10

INDEX NUMBER	(Column "C" continued)	INDEX NUMBER	(Column "D" continued)
7071	Cassleman John	7111	De Forrest Abraham
7072[f]	Coghill John	7112[f]	Denniston Robert
7073	Clendenning Abraham	7113	Dean*Aaron
7074	Coon John Serjt.	7114	Davis Isaac
7075[f]	75 Crantz Michael	7115	115 Dennis John
7076	Clement Joseph Lieut.	7116[f]	Doan* Joseph
7077	Clement James	7117	Depew John Sen[r].
7078	Crumb William	7118	Dacksteder John Lieut.
7079[f]	Crysler Adam Lieut.deceased	7119	De Cowe Jacob
7080	80 Cox Samuel	7120	120 Dugan* Cornelius
7081	Clement John Lieut.	7121	Davis Benjamin
7082	Colrake Peter	7122	Dacksteder, John Jun[r]. Corpl.
7083	Chisholm John		
7084	Cain Barnabas	7123	Dill Henry
7085	85 Clement Lewis Sen[r]. dec[d].		
7086	Collard John		E
7087[f]	Cooper James	7124	Emmit Stephen
7088[f]	Cooper Thomas	7125	125 Elsworth Francis
7089	Coghill George Jun[r].	7126	Evringham James
7090	90 Caldwell John		
7091	Crawford James		F
7092	Chisholm George	7127	Frelick John
7093	Coghill Peter	7128	Forbush Nickolas*
7094	Clendenning John	7129	Fields Gilbert
7095	95 Carle Jonas	7130	130 Frelick Benjamin Corp[l].
7096[f]	Cosby George		
7097	Cain John	7131	Frey Bernard Captain
7098	Coltman John Serjt.	7132	Feero Peter
7099	Chambers Ahijah* Serjt.	7133	Fields George Deceased
7100	100 Corus Cos	7134	Files* John
7101	Colins* Alexander	7135	135 Fairchild Benjamin Corp[l].
7102	Clench V. Benjamin		
	D	7136	Frost Edward
		7137	Forsyth George
7103[f]	Dame George Captain	7138	Forsyth James
7104	Depew* Charles	7139	Fowler John
7105	105 Dacksteder Fred[k]. dec[d].	7140	140 Force Phillip*
7106	Decker Thomas	7141	Frey Phillip* Ensign
7107	Dagherty Anthony	7142	Fulton James Capt.
7108	Depew* John Jun[r].		
7109	De pew* William		
7110[f]	110 Davies William		

NOTES:

1. Nos. 7072/7087/7088 - word "omitted" faintly written beside.
2. No. 7075 - quite definite as copied; more definite than Files 7 & 8.
3. No. 7079 - spelling corrected to more correct version.
4. No. 7096 - good 2nd choice CORBY.
5. No. 7103 - name, but not rank, stroked through; see No. 2805.
6. No. 7110 - correct as written;File 7 & 8 written DAVIS.
7. Nos. 7113/6 - correct interpretations; could be same name.

File 10

INDEX NUMBER	
	G
7143	Green Benjamin
7144	Gilbert Josiah
7145	145 Gould John
7146	Garner William
7147	Gardner* John
7148	Gahagan* Oliver
7149 f	Glover Jacob
7150	150 Gilman* Benjamin
7151	Greenlaw Jonathan
	H
7152	House Phillip*
7153	Hainer John
7154	Hagerman Arnold Serjt.
7155	155 Hainer Albert
7156	House Daniel
7157	Hodgekinson* W^m.
7158 f	Henry James
7159	Hayslip* James Corp^l.
7160	160 Hoghtellin James
7161	Hainer Richard
7162	Hanes* Nathaniel
7163	Hare Peter Captain
7164	Hare John Lieut. deceased
7165	165 Hare Peter Deceased
7166	Hare William
7167	Herkimer George Lieut. deceased
7168	House John
7169	House George
7170	170 House Harmanus
7171	Haverland Harmanus Senr.
7172	Haverland Harmanus Junr.
7173	Hill Carney
7174	Harris Henry
7175	175 Harris John
7176	Harris Thomas
7177	Howey Robert
7178	Hazen Daniel Serjt.
7179	Huffman Christopher

INDEX NUMBER	(Column "H" continued)
7180 f	180 Henn Michael
7181	Hendershotte* Peter
7182	Huffman Nickolas*
7183	Huffman Jacob
7184	Hodgekinson* John
7185 f	185 House Frederick
7186	Hosteder* (blank)
7187	Hagerty Hugh
7188	Hitchcock Miles
7189	Holmes Asa
7190	190 Hamilton Catherine Mrs.
7191	House Joseph
7192	Haines*Joseph Senr.
7193	Hill John Junr.
7194	Hardy John Serjt.
7195	195 Henry Phillip*
7196	Hare John Captain deceased
7197	Hill John Senr.
7198	Hunt Edward
7199	House James
7200	200 Hunter John
7201	Hardison Benjamin
7202	Huntsinger*John
	J
7203	Johnson Brant Lieut.
7204	Johnston William Lieut.
7205	205 Jones James deceased
7206	Johnston Ralph
7207	Johnson Coonrade*
7208 f	Johnson Jemima Miss
7209	Johnson Sarah Miss
7210	210 Johnson Mary Miss
7211	Johnston John Captain deceased
7212	Johnston John
7213	Johnston Jonas
7214	Jones Jane Mrs.
7215	215 Jones Ebenezer

NOTES:

1. The asterix means "Sic", ie, as written - a possible mistake.
2. There are a fair number of spelling variations on this page, eg, HENRY is likely spelled HENEREY/HENREY and No.7181.
3. No. 7150 - this is spelled GILMORE elsewhere.
4. The word "omitted" again appears beside Nos. 7156 & 7167.
5. No. 7159 - the change in spelling is quite significant.
6. No. 7186 - change in spelling significant & 1st name (JOHN) left off.
7. No. 7208 - the spelling of JOHNSON seems to be important as a "t" was scratched-out here.

File 10

INDEX NUMBER	
	K
7216	Kemp Mathew
7217[f]	Kilman Gacob*
7218	Kenny James
7219	Kilman John
7220	220 Keefer George Sen[r]. deceased
7221	Kettle Jeremiah Sen[r].
7222[f]	Kern Mattin*
	L
7223	Larroway Jonas
7224	Lambert Cornelius Corporal
7225	225 Lampman Frederick
7226	Land Abel
7227	Lockwood Benjamin
7228	Lippincott Richard
7229	Laurence Richard
7230	230 Lymburner Mathew dec[d].
7231	Lyons Benjamin
7232	Land Robert
7233	Lottridge* Robert Capt. deceased
7234	Larroway Abraham
7235	235 Laurence George
7236	Lutz Sampson
7237	Lampman Peter
7238[f]	Lymburner Mathew
7239	Lymburner John
	M
7240	240 May William
7241	McDonald John Corporal
7242	McDonald Christian
7243[f]	Miller George
7244	McMicking Peter
7245	245 McMichael Isaac
7246	McDonald Peter Serjt.
7247	Maby Lewis Serjt.
7248	McClellan William
7249[f]	Maracle Frederick

INDEX NUMBER	(Column "M" continued)
7250[f]	250 Maracle John Serjt.
7251[f]	Maracle James
7252	Martha John
7253	McDonald Ronald Serjt. deceased
7254	Mattice Abraham
7255	255 Murray Duncan Lieut. deceased
7256	Murray John Q[r]. Master deceased
7257	Millard Dan Corp[l].
7258	McDonell Allan Capt. deceased
7259	Millard Jesse
7260	260 McLaughlin* Edward
7261	McCool Arch[d]. Deceased
7262[f]	McGaw Patrick
7263	Millard Thomas
7264	Morden Moses
7265	265 Mathews James
7266	McNabb John
7267	McNabb Alexander
7268	Maby Frederick deceased
7269	McNabb James D[r]. deceased
7270	270 McLaughlin* James
7271	Marcelles Peter
7272	Morden John
7273	Morden Ralph deceased
7274	Malcolm Finlay
7275	275 Miller Peter deceased
7276[f]	McCall* Daniel Sen[r].
7277	McQuin Alex[r]. Sen[r].
7278	McCool William
7279	McDonald William
7280	280 Miller Andrew
7281[f]	Muck(le ?) John
7282	Miller Thomas
7283	Medaugh Stephen
7284	Meredith Charles
7285	285 Montross Silas
7286	Merit* Thomas Lieut.
7287	McMichael Edward

NOTES:

1. Some spelling changes noted this page include: No. 7217 GACOB quite definite and seen before; No. 7222 - MATTIN for MATHIAS; No. 7262 - McGaw for MAGAW
2. No. 7238 - deceased likely omitted.
3. No. 7243 - the word "omitted" beside this entry.
4. Nos. 7249/50/51 - MARACLE a spelling variant for MARAKLE/MARKLE/MERKLEY/MERICLE/MARQUEL et var.
5. No. 7276 - heavy overwrite on the "Mc" of McCALL.
6. No. 7281 - broken fold with mend obscures some letters.

File 10

INDEX NUMBER	(Column "M" continued)
7288	Medaugh James
7289	McMicking Thomas
7290	290 Murphy Timothy
	N
7291	Newberry William Serjt. deceased
7292	Newkirk James
7293	Neil George
7294	Nellis William
7295	295 Nellis Warner
7296	Nellis Abraham
7297	Nellis Wm. Henry Capt. decd.
7298	Nellis Robert Lieut.
7299	North Thomas
	O
7300	300 OConnelly James
7301	Osterhaut* William
7302	OCarr Peter
7303	Outhouse Nickolas*
7304	Overholt Abraham
	P
7305	305 Pauling* Benjamin Capt.
7306	Pauling* Jesse Qr. Master
7307	Page Joseph
7308	Price Christian
7309	Pickard Benjamin
7310	310 Pickard James
7311	Post Jacob
7312	Parepoint Richd. Black man
7313	Phelps Elijah
7314	Plato Christian
7315	315 Petry Joseph Serjt.
7316	Putman Henry
7317	Pickard William
7318	Petry John Jost
7319	Prout Sherman
7320	320 Powell John Captain
7321	Price David
7322	Pettit John

INDEX NUMBER	(Column "P" continued)
7323	Powell William Dummer
7324	Pell Joshua
7325	325 Pew Samuel
7326	Plater*George (see 2840)
7327	Pound Daniel
7328 f	Plato Peter
7329	Pettit Nathaniel
	Q
7330	330 Quick Benjamin
7331	Quick Solomon
7332	Quarry Joseph Negroe
	R
7333	Reily John Serjt.
7334	Reide George
7335	335 Ransier George
7336	Richards Christopher
7337	Ricely Christian Corpl.
7338	Rowe Frederick Corpl.
7339	Rowe John Serjt.
7340	340 Reynolds Caleb Lieut.
7341	Robertson James
7342	Robertson Prince
7343	Rooreback Berent Capt.
7344	Russell James
7345	Reide William
7346 f	345 Redoubt Mary Mrs.
7347	Rose Donald
7348	Rychman John Lieut.
	S
7349	Swayze Isaac
7350	Spurgin William
7351 f	350 Swayze Caleb
7352 f	Swayze Caleb Senr.
7353	Swayze Richard
7354	Smith Elias
7355 f	Secord* James Senr. Decd.
7356	355 Slingerlandt Anthony decd.
7357	Springer David Deceased

NOTES:

1. The archivist describes File 10 as "essentially duplicating... File 8". There are names on this list, not only not on File 8, they are not on any of the Files; eg, 7329 & 7352 - though File 11 will show 7352 was mistakenly left off.

2. The clerk, in a very crowded situation, miscounted; he is one short.

3. No. 7355 - note the quick change in spelling of SEACORD to SECORD as it is today; this continues on page 6.

File 10

INDEX NUMBER	(Column "S" continued)	INDEX NUMBER	(Column "S" continued)
7358	Skinner Timothy	7399 [f]	Servos Jacob Lieut.
7359	Secord Peter Sen[r].	7400	Secord Daniel
7360	Secord Peter Jun[r].	7401	400 Smith John
7361	360 Street Samuel Sen[r].	7402	Stone John
7362	Smith John Sen[r]. G. River	7403	Stewart Alex[r]. Lieut.
7363	Stewart Thomas	7404	Steel William
7364	Stiles Selah*	7405	Slighter John
7365	Stooks Edward	7406	405 Smith Hart
7366	365 Secord Solomon Lieut.	7407	Sheehan Walter Butler
7367 [f]	Smith John who died at Brunswick (?)	7408 [f]	Sipes* Jonas
7368	Schram Frederick Corporal		T
7369	Springsteen States*	7409	Ten Broek* Peter Captain
7370	Secord John Sen[r].	7410	Terry Pershall*
7371	370 Secord John Jun[r].	7411	410 Thompson Peter
7372	Secord Stephen Serjt.	7412	Thompson Andrew Capt.Dec[d].
7373	Spencer Robert	7413	Tederick* Lucas
7374	Slingerland* Richard	7414	Tederick* Jacob Serjt.
7375	Stevens John Sen[r].	7415	Tracey Timothy
7376	375 Schram Valentine	7416	415 Thomas Jacob
7377	Showers Michael Sen[r]. dec[d].	7417	Teeple Peter
7378	Stuart George	7418	Thompson Samuel
7379	Smith Nicholas	7419	Thather* John
7380	Smith John	7420	Trainer John
7381 [f]	380 Silas Secord Serjt.	7421	420 Thompson Archibald
7382	Stull Latham	7422	Thompson George
7383	Snider John	7423	Tice Gilbert Capt. dec[d].
7384	Secord David Sen[r].	7424	Thomson Arch[d].
7385	Shaw Michael	7425 [f]	425 Thompson Elizabeth Mrs.
7386	385 Smith Henry		V
7387	Schram Jeremiah	7426	425 Vollick Isaac
7388	Schram John	7427	Vrooman Adam Serjt.
7389	Springer Richard	7428	Vollick Sturm*
7390 [f]	Sypes*Jacob	7429	Vanevery Samuel
7391	390 Sims John Serjt.	7430	Vanalstine* Jacob
7392	Soper Samuel	7431	430 Vanevery William
7393	Seagor Frederick	7432	Vanevery David Serjt.
7394	Seagor Jacob	7433	Vanderlip Frederick deceased
7395	Snyther Jacob Corporal		
7396	395 Stoner John		
7397	Stevens Arent Commissary		
7398 [f]	Servos* Daniel Lieut.		

NOTES:

1. No. 7367 - there are quite a few JOHN SMITHs; this may help identify one of them.
2. No. 7381 - the clerk "reversed" the order of names.
3. No. 7425 - the clerk made an error in his numbering - but corrected it.
4. Nos. 7390 & 7408 - note the two spellings of SYPES/SIPES.
5. Nos. 7398/9 - note the quick change in spelling of SERVOSS to SERVOS as it is today.

File 10

INDEX NUMBER	(Column "V" continued)	
7434[f]	Vanderlip Elizabeth Miss	X
7435[f]	Vanderlip Mary Miss	X
7436	435 Vanderlip William	
7437[f]	Vanhoesen Richard	
7438	Vincent Elijah Ensign	
7439	Van Patten* Arent	
	W	
7440	Walker William	
7441	440 Williams Samuel	
7442	William_ Rachel	
7443	Wilmot Āllan	
7444	Wall Edward Deceased	
7445[f]	Warren Henry	X
7446[f]	445 Warren John Jun[r].	X
7447	Wilson Benjamin	
7448	Wilson John Irish	
7449	Wilson John	
7450	Woodley George	
7451	450 Wilson Jacob	
7452	Wilson Joseph	
7453	Wardle Cornelius	
7454	Whitsell Andrew	
7455	WestBrook* Anthony	
7456	455 Wrong John	
7457	Weaver Francis	
7458	Whitner Henry	
7459	Walker Jacob Deceased	
7460	Warner Christian Serjt.	
7461	460 Winney Cornelius Corp[l].	
7462	Windecker Henry	
7463	Wintermute Peter Corp[l].	
7464	Wintermute John D[o].	
7465	Wintermute Abraham D[o].	
7466	465 Wintermute Phillip	
7467	Wintermute Benjamin	
7468	Wilson John Serjt.	
7469	Wormwood Mathew	
7470	Wright Gabriel	
7471	470 Welch Thomas Q[r]. Master	
7472	Williams Frederick	
7473	Wardle Michael	

INDEX NUMBER	
	Y
7474	Young John Lieut.
7475	Young Abraham
7476	475 Young John Serjt.
7477	Young Henry
7478	Young Daniel Serjt.
7479	Younglove Ezekiel*
7480	Young John Jun[r].
7481	480 Young Phillip
7482	Young Adam Sen[r]. deceased
7483	Young George
7484	Young Jacob Serjt. Dec[d].
7485	Young Jacob

A true Copy from the list/ given in by the/ Clerk of the Peace and signed/

Robert Hamilton Chairman

Samuel Street J.P.

William Dickson J.P.

and likewise from an additional list /signed/

R. Hamilton J.P.

J. Muirhead J.P.

George Forsyth J.P.

together with addenda allowed by the Hon[bles]/ the Executive Council

David Burns/

Clk of the Council/

NOTES:

1. Nos. 7434/5 - 7445/6 - the Xs beside the entry likely mean the same as "omitted", ie, they were judged not to be eligible to be on the UE List.
2. No. 7437 - this is likely the correct interpretation of the writing, not only here on File 10, but in the other Files in which this name appears.

File 11

NATIONAL ARCHIVES OF CANADA (NAC)

UPPER CANADA (ONTARIO) DISTRICT LOYALIST ROLLS 1796-1803

Reference: NAC RG 1, L 7, vol. 52B (B as in Bravo) (Files 1 to 15)

FILE 11

Archivist's Description

Endorsed "Names of UE to be added to the List, Home District, 13 Apr[1] 1797". Original, 32x20 cm, haphazardly mended before being endorsed, obscuring the watermark. The list of 12 names should be compared to entries on the lists in Files 8 and 10.

Transcriber's Comments

Heading and endorsement as given above and in text. Very easy to read. The sheet has obviously suffered on the margins and the folds but there is no impairment in the reading. Possibly a small corner of the sheet is missing with one or more names.

File 11

INDEX NUMBERS	Home District	REMARKS
	List of Perons omitted in the Roll of U.E.s fyled in the Court of Kings Bench through mistake and now to be added 13th April 1797.	
7501f	Mrs. Elizabeth Thompson	
7502	X Mathias Buckner	
7503	X Mathew Kemp	
7504	X John Lymburner	
7505	X Henry Buckner	
7506	X Daniel McCall Senr.	
7507	X Caleb Swayze Senr.	
7508	X Alexr. McQuin Senr.	
7509	X John Boice Senr.	
7510	X Mattice Kern	
7511	X Greenlaw Jonathan R. Hamilton J.P.	) Individual
7512f	X Young Jacob J. Muirhead J.P.	) Signatures
	Geo. Forsyth J.P.	)

NOTES:

1. Beneath the signatures is a faint notation: " X all (entered ?) List dated 15 Oct 1797 (signed) (J. Muirhead ?)"
2. The sheet has been folded horizontally and vertically and shows the effects of this; there appears to be a portion of the lower left corner of the page missing. The missing portion is almost square in outline and comes just after No. 7512 and might have writing on the remaining portion. This suggests there could have been at least one more name, if not more, that are lost.
3. No. 7501 - the copy has quite a smudge where an "X" might be.

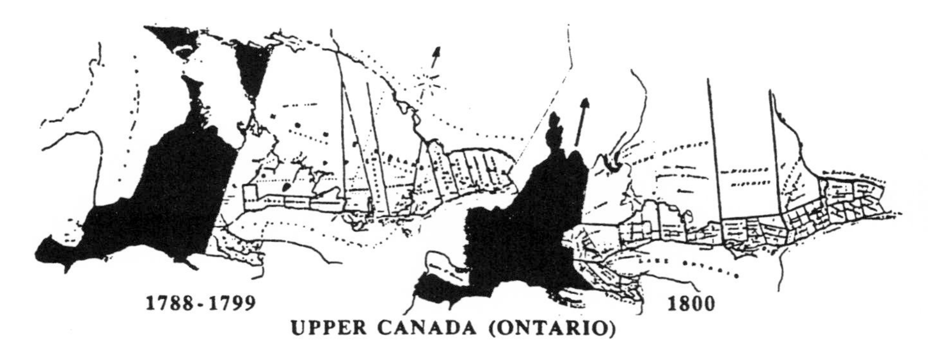

1788-1799 1800

UPPER CANADA (ONTARIO)

In 1796 the Western District, originally called the Hesse District, comprised all of the land west of a line drawn north from the tip of Long Point on Lake Erie. It included Essex, Kent, Middlesex, Norfolk and Oxford Counties. The district town was Sandwich, now Windsor. In 1800 Norfolk, Oxford and Middlesex Counties formed a separate district called the London District.

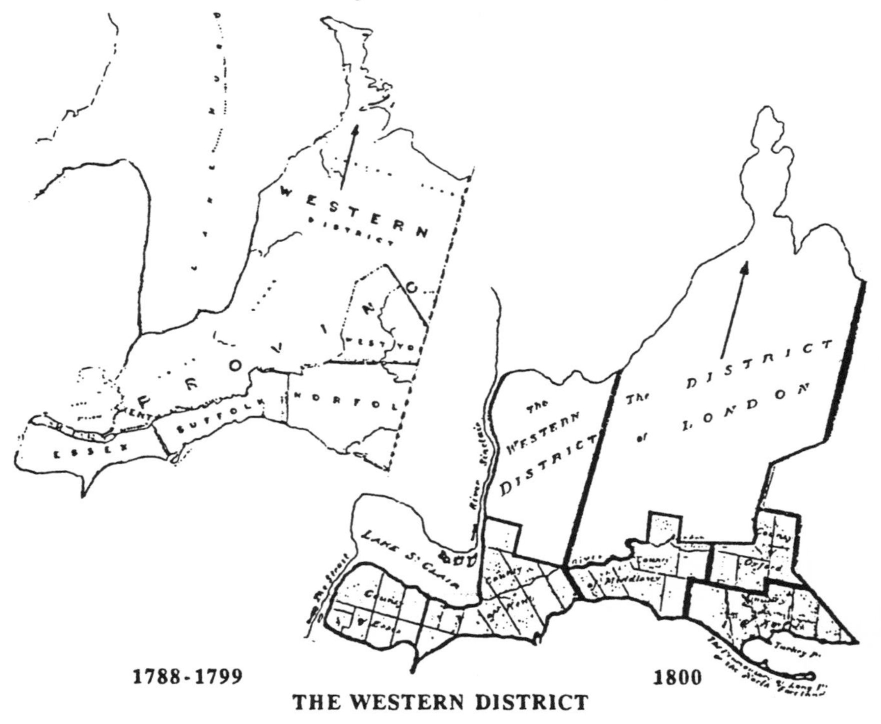

1788-1799 1800

THE WESTERN DISTRICT

File 12

NATIONAL ARCHIVES OF CANADA (NAC)

UPPER CANADA (ONTARIO) DISTRICT LOYALIST ROLLS

Reference: NAC RG 1, L 7, vol. 52B(B as in Bravo) (FILES 1 to 15)

FILE 12

Archivist's Description

WESTERN DISTRICT

Not endorsed, but bearing an extensive title "Roll of persons ..... of the Western District...". A contemporary copy, undated and not watermarked by date, on a single sheet 40x33 cm, bearing evidence of having once been attached by wax to another document; much worn on folds and margins. The list gives 41 names.

Transcriber's Comments

The heading, on six lines across the top of the sheet, reads: "Roll of Persons verified and vouched for by the different Magistrates of the Western District of the/ Province of Upper Canada, of having adhered to the Unity of the Empire, by joining the Royal/ Standard in America prior to the Treaty of separation in the year one thousand seven/hundred and eighty three agreeable to the Proclamation of His Excellency John Graves Simcoe/ Esquire Lieutenant Governor of the said Province &c &c &c bearing date the sixth day/ of April last."

The sheet is divided into four columns;the first and third columns are used for names, whilst the second and fourth are used for addresses/locations. There are no column headings. The writing is extremely easy to read, the capital letters being up to ½ inch high and lower case at least ¼ inch high. Spacing on the sheet is very generous.

File 12

7601	Joseph Abbot Esquire	River Thames 3^{d} Township
7602	John Cornwall senior	Township of Malden
7603	John Carpenter	River Thames 3^{d} Township
7604	Robert Dowlar	Parish of L'Assomption
7605	Matthew Dalson	River Thames 1st Township
7606	Isaac Dalson	River Thames 1st Township
7607	Timothy Disman	D^{o} D^{o} 3^{d} Ditto
7608	Matthew Elliot Esquire	Township of Malden
7609	Daniel Fields	River Thames 1st Township
7610	Nathan Fields	D^{o} D^{o} 2^{d} Ditto
7611	Matthew Gibson	D^{o} D^{o} D^{o} Ditto
7612	John Gordon	D^{o} D^{o} D^{o} Ditto
7613	Andrew Hamilton	D^{o} D^{o} D^{o} Ditto
7614	William Harper	D^{o} D^{o} 3^{d} Ditto
7615	Samuel Hall	New Settlement on Lake Erie
7616	Edward Harel	Township of Malden
7617	William Jemmison	River Thames 1st Township
7618	John Julian	D^{o} D^{o} 3^{d} Ditto
7619	Benjamin Knapp	New Settlement on Lake Erie
7620	Stephen Kissler	River Thames 3^{d} Township
7621	John Little senior	Detroit
7622	William Monger	New Settlement on Lake Erie
7623	John McLean	Ditto
7624	Edward Neville	Ditto
7625	Jacob Quant	River Thames 3^{d} Township
7626	Thomas Parsons	D^{o} D^{o} 1st Ditto
7627	Coleman Roe	D^{o} D^{o} D^{o} Ditto

NOTES:

1. While undated, we know that Lt. Gov. Simcoe's Proclamation was dated 6 April 1796 and the heading uses "last" to designate the year the list was made. Thus, the original was made sometime in 1796 - likely Oct/Nov as all the others in the various districts were made at that time.
2. Note the preponderance of Anglo-Saxon names - unlike other districts.

File 12

7628	John Stockwell	New Settlement on Lake Erie
7629	Leonard Scratch	Ditto
7630	James Stewart	Ditto
7631	Thomas Smith Esquire	Parish of L'Assomption
7632	Robert Surplet	River Thames 1st Township
7633	Joseph Springfield	Do Do Do Ditto
7634	William Shaw Esquire	Do Do 3d Ditto
7635	Edward Turner	Do Do 2d Ditto
7636	John Topp	Township of Malden
7637	Elisha Wilcox senior	New Settlement on Lake Erie
7638	John Wheaton	River Thames 1st Township
7639	Thomas Williams	Do Do Do Ditto
7640[f]	Simon Girty	Township of Malden
7641[f]	James Girty	Do Ditto

Copy of the names of the U.E. Loyalists in the Western District transmitted by the Clerk of the Peace

/signed/

F. Baby, J.P.W.D.

Paul Selby Chairman J.P.W.D.

Geo. Sharp J.P.W.D.

David Burns

Clk of the Crown &c

NOTES:

1. The reader is referred to the following for additional information:
   (a) Fred Coyne Hamil: The Valley of the Lower Thames (University of Toronto Press: 1951.
   (b) The Papers of John Askin of Detroit and Sandwich, edited by Milo M. Quaife (Detroit Library Commission: 1931).
2. Nos. 7640/1 - Simon Girty had the name "the White Savage"; his brother was James. Simon died at Amhertsburg in 1816.
3. No. 7629 - originally Kratz, a soldier in Butler's Rangers.

File 13

NATIONAL ARCHIVES OF CANADA (NAC)

UPPER CANADA (ONTARIO) DISTRICT LOYALIST ROLLS 1796-1803

Reference: NAC RG 1, L 7, vol. 52B (B as in Bravo) (Files 1 to 15)

FILE 13

Archivist's Description

Endorsed "The U.E. List of the West^{n} District for the year 1797". Original, on paper watermarked 1796, folded in two (32x20 cm), of which three out of four pages are used. The list gives 15 names. (Actually only 13 as two husband's names are repeated twice).

Transcriber's Comments

Endorsement as described above quite accurate. The heading is reproduced above the list. The writing looks like a copy as a professional scribe must have written it; the letters are extremely clear and large - nothing is in doubt. The 13 names it contains are those of File 15 less those of that File that have an "X" before the entry, ie, less those who were resident in the Western District before 1775.

The Archivist describes this File as the original and File 15 as the copy; personally, one must consider the reverse to be the case.

File 13

Roll of Persons residing in the Western District, who have either been verified on Oath, or vouched for by some Magistrate of the said District, of having adhered to the Unity of the Empire, and joined the Royal Standard in America, prior to the Treaty of Separation in the year 1783.

	Names	Place of Residence
7701	Jacob Arnold	Settlement on Lake Erie
7702	George Jacob Rudhart	d° d°
7703	Ebenezer Loveless	d° d°
7704	William Caldwell Esquire	Maldin
7705	Alexander McKee Esquire	d°
7706	Thomas McKee	d°
7707	Abraham Iredelle Esquire	River Thames
7708	Hester Marsh (wife of Abraham Iredelle Esqr.)	
7709	Edward Richardson	River Thames
7710	Esther Richardson (wife of Edward Richardson)	
7711 ff	Alexander Mackenzie	Maldin
7712	Joseph Jackson	Sandwich
7713	John Clearwater	Settlement on Lake Erie
		P. Selby Chairman
		William Park J.P.
		A. Iredelle J.P.

NOTES:

1. No. 7711 ends the first page of this copy. It has the traditional "JOSEPH" at the bottom right-hand corner of the page, indicating the first word of the following page.
2. Under No. 7711 is the word "unanimous". It is written strayly across the page - connected to nothing in particular.

File 14

NATIONAL ARCHIVES OF CANADA (NAC)

UPPER CANADA (ONTARIO) DISTRICT LOYALIST ROLLS 1796-1803

Reference: NAC RG 1, L 7, vol. 52B (B as in Bravo) (Files 1 to 15)

FILE 14

Archivist's Description

Endorsed "U E Roll, Western District", 1796. A contemporary copy, essentially duplicating File 12, but on paper without watermark as to date, 33x21 cm. The list gives 41 names. The paper is badly broken along folds and margins.

Transcriber's Comments

Very easy reading. There is much faint writing on the sheet and it is frustratingly unreadable; possibly the original is better than the photocopies the transcriber had to work.

The words lost on the broken folds and margins are assumed from File 12 and inserted in brackets. This large, single sheet has the heading across its width at the top and the entries in three columns of: number (not recorded as most are lost); name; and, place of residence. The transcription had to be done on two pages. There is no obvious explanation for the "o"s after some names.

As with other transcriptions in this volume, the original writing is enclosed in double lines; anything outside those lines is transcriber's comment. The asterix, "*", is used to indicate Sic, ie, as written, a possible mistake in the original.

File 14

(Ro)ll of Persons verified and vouched for by the Different Magistrates of the Western(District)/ of the Province of Upper Canada, of having adhered to the Unity of the Empire, by (joining/ the) Royal Standard in America, prior to the Treaty of Separation in the (year one/ thou)and, seven hundred and eighty three agreeable to the Proclamation (of His/ Exce)llency John Graves Simcoe Esquire, Lieutenant Governor of said (Province &c &c/ bea)ring date the sixth day of April last.

INDEX NUMBER	NAMES		PLACE OF RESIDENCE
7801[f]	Joseph Abbot Esq[r]		River Thames 3[d] Town(ship)
7802	John Cornwall senior		Township of Malden
7803	John Carpenter		River Thames 3[d] Townsh(ip)
7804	Robert Dowlar		Parish of L'Assomption
7805	Matthew Dalson	o	River Thames 1st Township
7806	Isaac Dalson	o	Ditto
7807	Timothy Disman		3[d] Township
7808	Matthew Elliot Esq[r]	o	Township of Malden
7809	Daniel Fields	o	River Thames 1st Township
7810	Nathan Fields	o	2[d] Ditto
7811	Matthew Gibson	o	Ditto
7812	John Gordon	o	3[d] Ditto
7813	Andrew Hamilton	o	1st Ditto
7814	William Harper	o	3[d] Ditto
7815	Samuel Hall		New Settlement on Lake Erie
7816	Edward Harel	o	Township of Malden
7817	William Jemmison		River Thames 1st Township
7818	John Julian		3[d] Ditto
7819	Benjamin Knapp	o	New Settlement on Lake Erie
7820[f]	Stephen Kissler		River Thames 3[d] Ditto
7821	John Little senior		Detroit
7822	William Monger		New Settlement on Lake Erie

NOTES:

1. There is no explanation given for the "o"s after some names.
2. The clerk gave a number to each entry but they have almost all been lost by the broken margin.
3. After No. 7801 is faint writing; possibly "Dis 26th" with only the 26th being definite. British Regiment ?

File 14

7823	John McLean		Ditto (ie, Lake Erie - EKF)
7824	Edward Neville	o	Ditto
7825	Jacob Quant		River Thames 3d Dittof
7826	Thomas Parsons		1st Dittof
7827f	Coleman Roe		Do Dittof
7828	John Stockwell	o	New Settlement on Lake Erie
7829	Leonard Scratch		Ditto
7830	James Stewart		Ditto
7831	Thomas Smith Esqr.	o	Parish of L'Assomption
7832	(R)obert Surplet	o	River Thames (1st Township)
7833	(J)oseph Springfield		Do Ditto
7834f	William Shaw Esqr.	o	3d Ditto
7835	Edward Turner	o	2d Ditto
7836	John Topp		Township of Malden
7837	Elisha Wilcox senior	o	New Settlement on Lake Erie
7838	John Wheaton	o	River Thames 1st Dittof
7839	Thomas Williams		Do Dittof
7840	Simon Girty	o	Township of Malden
7841	James Girty	o	Do Ditto

(List) of U.E. loyalists* Western District/signed/ F. Baby W.D.J.P. P. Selby (Chairm)an J.P.W.D. Geo. Sharp J.P.W.D. (signed) David Burns/ Clk. of the Council &c &c.

NOTES:

1. No. 7820 - faint writing after name; possibly "Discharged from the (3 more words ?)".
2. No. 7827 - after name faint writing "marine ?".
3. No. 7834 - after name faint "D".
4. The spacing on the various lines places the word "Ditto" usually under "Township" not under "Lake Erie".

File 15

NATIONAL ARCHIVES OF CANADA (NAC)

UPPER CANADA (ONTARIO) DISTRICT LOYALIST ROLLS

Reference: NAC RG 1, L 7, vol. 52B(B as in Bravo) (FILES 1 to 15)

FILE 15

Archivist's Description

Not endorsed, but titled in the same style as File 13, which it duplicates and supplements. Contemporary copy, undated (1796 ?), breaking along folds; 37x23 cm, containing 32 names (actually 28 as five husbands are mentioned twice), overlapping those in the list in File 13.

Transcriber's Comments

Actually very difficult to read if one did not have File 13 to use as a guide - even though File 13 only has 13 of the names on it. In spite of this, there are only two or three words transcribed without confidence. There is an interesting principle made in a note at the end.

The asterix "*" continues to be used to denote "Sic", or as written, a possible mistake. The double lines enclose all that is on the original document. Whilst undated, there is reasonable assurance that it is dated late (Oct/Nov) 1796.

There are an unusual number of "Esquires" in such a short list; one wonders if it was presumptuous of those on the list or if the local magistrates only enrolled the "gentry".** The listing of the maiden names of some wives is an interesting genealogical finding. Also the fact that some were residents before 1775 is likely not to be found elsewhere.

** NOTE: Orlo Miller, a genealogist of note, offers a possible explanation. The British granted Fort Detroit to the Americans in 1797. The "gentry" of Detroit, being mainly "Loyalist", moved across the river to the Windsor/Sandwich area to remain under British rule.

File 15

INDEX NUMBER	Roll of Persons who have either been verified on Oath, or vouched for by some Majestrate of the Western District of having adhered to the Unity of the Empire and joined the Royal Standard in America prior to the Treaty of Separation in the year 1783.	
	Names	Place of Residence
7901	Jacob Arnold	Settlement on Lake Erie
7902	Geo. Jacob Rudhart	d^o d^o
7903	Ebenezer Loveless	d^o d^o
7904	X Paul Selby	Sandwich
7905	X W^m. Caldwell Esqr.	Malden
7906	X Alex^r. McKee Esqr.	River Thames
7907	X Capt. Thos. McKee	Sandwich
7908[f]	Abr^m. Iredele Esqr.	River Thames
7909	X Hester Marsh wife of Abr^m. Iredele	
7910[f]	X Rich^d. Pollard Esqr.	Sandwich
7911	Edwd. Richardson	River Thames
7912	Ester Richardson wife of Edwd. Richardson	
7913	X Walter Roe Esqr.	Sandwich
7914	X Ann Laughton wife of W. Roe Esqr.	
7915	X Willm. Park Esqr.	d^o
7916	X Geo. Meldrum Esqr.	Sandwich
7917	X Thos. Reynolds	Amherstburg
7918	X Margaret Reynolds wife of Thos. Reynolds	
7919	X John Sparkman	d^o
7920	X Susannah Stedman wife of J. Sparkman	
7921[f]	X (Genl. ?) Alex^r. Grant	Malden (See note page 2)

NOTES:

1. No. 7908 - signature is IREDELLE on File 13.
2. No. 7921 - the first word is puzzling.
3. No. 7910 - Richard Pollard former sheriff of Detroit who took Holy Orders and became the first Anglican Priest in the Western District in 1802.

File 15

INDEX NUMBER	Names	Place of Residence
7922	Alex^r. Mackenzie	Malden
7923	X Gregor McGregor Esqr.	Sandwich
7924	Joseph Jackson	d^o
7925	X John Drake Esqr.	River Thames
7926	X Joseph Abbott Esqr.	d^o
7927	X John Arkin Esqr. (ASKIN ?)	(blank - River Thames ?)
7928	John Clearwater	Settlement on Lake Erie

Signed P. Selby
J.P.W.D. Chairman
of the Quarter
Sessions
Thos. Smith J.P.W.D.
Gregor McGregor J.P.

(Quen ?) Whither
Those marked with an asterish*^f
(were ?) resident within the
(settled ?) Colonies before and
at the time of the breaking out
of the Rebellion in 1775.
Because if they were not they
do not come within the description
of U.E. The same inquiry should
also be made (for ?) the others.
Signed Peter Russell

No. 7921 - the Honourable ALEXANDER GRANT, Commodore of H.M. Fleet on the Upper Lakes at the outbreak of the War of 1812 when he was 85, according to one source. However, a more accurate record gives his dates as 1734-1813. See Macdonald, G.F., Commodore Alexander Grant, Papers & Records Ont. Historical Society 1925.

NOTES: 1. The note immediately above is in rather odd grammar but it puts its point across. It seems like a personal note to a known person of some authority. The "asterish" are the large Xs beside the majority of the names.

- *The Old United Empire Loyalists List* with an introduction by Milton Rubincam. Baltimore, Maryland: Genealogical Publishing Co., Inc., 1976.

Allen, Robert S. *Loyalist Literature.* Toronto, Ontario: Dundurn Press Limited, 1982.

Armstrong, Frederick H. *Handbook of Upper Canadian Chronology.* Toronto, Ontario: Dundurn Press, 1985.

DeMarce, Virginia. *German Military Settlers in Canada after the American Revolution.* Sparta, Wisconsin: Joy Reisinger, 1984.

Fitzgerald, E. Keith. *Loyalist Lists.* Toronto, Ontario: Ontario Genealogical Society, 1984.

- . "Loyalist Stragglers in Montreal, September-October 1784." *Families* (Volume 24 No. 1 February 1985): 2-22. Toronto, Ontario: Ontario Genealogical Society.
- . "The Anglicization of German Surnames." *Families* (Volume 22 No. 2 May 1983): 97- 99. Toronto, Ontario: Ontario Genealogical Society.

Hamil, Fred Coyne. *The Valley of the Lower Thames.* Toronto, Ontario: University of Toronto Press, 1951.

Mathews, Hazel C. *The Mark of Honour.* Toronto, Ontario: University of Toronto Press, 1965.

Penrose, Marily B. *The Mohawk Valley in the Revolution.* Franklin Park, N.J.: Liberty Bell Associates, 1978.

Pringle, J. F. *Lunenburgh or the Old Eastern District.* Cornwall, Ontario: Standard Printing House, 1890.

Quaife, Milo M., ed. *The John Askin Papers.* Detroit:Detroit Library Commission, 1928-1931.

Rooney, Doris Dockstader. *The Dockstader Family.* Dodge City, Kansas: DDR, 1987.

Smith, Alexander. "Some Hessians of the U. E. L. Settlement in Marysburgh." *Papers and Records* (Volume 21) 259-261. Toronto, Ontario: Ontario Historical Society, 1924.

Wilson, Bruce. *As She Began.* Toronto, Ontario: Dundurn Press, 1981.

Wrong, Norman M. "My United Empire Loyalist Ancestors." *The Medical Graduate* (Fall 1983) 9-10. Toronto, Ontario: Medical Alumni Association.

Young, A.H. " 'Bishop' Peters." *Papers and Records* (Volume 27) 583-623. Toronto, Ontario: Ontario Historical Society, 1931.

LOCATIONS IN UPPER CANADA

The following list of place names mentioned in the court records is intended to help the reader who is not familiar with the structure of counties and townships in early Upper Canada. These places do not show on the maps of the districts but can be located, at least approximately, with the notations provided.

ADOLPHUS TOWN, page 122, westernmost township on Lake Ontario and the Bay of Quinte in Lennox and Addington Counties

AMELIASBURG, page 122, westernmost township on the Bay of Quinte in Prince Edward County

AMHERSTBURG, page 216, settlement on the Detroit River in the southwest corner of Essex County

AUGUSTA, page 9, westernmost township on the St. Lawrence River in Grenville County

BASTARD, page 9, township between Crosby and Kitley Townships in Leeds County

CHARLOTTENBURG, page 9, westernmost township on the St. Lawrence River in Glengarry County

CORNWALL, page 9, easternmost township on the St. Lawrence River in Stormont County

EDWARDSBURG, page 9, easternmost township on the St. Lawrence River in Grenville County

ELISABETHTOWN/ELIZABETHTOWN, page 9, easternmost township on the St. Lawrence River in Leeds County

ERNEST TOWN, page 122, easternmost township on Lake Ontario in Lennox and Addington Counties

ESCOTT, page 9, the middle township on the St. Lawrence River between Yonge and Lansdowne Townships in Leeds County

FREDERICKSBURG, page 122, the middle township on the Lake Ontario between Adolphustown and Ernestown Townships in Lennox and Addington Counties

GRAND RIVER, pages 9 and 177 - in Eastern Ontario it is an old name for the Ottawa River; in Western Ontario the Grand River flows through Brantford in Brant County

HAWKSBURY/HAWKESBURY, page 9, the easternmost township on the Ottawa River in Prescott County

KINGSTON, page 122, the westernmost township on Lake Ontario in Frontenac [Frontignac] County

KITLEY, page 9, the township north of Elizabethtown Township in Leeds County

LAKE, page 9 - an old name for Lancaster Township in Glengarry County

LAKE ERIE SETTLEMENTS/NEW SETTLEMENTS, page 216, Colchester and Gosfield Townships, east of Malden Township on Lake Erie in Essex County

LANCASTER, page 9, easternmost township on the St. Lawrence River in Glengarry County
LANSDOWNE, page 9, the township east of Leeds Township on the St. Lawrence River in Leeds County
LEEDS, page 9, westernmost township on the St. Lawrence River in Leeds County
L'ASSOMPTION PARISH, page 216, an early name for Sandwich, later Windsor, on the Detroit River in the western part of Essex County
MALDEN, page 216, southwestern township in Essex County

MARYSBURG, page 122, easternmost township in Prince Edward County

MATILDA, page 9, westernmost township on the St. Lawrence River in Dundas County
MONTAGUE, page 9, northwestern township in Grenville County

OSNABRUCK, page 9, westernmost township on the St. Lawrence River in Stormont County
RICHMOND, page 122, township north of Fredericksburg Township in Lennox and Addington Counties
RIVER THAMES, page 177 - it flows through Chatham in Kent County and London in Middlesex County; the 1st, 2nd, and 3rd townships are possibly Harwich, Howard and Tilbury Townships on Lake Erie in Kent County. Howard is the second township west of the eastern boundary of the county, Harwich is west of Howard, and Tilbury is second township east of the western boundary of the county.
ROXBURY/ROXBOROUGH, page 9, northeastern township of Stormont County
SANDWICH, page 216, northwestern township of Essex County

SOPHIASBURG, page 122, north central township in Prince Edward County east of Ameliasburg Township
THURLOW, page 122, middle township in Hastings County on the Bay of Quinte
WILLIAMSBURG, page 9, easternmost township on the St. Lawrence River in Dundas County
YONGE, page 9, township west of Elizabethtown Township on the St. Lawrence River in Leeds County

In later years there were numerous changes to the county/township structure - for example, Montague Township, shown here in Grenville County, became a part of Lanark County when Lanark County was established in 1824.

INDEX